First Impressions

Dining with Distinction

front cover sponsored by:
The Cookbook Development
Committee

back cover sponsored by:
Roswitha Marold
Kathryn Marold Fain
Jeannie Robertson

First Impressions

Dining with Distinction

A Collection of Memorable Recipes from the
Junior League of Waterloo-Cedar Falls, Iowa

First Impressions
Dining with Distinction

Copyright© 2001 by
The Junior League of
Waterloo-Cedar Falls, Iowa, Inc.
P.O. Box 434, Waterloo, Iowa 50704
319-232-8687

This cookbook is a collection of
favorite recipes, which are not
necessarily original recipes.

Library of Congress
    Catalog Number: 00-131129
ISBN: 0-9676325-0-1

Edited, Designed, and
Manufactured by
Favorite Recipes® Press
an imprint of

FRP™

P.O. Box 305142
Nashville, Tennessee 37230
800-358-0560

Managing Editor: Mary Cummings
Art Director and Designer:
    Steve Newman
Book Project Managers:
    Ginger Ryan Dawson and
    Judy Jackson
Editor: Jane Hinshaw
Production Manager: Mark Sloan

Manufactured in the
United States of America
First Printing: 2001   30,000 copies

COOKBOOK DEVELOPMENT COMMITTEE

Chairperson
Jeannie Robertson

Assistant Chairperson
Kathryn Marold Fain

Non-Recipe Text Editors
Linda Hanson
Anne Gallagher Nass

Sustainer Advisor
Julie Westin

Recipe Testing
Peg Ascherl
Ann Aulwes
Margaret Kaliban

Marketing
Becky Poe, Chairperson
Laura Dobson
Stacy Gary
Carol Heth

SUBCOMMITTEES

Recipe Development
Kathryn Marold Fain
Linda Hanson
Anne Gallagher Nass
Jeannie Robertson
Sustainer Advisor
Carol Luce

Recipe Testing
Peg Ascherl
Ann Aulwes
Margaret Kaliban
Sustainer Advisor
Mary Esther Pullin

Photography
Kathryn Marold Fain
Jeannie Robertson

Marketing
Laura Dobson, Chairperson
Peg Ascherl
Kathy Bailey
Suzanne Benda
Kim Bigler
Laura Buser
Carol Heth
Sally Hollis
Joanna Landau
Lisa McManus
Becky Poe
Kendra Richman
Anne Wilson

PROFESSIONAL CREDITS

Food Photographer
Dean Tanner
Primary Image
Des Moines, Iowa

Food Photo Stylist
Dana Etzel
The Prop House
2212 Ingersoll Avenue
Des Moines, Iowa
50312
515-288-3656

Food Stylist
Glenda Dawson
Des Moines, Iowa

Scenic Photography
Larsh Bristol Photography
1207 Old Stage Road
Waukon, Iowa 52172

Scenic Photography
David Cavagnaro
1575 Manawa Trail
Decorah, Iowa 52101

Food Stylist Assistant/Home Economist
Tami Leonard
Marion, Iowa

The Junior League of Waterloo-Cedar Falls wishes to recognize the extraordinary talent evident in each photograph in this fine book and thank each of these established professionals who donated all or part of their costs to make this book possible. We wish to further recognize Dean Tanner and Dana Etzel for their invaluable design assistance throughout the development of this book.

Table of Contents

Our Junior League

The Junior League of Waterloo-Cedar Falls, Iowa, Inc., is an organization of women committed to promoting voluntarism, developing the potential of women, and improving communities through the effective action and leadership of trained volunteers. Its purpose is exclusively educational and charitable.

The Junior League of Waterloo-Cedar Falls strives to improve the lives of children by embracing diverse perspectives, building partnerships, and inspiring shared solutions.

Serving the community since 1938, the Junior League of Waterloo-Cedar Falls, Iowa, Inc., has been instrumental in establishing the following agencies:

Minnie Crippen Home for Children
Byron Avenue Day Care Center
United Way
Exceptional Persons, Inc.
Community Foundation of Waterloo & Northeast Iowa
Goodwill Industries
Waterloo Recreation and Arts Center
Rensselaer Russell House Museum
Black Hawk Children's Theater
Junior Art Gallery
Green Scene
Grin and Grow Day Care
Family and Children's Council
Hartman Reserve Nature Center Expansion Project
Children's Garden at the Cedar Valley Arboretum & Botanic Garden
Traveling Tales
Adults, Inc.
Newel Post

Introduction

FIRST IMPRESSIONS

YOU KNOW IT WHEN YOU SEE IT. It has that special something—quiet elegance, simplicity, tradition, familiarity, comfort, beauty, grace, or abundance.

It can be as simple as an indescribable sunset with pigments that leave you breathless or as beautiful as the drop of dew on a rosebud that sparkles like a diamond. Whatever the situation, everything makes a "First Impression."

YOU KNOW IT WHEN YOU TASTE IT. It has that special something—creamy, rich, sweet, and excessive; tart, sharp, tangy, and stimulating; or meaty, choice, sumptuous, and grand. Whatever the occasion, all foods make a "First Impression."

We bring to you recipes of distinction. All are foods from family traditions spanning the years and recipes that nurture. Much like the people who live here, this book demonstrates the diversity and discerning nature of its residents.

We invite you to immerse yourself into the radiance and delicious culture that brings you *First Impressions*.

Menus and Place Settings

Brunch on the Porch

Sunrise Mimosa
Hazelnut Coffee
Pecan and Cranberry Biscotti
Fruit Compote
Raspberry Cream Cheese Coffee Cake
Dutch Babies Baked Pancake
Sausage and Egg Strata
Crepes Iceland

Picnic by the Lake

Curried Deviled Eggs
Iced Tea
Arugula Salad with Pears and Beets
Garlic Tomatoes
Turkey and Apple Pitas
Lemon Pistachio Cookies
Almond Macaroons

Breakfast

A. Napkin
B. Luncheon Plate
C. Cereal Bowl
D. Bread and Butter Plate
   with Butter Knife
E. Cup and Saucer with
   Teaspoon
F. Water Glass
G. Juice Glass
H. Fork
I. Knife
J. Teaspoon

Menus and Place Settings

MIDSUMMER LUNCHEON

Chablis
Crab Bruschetta
Blueberry Spinach Salad
Iced Parsley Soup
Chenin Blanc or Iced Tea
Grilled Asparagus Pâté Sandwiches
Vanilla Coffee
Peach and Berry Shortcakes with
warm Cream Sauce

TAILGATE PARTY

Corona Beer with Lime
Mexican Spinach Dip
Tortilla Stacks
Texas Caviar
Margaritas Supreme
Chili Blanco
Pressed Picnic Sandwiches
Cafe au Lait
Cappuccino Brownies
Pecan Clusters

LUNCHEON

A. Napkin
B. Luncheon Plate
C. Soup Bowl (or other first
    course plate) on a
    Liner Plate
D. Bread and Butter Plate with
    Butter Knife
E. Water Glass
F. Wine Glass
G. Luncheon Fork
H. Knife
I. Teaspoon
J. Soup Spoon

Menus and Place Settings

BUFFET

Curried Chicken Canapés
Grilled Shrimp Dijonnaise
Cranberry and Apple Salad
Tomato and Cucumber Bread Salad
Swiss Crab Bake
Roast Lamb with Potato and Tomato Gratin
Roast Pork with Fruit Stuffing
Barbecued Beef Brisket
Risotto
Potato and Carrot Bake
Cider-Roasted Squash
Flourless Chocolate Cake
Irish Cream Chocolate Chip Cheesecake
Best-Ever Cream Puffs
Various Red and White Wines

WEEKEND COMFORT

Semidry Rosé
Sausage-Stuffed Mushrooms
Grilled Vegetable Salad with Pesto Vinaigrette
Creamy Sweet Potato Soup
Pouilly-Fuissé
Grilled Chicken Grand Marnier
Honey-Glazed Carrots
Scalloped Corn
Coffee
Double-Decadent Brownie Torte
Rich Homemade Vanilla Ice Cream

FAMILY DINNER

A. Napkin
B. Dinner Plate
C. Salad Plate
D. Bread and Butter Plate with Butter Knife
E. Water Glass
F. Fork
G. Knife
H. Teaspoon

Menus and Place Settings

CELEBRATION DINNER

Champagne/Sparkling Wine
Roquefort Grapes
Seafood Tartlets
Salad with Hot Brie Dressing
Chardonnay
Roasted Garlic Soup with
Prosciutto and Gruyère
Strawberry Grand Marnier Sorbet
Pinot Noir
Carrots in Port Sauce
Scalloped Broccoli
Normandy-Style Pork Loin
Sauternes
Glazed Cardamom Pears with
Honey Cream Sauce

HOLIDAY CHEER

Poinsettia Punch
Holiday Punch
Iowa Maytag Tart
Stuffed Phyllo Cups
Apple Walnut Salad with Bacon Vinaigrette
White Zinfandel
Strawberry Cantaloupe Soup
Merlot
Sweet Potato Puff
Onion Casserole
Beef Tenderloin with Bordelaise Sauce
Hazelnut Coffee or Asti Spumonti
Pumpkin Cheesecake with Cranberry Glaze
Bûche de Noël (Yule Log)

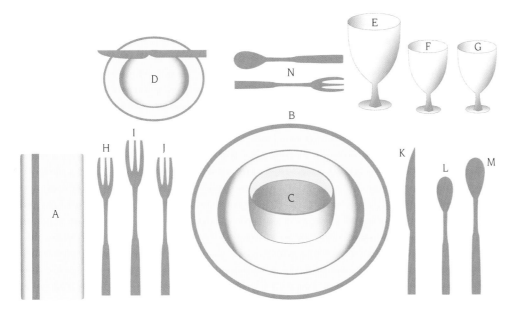

FORMAL DINNER

A. Napkin
B. Service Plate
C. Soup Bowl on a Liner Plate
D. Bread and Butter Plate with
    Butter Knife
E. Water Glass
F. Wine Glass
G. Wine Glass
H. Salad Fork
I. Dinner Fork
J. Fruit Fork
K. Knife
L. Teaspoon
M. Soup Spoon
N. Dessert Fork and Spoon

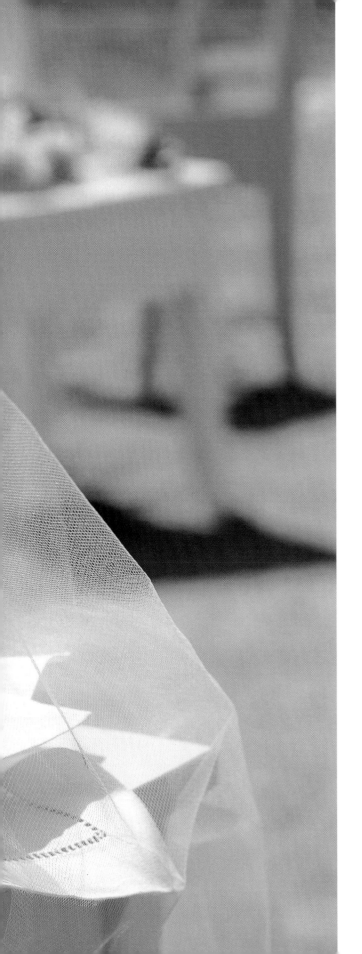

At First Glance...

APPETIZERS & BEVERAGES

At First Glance...

Just as appetizers prepare one's appetite for the courses to follow, organizational skills ready a culinary event for success. Certain tasks, done in advance, allow the hostess and host the ability to enjoy their guests and their labor of love, which is dining. Whether it be an evening meal with one's family, a brunch with friends, or a cocktail party for twenty-five, preplanning allows for stress-free entertaining.

A first consideration is when will this dining experience take place? If it's your daily meal, then, of course, this is predetermined. A special dinner or event, however, deserves a discerning look ahead. Do you have enough time to pull it all together? Will your guests be available? Do you need to reserve tables, chairs, serving pieces, or dishes? Do you need to preorder meat, food items, or flowers?

Another important concern should include a review of the guest list. Will the guests complement one another? Are they interesting people? Are there any individuals or groups that should not be integrated? By taking a few moments to review one's intended audience, possible conflicts or lackluster events may be avoided.

After the guest list has been defined, it's time to contemplate invitations. Even dinner on weeknights with the kids offers an opportunity for a friendly and inviting call to dine. How casual or formal is the event? Will a phone call suffice for a few friends with a casual menu and theme, or are formal printed invitations necessary? Casual events may need only a verbal invitation, but a written note confirming the day, time, and purpose serves as a nice reminder. A follow-up call will allow you to confirm their attendance. A formal affair requires a printed invitation, which includes your name, the phrase "request the pleasure of your company," the date, time, occasion, attire, and an R.S.V.P. including your phone number. If your invited guests fail to respond, do not hesitate to call for a confirmation. After all, you have an event to plan. Unfortunately, in these busy times, etiquette is often overlooked or ignored. Don't think that because they failed to respond that they are not coming, unless they have indicated so.

A final issue to be decided well in advance of the dining occasion is the theme. This helps to establish the entire tone of the event. A theme potentially determines the dishware, flowers, lighting, music, color scheme, invitations, and attire. Knowing the general theme allows you the advantage of time—to plan, evaluate, and process the experience.

ANTIPASTO APPETIZER

Provolone is a cheese made from cow's milk with a firm texture and a mild, smoky taste. A product of southern Italy, this cheese has a golden rind.

    1 (16-ounce) can artichoke hearts, drained
    4 ounces fresh mushrooms
    1/2 cup black olives
    2 cups (1/2-inch) cubes provolone cheese
    1 or 2 garlic cloves, finely chopped
    1/4 cup chopped fresh parsley
    1 tablespoon crushed sun-dried tomato
    1/2 to 1 cup extra-virgin olive oil

Cut the artichoke hearts into quarters. Cut the mushrooms and black olives into halves lengthwise. Combine the artichoke hearts with the mushrooms, olives, cheese cubes, garlic, parsley and sun-dried tomato in a container with a lid. Add the olive oil and mix well.

Marinate, covered, in the refrigerator from 3 to 24 hours, turning several times. Drain and spoon into a serving dish. Serve with wooden picks.

Yield: 12 servings

CRAB BRUSCHETTA

    1 (6-ounce) can crab meat
    2 tablespoons chopped green onions
    1 teaspoon minced garlic
    1/2 cup shredded Cheddar cheese
    1/2 cup mayonnaise
    1/4 teaspoon seasoned salt
    1/8 teaspoon pepper
    1 small loaf French bread

Drain the crab meat, pressing to remove the excess moisture. Combine with the green onions, garlic, cheese, mayonnaise, seasoned salt and pepper in a bowl and mix well.

Cut the bread into 1/2-inch slices. Spread the crab mixture on the bread and arrange on a baking sheet. Bake at 400 degrees for 15 minutes. Serve hot. Do not use imitation crab meat in this recipe.

Yield: 7 servings

FIRST-PRESSED OLIVE OIL *is oil pressed from tree-ripened olives. Oils are graded, with the highest quality being cold-pressed extra-virgin. It is naturally low in acidity. Extra-virgin oils vary in color from pale yellow to deep green. The darker the oil, the more potent the flavor.*

Greek-Style Bruschetta

1½ ounces drained water-pack white tuna
1½ tablespoons minced red onion
3 tablespoons drained capers
1½ teaspoons minced garlic
1½ tablespoons minced parsley
3 tablespoons minced kalamata olives
2 teaspoons soy sauce
¾ teaspoon each lemon juice and minced lemon zest
¼ teaspoon olive oil
8 (¼-inch) slices French bread
2 tablespoons butter, softened

Combine the tuna, onion, capers, garlic, parsley and olives in a small bowl. Add the soy sauce, lemon juice, lemon zest and olive oil and mix well. Store, covered, in the refrigerator until serving time.

Arrange the bread on a baking sheet just before serving time. Toast until crisp. Spread with the butter and the tuna mixture. Garnish with freshly grated Parmesan cheese.

Yield: 8 servings

CAPERS *are pickled flower buds with a salty, tart flavor. Capers vary in size from very small to the size of a large pea. They are generally sold packed in brine but may be sun dried. Rinse before using.*

Curried Chicken Canapés

An average-size lemon will yield 2 to 3 tablespoons of juice. To access the maximum amount of juice from a lemon, pierce the lemon with a knife and microwave for one minute. Then juice as usual.

1 cup minced cooked chicken breast
¾ cup shredded Monterey Jack cheese
2 large shallots, minced, or ¼ cup minced onion
¼ cup chopped parsley
⅓ cup ground almonds
1 cup mayonnaise
2 teaspoons fresh lemon juice
¼ to ½ teaspoon Tabasco sauce
1½ teaspoons curry powder
¼ to ½ teaspoon cayenne pepper
1 loaf cocktail bread

Combine the chicken, cheese, shallots, parsley and almonds in a bowl. Add the mayonnaise, lemon juice, Tabasco sauce, curry powder and cayenne pepper and mix well. Chill, covered, in the refrigerator for 1 hour or longer.

Spread the chicken mixture on the bread slices, spreading to the edges of the bread. Arrange on a baking sheet. Bake at 500 degrees for 5 minutes.

Yield: 16 servings

ROQUEFORT GRAPES

    1 pound large seedless red grapes, about 50 grapes
   10 ounces pecans
    4 tablespoons Roquefort cheese, crumbled
    8 ounces cream cheese, softened
    2 tablespoons heavy cream

Wash the grapes and pat dry. Crush the pecans on a platter or sheet of waxed paper.

Combine the Roquefort cheese, cream cheese and cream in a bowl and mix well. Roll the grapes in the cheese mixture and then in the pecans, coating well. Chill, covered, until serving time.

Yield: 50 servings

CURRIED DEVILED EGGS

    8 eggs, hard-cooked, peeled
  1/3 cup mayonnaise
  1/4 teaspoon curry powder
  1/4 teaspoon dry mustard
  1/2 teaspoon salt
       Paprika to taste

Cut the eggs into halves lengthwise and remove the yolks to a bowl. Mash the egg yolks and add the mayonnaise, curry powder, dry mustard and salt; mix well.

Spoon the egg yolk mixture into the egg whites and arrange on a serving plate; sprinkle with paprika.

Note: *When hard-cooking eggs, add salt to harden the shell and promote easier peeling. Hard-cooked eggs should be refrigerated and are best used within one week. Storage in the refrigerator should not exceed five weeks.*

Yield: 8 servings

ROQUEFORT CHEESE *is a bleu cheese made from sheep's milk and a mold (Penicillium roqueforti) that is aged for three months or more. Genuine Roquefort is from France and the name is protected by law. It has a creamy, rich texture and a salty intense flavor. It's often used in salad dressings and spreads.*

SAUSAGE-STUFFED MUSHROOMS

  16 ounces (1$^{1}/_{2}$-inch) fresh button mushrooms
    8 ounces seasoned pork sausage
    1 cup freshly grated Parmesan cheese
    1 cup cracker crumbs or fine bread crumbs

Wipe the mushrooms and remove the stems, reserving the caps and $^{1}/_{3}$ of the stems. Chop the reserved mushroom stems and combine with the sausage, cheese and cracker crumbs in a bowl; mix well. Spoon the mixture into the reserved mushroom caps until well rounded.

     Arrange the stuffed mushroom caps on a microwave-safe plate. Microwave on High for 7 minutes or until the sausage is cooked through. Let stand for 2 minutes. Serve hot.

     Yield: 8 servings

GRUYÈRE-STUFFED MUSHROOMS

GRUYÈRE CHEESE, *a cheese made from cow's milk, has a rich, nut-like flavor. It is aged ten to twelve months, a process that produces a pale yellow cheese with a golden ring and medium-size holes. It is often produced in Switzerland or France.*

  12 to 14 large mushrooms
    1 small onion, chopped
    3 tablespoons butter
  $^{1}/_{3}$ cup bread crumbs
    2 tablespoons crumbled Gruyère cheese
       Salt and cayenne pepper to taste
  $^{1}/_{4}$ cup ($^{1}/_{2}$ stick) butter, melted
       Paprika to taste

Wipe the mushrooms and remove the stems, reserving the stems and caps; chop the stems. Sauté the stems with the onion in 3 tablespoons butter in a small skillet. Add the bread crumbs, cheese, salt and cayenne pepper.

     Dip the mushroom caps in the melted butter and arrange in a shallow baking dish. Spoon the sautéed mixture into the caps and sprinkle with paprika. Bake, uncovered, at 350 degrees for 20 to 25 minutes or until brown.

     You may substitute button mushrooms for the large mushrooms for smaller servings.

     Yield: 14 servings

HOT MARINATED MUSHROOMS

    2 pounds whole large mushrooms
    1 garlic clove, minced
    1 tablespoon chopped fresh dill
    1 cup (2 sticks) unsalted butter
  1/2 (750-milliliter) bottle dry white wine
    2 teaspoons Worcestershire sauce
    1 cup boiling water
    2 teaspoons instant beef bouillon
    2 teaspoons instant chicken bouillon
 1 1/2 teaspoons meat tenderizer
  1/2 teaspoon freshly ground pepper

Combine the mushrooms, garlic, dill, butter, wine, Worcestershire sauce, boiling water, beef bouillon, chicken bouillon, meat tenderizer and pepper in a large saucepan. Cook, covered, over low heat for 5 hours. Cook, uncovered, for 3 hours longer or until the liquid is reduced. Serve hot.

Note: *Unsalted butter contains absolutely no salt. Because it contains no salt (which acts as a preservative) and is more perishable than salted butter, it may be found in the freezer section of some grocery stores.*

Yield: 24 servings

PARMESAN KNOTS

 1 1/2 cups olive oil
  1/2 cup grated Parmesan cheese
 2 1/2 teaspoons garlic powder
    1 tablespoon parsley flakes
    1 tablespoon oregano
  1/4 teaspoon pepper
    3 (10-count) cans refrigerator buttermilk biscuits

Combine the olive oil, Parmesan cheese, garlic powder, parsley flakes, oregano and pepper in a bowl and mix well; set aside.
    Cut each biscuit into 3 equal pieces. Stretch and roll each piece into a rope and tie into a knot. Place on an ungreased baking sheet. Bake until brown, using the package directions and reducing the baking time by 2 to 4 minutes.
    Place the knots immediately in the olive oil mixture and let stand until the mixture is absorbed. Return the knots to the baking sheet. Bake at 350 degrees for 11 to 14 minutes. You may freeze the knots in airtight containers. Let stand for 5 minutes at room temperature. Reheat at 350 degrees for 10 to 12 minutes.

Note: *Make and use the delicious recipe at right for your own buttermilk biscuits—when time permits.*

Yield: 90 servings

BUTTERMILK BISCUITS

Mix 2 cups unbleached flour, 2 1/4 teaspoons baking powder, 1/4 teaspoon baking soda and 1 teaspoon salt in a bowl. Cut in 6 tablespoons butter. Add 3/4 cup buttermilk; mix lightly. Knead 6 times lightly on a floured surface; roll 1/2 inch thick. Cut out; place on a greased baking sheet. Bake at 450 degrees for 12 minutes or until light brown.

Country Pâté

Sherry *is a fortified wine. Produced around the world, sherries vary from inexpensive to connoisseur. They also vary greatly in dryness and flavor. Flavors range from very sweet to dry and nutty. Aged sherries are generally more costly.*

4 ounces mushrooms, chopped
1 medium onion, minced
1 small garlic clove, minced
2 tablespoons vegetable oil
1/4 cup dry sherry or cooking sherry
1/2 teaspoon dried thyme leaves
1/8 teaspoon ground nutmeg
1 teaspoon salt
1/2 teaspoon cracked pepper
8 ounces ground pork
8 ounces ground chicken
4 ounces ground pork fat
1/4 cup shelled pistachios
1 egg
2 tablespoons chopped parsley
8 ounces sliced bacon
3 tablespoons chopped parsley

Cook the mushrooms, onion and garlic in the heated oil in a 3-quart saucepan over medium heat for 5 minutes or until tender, stirring occasionally. Add the sherry, thyme, nutmeg, salt and pepper. Bring to a boil and reduce the heat to low. Simmer for 5 minutes, stirring occasionally; remove from the heat.

Add the ground pork, ground chicken, ground pork fat, pistachios, egg and 2 tablespoons parsley and beat with a wooden spoon until well mixed.

Reserve several slices of bacon for the top of the pâté. Line the bottom and sides of a 4 1/2 x8 1/2-inch loaf pan with the remaining bacon, allowing the slices to hang over the sides. Spoon the pâté mixture into the prepared pan and press to pack firmly. Fold the bacon slices over the mixture and top with the reserved bacon.

Bake at 350 degrees for 1 1/4 hours. Chill, covered, in the refrigerator for 8 hours.

Dip the loaf pan in 2 inches hot water for 15 seconds. Loosen the sides of the pâté from the pan with a spatula and invert onto a serving plate. Sprinkle with 3 tablespoons parsley.

Yield: 16 servings

CREAMY GARLIC SNOW PEAS

  100 fresh snow peas or sugar peas
    8 ounces cream cheese, softened
  1/4 cup (1/2 stick) butter, softened
    2 tablespoons half-and-half
    2 tablespoons chopped parsley (optional)
    1 teaspoon dry mustard
  1/4 to 1/2 teaspoon garlic powder, or to taste
  1/2 teaspoon salt

Pour boiling water over the peas in a bowl and let stand for 1 to 2 minutes to blanch. Drain and place in a bowl of ice water for 3 to 5 minutes or until cool. Drain and pat dry. Chill in the refrigerator for 30 minutes or longer.

Combine the cream cheese, butter, half-and-half, parsley, dry mustard, garlic powder and salt in a bowl and mix until smooth. Spoon into a pastry bag fitted with a 1/8-inch decorating tip.

Cut 1/4 inch from the stem end of each pea and gently open the peas lengthwise. Pipe the cream cheese mixture into the peas and arrange on a plate. Chill, covered, in the refrigerator for 4 to 24 hours.

You may also pipe the cream cheese mixture into other vegetables or onto bagel chips.

Yield: 100 servings

BLANCHING means to briefly immerse a vegetable or fruit in boiling water and then into ice water to prevent further cooking. This process loosens the skin and brightens the color.

HERBED CHEESE SPREAD

    4 ounces cream cheese, softened
  1/3 cup sour cream
    2 cups shredded Colby/Monterey Jack cheese
    2 tablespoons minced parsley
    2 tablespoons minced green onions
  1/2 teaspoon paprika
  1/4 teaspoon Tabasco sauce

Combine the cream cheese and sour cream in a mixing bowl and beat until smooth. Stir in the cheese, parsley, green onions, paprika and Tabasco sauce. Spoon into a small crock and chill, covered, until serving time.

Yield: 16 servings

MEDITERRANEAN FETA STUFFED MUSHROOMS

16 ounces fresh button mushrooms
 3 green onions, chopped
1/4 cup (1/2 stick) butter
1/2 cup fine fresh bread crumbs
 3 tablespoons Mediterranean feta cheese, crumbled
 1 tablespoon minced fresh parsley
 1 tablespoon lemon juice
1/2 teaspoon salt
    Paprika to taste

Remove the stems from the mushrooms, reserving the stems and caps; chop the stems. Sauté the stems with the green onions in the butter in a skillet. Add the bread crumbs, feta cheese, parsley, lemon juice and salt and mix well. Spoon into the reserved mushroom caps.

Arrange the stuffed caps in a shallow baking dish and sprinkle with paprika. Bake at 450 degrees for 8 minutes or until light brown.

Yield: 12 servings

MEXICAN CHICKEN PIZZA

 2 boneless skinless chicken breasts, cooked, chopped
1 1/2 cups thick and chunky salsa
 1 (12-inch) Italian bread shell
1/2 cup red bell pepper strips
1/2 teaspoon chopped cilantro
 1 cup shredded mozzarella cheese
 1 cup shredded Cheddar cheese

Heat a large skillet that has been sprayed with nonstick cooking spray. Add the chicken. Cook over medium heat for 5 minutes or until heated through. Add the salsa. Cook over low heat for 5 minutes. Place the bread shell on a 12-inch round pizza pan or pizza stone. Spoon the chicken mixture over the bread shell. Top with the red pepper strips and cilantro. Top with the cheeses.

Bake at 400 degrees for 10 to 15 minutes or until the cheese is melted and bubbly. You may use thick and chunky mild salsa with cilantro and omit the fresh cilantro.

Yield: 12 servings

ICED TEA flavor is improved by partially filling iced tea glasses with crushed ice or ice cubes and filling with hot, strong, freshly brewed tea. This brings out the best flavor, as tea loses some of its flavor when cooled. Serve with a slice of lemon or orange. A sprig of mint or lemon slices frozen in ice cubes also make a refreshing garnish.

MEDITERRANEAN PIZZAS

Pita rounds
Refrigerator commercial pesto, or Basil Pesto (below)
Sliced Roma tomatoes
Sliced pitted kalamata olives
Crumbled feta cheese
Grated Parmesan cheese (optional)
Chopped red onions (optional)

Arrange the pita rounds on a baking sheet. Spread with a thin layer of pesto. Top with the sliced tomatoes and olives. Sprinkle with the cheeses and onions. Broil for 8 to 10 minutes or just until bubbly.

Yield: variable

BASIL PESTO

4 cups packed rinsed fresh basil leaves
Salt to taste
1/2 cup toasted pine nuts, cooled, finely chopped
1/2 cup grated Parmesan cheese
2 large garlic cloves, minced
1/2 cup minus 1 tablespoon extra-virgin olive oil
Pepper to taste

Blanch the basil 1 cup at a time in salted boiling water in a saucepan for about 2 seconds; remove to a bowl of ice water with a slotted spoon. Drain in a colander and pat dry.

Combine the basil with the pine nuts, Parmesan cheese, garlic and olive oil in a food processor container and process until smooth. Season with salt and pepper.

Spoon into a bowl and place a sheet of plastic wrap directly on the surface to cover. Store in the refrigerator for up to 2 days.

Yield: 10 servings

FETA CHEESE is a Greek cheese traditionally made from goat or sheep milk that is now made commercially from cow milk. Cured and stored in its own brine, it is white and crumbly and generally is pressed into squares. It ranges from soft to semidry.

POT STICKERS WITH ASIAN SAUCE

Chili oil can be found in the Asian food section of supermarkets.

Pot Stickers

8	cups finely chopped Chinese cabbage, about 1 pound
1	teaspoon salt
1	pound ground pork
1½	cups chopped green onions
1	egg, beaten
¼	cup chopped gingerroot
2	teaspoons sugar
2	tablespoons soy sauce
¾	teaspoon salt
50	won ton wrappers

Asian Sauce

⅔	cup vinegar
1	cup soy sauce
1	cup water
1	teaspoon chili oil
½	cup sugar

For the pot stickers, sprinkle the cabbage with 1 teaspoon salt in a bowl and let stand for 10 minutes. Press to remove the liquid. Combine with the pork, green onions, egg, gingerroot, sugar, soy sauce and ¾ teaspoon salt in a bowl and mix well. Sauté in a large saucepan until the pork is no longer pink; drain.

Cut the won ton wrappers into circles. Spoon a small amount of the pork mixture onto each circle. Moisten the edges of the wrappers with water and pinch to seal and enclose the filling. Simmer in water in a saucepan for 10 minutes, turning once. Remove pot stickers to a serving platter with a slotted spoon.

For the dipping sauce, combine the vinegar, soy sauce, water, chili oil and sugar in a saucepan and mix well. Simmer until the flavors blend. Serve with the pot stickers.

Yield: 50 servings

DRINK GLASSES *vary for different drinks. They ascend in size in this order: liqueur, port, sherry, white wine, red wine, and water. Champagne should be served in a fluted glass, not a wide shallow one.*

MINIATURE FOCACCIA SANDWICHES

       1 (12-ounce) focaccia, 8 inches in diameter and 1$1/2$ inches thick
       8 ounces cream cheese, softened
       2 to 3 tablespoons 2% milk
    $1/4$ cup oil-pack sun-dried tomatoes, drained, chopped
       4 teaspoons chopped fresh basil
       4 teaspoons chopped fresh thyme
       1 small garlic clove, minced
    1$1/2$ cups packed stemmed fresh spinach leaves
       8 ounces thinly sliced smoked deli turkey

Split the focaccia into halves horizontally with a long sharp serrated knife. Arrange cut sides up on a work surface.

Combine the cream cheese and milk in a small bowl and mix until smooth. Add the sun-dried tomatoes, basil, thyme and garlic and mix well. Spread $1/4$ of the mixture on each focaccia round, spreading to the edges.

Layer the spinach and turkey over the cream cheese mixture and spread the remaining cream cheese mixture over the tops. Wrap each round individually in plastic wrap and chill for 1 to 12 hours.

Cut each focaccia round into 5 strips and cut each strip into 1$1/2$-inch pieces to serve.

Yield: 48 servings

FOCACCIA is an Italian bread that is round and flat. Focaccia is brushed with olive oil and may also include various herbs stuffed into the dough before baking. This versatile bread may be served alone or with your favorite dishes.

WON TON SAUSAGE STARS

       2 cups drained cooked sausage
    1$1/2$ cups shredded sharp Cheddar cheese
    1$1/2$ cups shredded Monterey Jack cheese
       1 cup ranch salad dressing
    $1/2$ cup chopped red bell pepper
       1 (50-count) package won ton wrappers
          Vegetable oil

Combine the sausage with the cheeses, salad dressing and bell pepper in a bowl and mix well; set aside.

Press the won ton wrappers into lightly greased muffin cups and brush with oil. Bake at 350 degrees for 5 to 10 minutes or until golden brown. Remove to a baking sheet. Spoon the sausage mixture into the won ton cups. Bake for 5 minutes or until bubbly.

You may substitute egg roll wrappers cut into quarters for the won ton wrappers.

Yield: 50 servings

CURRIED CHICKEN PUFFS

Puffs
- 1/2 cup water
- 1/3 cup butter or margarine
- 2/3 cup flour
-   Salt to taste
- 2 eggs

Curried Chicken Filling
- 8 ounces cream cheese, softened
- 1/4 cup milk
- 1/2 to 1 teaspoon curry powder
-   Pepper to taste
- 1/4 teaspoon salt
- 1 1/2 cups chopped cooked chicken
- 1/3 cup slivered almonds, toasted
- 2 tablespoons sliced green onions

For the puffs, bring the water and butter to a boil in a saucepan. Reduce heat to low. Add the flour and salt, stirring until the mixture forms a ball and leaves the side of the saucepan; remove from the heat. Beat in the eggs one at a time.

Spoon the mixture by teaspoonfuls onto an ungreased baking sheet. Bake at 400 degrees for 25 minutes. Cool to room temperature.

For the filling, combine the cream cheese, milk, curry powder, pepper and salt in a bowl and mix until smooth. Add the chicken, almonds and green onions and mix lightly.

Cut the tops from the puffs and fill with the chicken mixture. Replace the tops and bake at 375 degrees for 5 minutes or until heated through.

You may fill the unfilled puffs immediately or freeze in airtight containers for several weeks until needed.

Yield: 18 servings

CURRY POWDER *is a combination of up to twenty spices, herbs, and seeds, including cardamom, chiles, cinnamon, cloves, coriander, cumin, fennel seeds, fenugreek, mace, nutmeg, red pepper, black pepper, poppy seeds, sesame seeds, saffron, tamarind, and turmeric. Commercially produced curry powder comes in two styles, standard and Madras (a hotter variety). Curry powder loses its snap quickly and should be stored, airtight, no longer than two months.*

Iowa Maytag Tart

Basic Pie Pastry
- 1 1/3 cups flour
- 1 tablespoon sugar
- 1/4 teaspoon salt
- 1/4 cup shortening, chilled, chopped
- 1/4 cup (1/2 stick) unsalted butter, chilled, chopped
- 1/2 large egg
- 1 1/2 tablespoons (or more) ice water

Filling
- 1/4 cup sour cream
- 1/4 cup heavy cream
- 4 ounces Maytag bleu cheese, crumbled
- 1 large egg
- 1 egg yolk
- 2/3 cup chopped walnuts

For the pastry, combine the flour, sugar and salt in a food processor container. Add the shortening and butter and pulse until the mixture resembles coarse meal.

Beat the egg with the ice water in a small bowl. Add to the flour mixture and process until the mixture begins to form a ball, adding additional water if needed. Shape into a ball and wrap in plastic wrap. Chill for 1 to 24 hours.

Let the pastry stand at room temperature for 10 to 15 minutes. Press into a 9-inch tart pan and prick the side and bottom with a fork. Bake at 400 degrees for 15 minutes or just until golden brown. Cool on a wire rack. Reduce the oven temperature to 375 degrees.

For the filling, combine the sour cream and heavy cream in a mixing bowl and mix until smooth. Process the bleu cheese, egg and egg yolk in a food processor or blender until smooth. Add the cream mixture and process until just combined.

Spoon the filling into the tart shell. Sprinkle with the walnuts. Bake for 20 minutes or until the filling is golden brown. Cool for 10 minutes. Slice and serve warm or at room temperature.

You may double the pastry recipe for a double-crust pie or substitute one 9-inch refrigerator pie pastry for the pastry in this recipe if preferred.

Yield: 8 first-course servings or 16 appetizer servings

MAYTAG CHEESE *is a bleu cheese manufactured in Newton, Iowa. Originally made in stainless steel Maytag washer tubs, it is known throughout the country for its rich flavor.*

SEAFOOD TARTLETS

22 thin slices sandwich bread
1/3 cup butter, melted
1 (4 1/2-ounce) can tiny shrimp, drained, rinsed
3/4 cup mayonnaise
1/3 cup each grated Parmesan cheese and shredded Swiss cheese
1/4 teaspoon Worcestershire sauce
1/8 teaspoon hot sauce
Paprika to taste

Roll each bread slice 1/4 inch thick and cut with a 2 1/2-inch round or daisy-shape cutter. Brush both sides with butter and press into miniature tart shells. Bake at 400 degrees for 8 to 10 minutes or until light brown.

Soak the shrimp in ice water in a bowl for 20 minutes; drain well. Mix with the mayonnaise, cheeses, Worcestershire sauce and hot sauce in a bowl.

Spoon the shrimp mixture into the tart shells and sprinkle with paprika. Bake at 400 degrees for 8 to 10 minutes or until bubbly. Garnish with parsley.

Yield: 22 servings

STUFFED PHYLLO CUPS

Walnut oil is a nutty flavored oil pressed from walnut meats and commonly used in salad dressings and sauces. It should be refrigerated.

12 sheets phyllo dough
1/4 cup walnut oil
8 ounces mild goat cheese
4 ounces cream cheese, softened
3 eggs
1/3 cup toasted pine nuts
1/4 cup finely chopped sun-dried tomatoes
6 scallions, finely chopped
Salt and pepper to taste

Cut the phyllo dough into 4-inch squares. Brush each square with the walnut oil and stack 4 squares together for each cup. Press each stack into a miniature muffin cup sprayed with nonstick cooking spray; allow the corners to stand up forming petal points. Cover with plastic wrap and chill for 1 hour or longer.

Mix the goat cheese and cream cheese in a mixing bowl. Add the eggs one at a time and mix well. Add the pine nuts, sun-dried tomatoes, scallions, salt and pepper; mix well. Let the phyllo cups return to room temperature before filling. Spoon the cheese mixture into the cups, filling 3/4 full. Bake at 350 degrees for 12 to 15 minutes or until the phyllo is golden brown and the filling is puffed.

Photograph for this recipe is on page 14 and opposite.

Yield: 36 servings

PHYLLO *(also spelled filo) is tissue-thin layered pastry dough that was developed in Greece. It is available in frozen form and may be stored in the refrigerator for up to one month unopened or for two to three days after opening. Frozen it may keep for one year.*

GRILLED SHRIMP DIJONNAISE

  1 cup dry white wine
  1 cup olive oil
¼ cup fresh lemon juice
  2 tablespoons Dijon mustard
½ cup chopped fresh basil
¼ teaspoon freshly ground pepper
24 jumbo shrimp, peeled, deveined
24 whole basil leaves
24 slices prosciutto

Combine the wine, olive oil, lemon juice, Dijon mustard, chopped basil and pepper in a shallow bowl and mix well. Add the shrimp and mix to coat well. Marinate, covered, in the refrigerator for 3 hours or longer.

Soak wooden skewers in water for 1 hour or longer. Drain the shrimp, reserving the marinade. Wrap each shrimp with a basil leaf and then with a slice of prosciutto. Thread onto the skewers.

Grill the shrimp over hot coals for 2 to 3 minutes on each side or until opaque, basting occasionally with the reserved marinade.

Note: *Deveining is the process of removing the gray-black vein from the back of a shrimp. This can be done with a sharp knife or a tool called a deveiner. On small and medium shrimp, this technique only needs to be done for appearance. However, the intestinal vein of large shrimp contains grit and should be removed.*

Yield: 24 servings

PROSCIUTTO is Italian ham that has been seasoned, salt-cured, and air-dried. It is pressed to a dense texture. Prosciutto cotto is cooked and prosciutto crudo is uncooked, although cured and ready to eat.

CHUTNEY CHEESE SPREAD

   8 ounces cream cheese, softened
   1 cup finely shredded Cheddar cheese, at room temperature
   2 tablespoons sherry
   1 teaspoon curry powder
$1/2$ (9-ounce) bottle chutney
$1/2$ cup chopped green onions with tops

Combine the cream cheese, Cheddar cheese, wine and curry powder in a bowl and mix until smooth. Spread the mixture on a platter. Chill, covered, until serving time.

Spread the chutney over the cheese mixture and sprinkle with the green onions. Serve with crackers.

Yield: 8 servings

CRAB RANGOON SPREAD WITH WON TON CRACKERS

Won Ton Crackers
20 won ton wrappers
  3 to 4 tablespoons butter, melted
  6 tablespoons grated Parmesan cheese

Spread
  8 ounces cream cheese, softened
  2 tablespoons milk
$1/4$ teaspoon garlic powder
  6 ounces crab meat or imitation crab meat, flaked
  1 tablespoon chopped green onions

For the crackers, cut the won ton wrappers diagonally into triangles. Brush with the melted butter and sprinkle with the cheese. Arrange on a buttered baking sheet. Bake at 375 degrees for 5 to 7 minutes or just until light brown. Cool on a wire rack.

For the spread, combine the cream cheese, milk and garlic powder in a bowl and mix until smooth. Add the crab meat and green onions and mix well.

Spoon into a baking dish or microwave-safe dish. Bake at 375 degrees for 10 to 15 minutes or microwave on High for 1 to 4 minutes or until bubbly. Serve warm with the crackers.

Yield: 20 servings

WON TONS *are Chinese bite-size dumplings consisting of paper-thin dough pillows filled with a minced mixture of meat, seafood, and/or vegetables. The dough comes prepackaged as won ton skins. Won tons may be prepared by boiling, steaming, or deep-frying and served as an appetizer, snack, or side dish.*

GUACAMOLE

    3   tablespoons chopped white onion
    1   teaspoon chopped jalapeño pepper
    4   teaspoons chopped cilantro
  $1/2$ teaspoon salt
    1   avocado
    2   tablespoons seeded chopped tomato

Combine 1 tablespoon of the onion, $1/2$ teaspoon of the jalapeño pepper, $1/2$ teaspoon of the cilantro and the salt in a small bowl. Press with the back of a wooden spoon to mash well.

Cut the avocado into halves lengthwise and remove the seed. Slice lengthwise and then crosswise into $1/8$-inch squares and scoop into the bowl with the mashed ingredients.

Add the remaining 2 tablespoons onion, $1/2$ teaspoon jalapeño pepper, $3^{1}/2$ teaspoons cilantro and the tomato and mix well.

    Yield: 2 servings

CREAMY KAHLÚA FRUIT DIP

Kahlúa is a liqueur from Mexico with a smooth coffee flavor.

    8   ounces cream cheese, softened
    1   cup whipped topping
  $3/4$ cup packed brown sugar
    1   cup sour cream
  $1/4$ cup Kahlúa

Combine the cream cheese, whipped topping, brown sugar, sour cream and Kahlúa in a bowl and mix until smooth. Serve with apples, grapes, pineapple, strawberries, bananas or other fresh fruit for dipping.

    Yield: 14 servings

AVOCADOS *are nutty, buttery fruits ranging in color from green to dark purplish black with either a smooth or pebbled skin. Ripe avocados yield to gentle pressure. Unripened fruit will ripen in two to four days in a paper bag. Once ripe, fruit should be refrigerated. Lemon or lime juice will prohibit browning once fruit is peeled, cubed, or mashed.*

Savory Hot Mushroom Dip

    4 slices bacon
    8 ounces fresh mushrooms, sliced
    1 medium onion, finely chopped
    1 garlic clove, minced
    2 tablespoons flour
 $1/4$ teaspoon salt
 $1/8$ teaspoon freshly ground pepper
    8 ounces cream cheese, chopped
    2 teaspoons Worcestershire sauce
    2 teaspoons soy sauce
 $1/2$ cup sour cream

Fry the bacon in a large skillet over medium heat until crisp; remove to a paper towel with a slotted spoon. Drain the skillet, reserving 2 tablespoons of the drippings in the skillet. Crumble the bacon and set aside.

Add the mushrooms, onion and garlic to the drippings in the skillet. Sauté over medium heat for 6 to 8 minutes or until the vegetables are tender and most of the liquid from the mushrooms has evaporated.

Stir in the flour, salt and pepper. Add the cream cheese, Worcestershire sauce and soy sauce and mix well. Cook over low heat until the cream cheese melts, stirring constantly. Remove from the heat and stir in the sour cream and bacon. Serve warm with crackers and breadsticks.

Yield: 12 servings

Reuben Dip

Maytag baby Swiss cheese is a mild Swiss cheese produced in Newton, Iowa.

   16 ounces cream cheese, softened
    8 ounces (1 cup) sour cream
    4 to 6 ounces sauerkraut, drained
   12 to 16 ounces corned beef, cut into small pieces
    6 ounces Maytag baby Swiss cheese, shredded
      Milk

Combine the cream cheese and sour cream in a saucepan and heat until the cream cheese melts, stirring to blend well. Stir in the sauerkraut.

Add the corned beef and Swiss cheese. Cook until the Swiss cheese melts, adding a small amount of milk if needed for the desired consistency, stirring occasionally. Serve warm with party rye or crackers.

Yield: 20 servings

AMANA SAUERKRAUT *is a high-quality product made in a conglomerate of seven scenic small communities in eastern Iowa known as the Amana Colonies. It consists of shredded cabbage that is fermented in a salt or vinegar brine-like mixture.*

Texas Caviar

1 (16-ounce) can white Shoe Peg corn, drained
1 (16-ounce) can black beans, drained
1 (16-ounce) can black-eyed peas, drained
1 green bell pepper, chopped
1 bunch green onions, chopped
3 tomatoes, chopped
1 (8-ounce) bottle Italian salad dressing
1/2 cup nonfat Italian salad dressing

Combine the corn, beans and peas in a bowl. Add the bell pepper, green onions and tomatoes. Add the salad dressings and mix gently. Chill, covered, for 2 hours or longer. Serve with corn chips.

You may use either the regular or nonfat salad dressing or any combination you prefer.

Yield: 12 servings

Tortilla Stacks

16 ounces cream cheese, softened
1/2 cup mayonnaise
1 green bell pepper, finely chopped
3 green onions, finely chopped
2 (2-ounce) packages dried beef, chopped
10 large flour tortillas

Blend the cream cheese and mayonnaise in a bowl. Add the bell pepper, green onions and dried beef and mix well.

Reserve 1 tortilla and spread the cheese mixture on 1 side of each of the remaining tortillas. Stack the tortillas, topping with the reserved tortilla. Chill in the refrigerator. Cut into small squares to serve.

Yield: 10 servings

Flour Tortillas

Cut 1/4 cup chilled shortening into 2 cups flour in a bowl until the mixture resembles fine meal. Add a mixture of 2/3 cup warm water and 1 teaspoon salt and toss to mix well. Knead on a lightly floured surface for 2 to 3 minutes or until smooth. Shape into 12 balls and let rest, covered with plastic wrap, for 30 to 60 minutes. Shape each ball into a 7-inch circle on a lightly floured surface. Bake on a heated griddle for 1 to 1 1/2 minutes or until puffed and golden brown, turning once. Stack heated tortillas and cover with a towel. Serve immediately or store in a sealable plastic bag in the refrigerator for up to 24 hours. You may make four 10-inch tortillas if preferred.

ROASTED RED PEPPER DIP

   6 ounces roasted red bell peppers
   6 to 8 ounces jalapeño peppers, chopped
   1 cup sour cream
   1 cup mayonnaise
   1 tablespoon fresh lemon juice
  $^1\!/_8$ teaspoon sugar
  $^1\!/_2$ teaspoon garlic salt

Purée the bell peppers in a food processor or blender. Combine the purée with the jalapeño peppers, sour cream, mayonnaise, lemon juice, sugar and garlic salt in a bowl and mix well. Chill, covered, for 8 to 12 hours. Serve with vegetables or chips for dipping.

     Note: *To roast bell peppers, cut the peppers into halves, discarding the seeds and membranes. Rinse the peppers and pat dry. Place cut side down on a baking sheet or grill. Roast at 400 degrees until the skin is puffed and brown or grill until charred. Place in a paper bag and seal; let stand for 10 to 15 minutes. Remove and discard the skin.*

     Yield: 8 servings

HOT SPINACH DIP

   2 (4-ounce) cans chopped green chiles
   1 small onion, chopped
   3 Roma tomatoes, chopped, seeded
   1 (10-ounce) package frozen chopped spinach, thawed
   1 (4-ounce) can jalapeño peppers, chopped
   1 tablespoon red wine vinegar
   8 ounces cream cheese, chopped
   2 cups shredded Monterey Jack cheese
   1 cup half-and-half
   1 teaspoon Worcestershire sauce

Sauté the green chiles and onion in a nonstick skillet until the onion is translucent. Add the tomatoes. Cook for 2 minutes, stirring constantly.
     Press the spinach to remove the excess moisture. Add to the skillet with the jalapeño peppers, vinegar, cream cheese, Monterey Jack cheese, half-and-half and Worcestershire sauce; mix well.
     Spoon into a buttered 9×13-inch baking dish. Bake at 350 degrees for 20 to 25 minutes or until bubbly. Serve with tortilla chips or toasted French bread rounds.

     Yield: 16 servings

VINEGAR *is a product of bacterial activity that converts liquids that have fermented into a weak acetic acid solution. Vinegars vary greatly, from French wine vinegars to fruit-flavored or white vinegar. Vinegars are used in many marinades and salad dressings. Store in a dark cool place in an airtight container.*

Mexican Spinach Dip

  1   medium onion, chopped
  2   tablespoons vegetable oil
12   ounces fresh tomatoes, chopped
  2 to 4 tablespoons canned drained chopped jalapeño chiles, or to taste
  1   (10-ounce) package frozen chopped spinach, thawed
  2   cups shredded Monterey Jack cheese
  8   ounces cream cheese, cut into 1/2-inch cubes, softened
  1   cup half-and-half
  2   (2-ounce) cans sliced black olives, drained
  1   tablespoon red wine vinegar
     Salt and fresh ground pepper to taste

Sauté the onion in the heated oil in a heavy medium skillet over medium heat for 4 minutes or until tender. Add the tomatoes and jalapeño chiles. Cook for 2 minutes.

Press the spinach to remove the excess moisture. Add to the skillet with the Monterey Jack cheese, cream cheese, half-and-half, olives and vinegar; mix well. Season with salt and pepper.

Spoon into a shallow baking dish. Bake at 400 degrees for 20 to 25 minutes or until the top is brown. Serve with tortilla chips.

You may prepare the dip in advance and chill for up to 2 days before baking; bake for 35 minutes.

Yield: 16 servings

JALAPEÑO CHILES *are dark green chiles with a smooth skin that vary from hot to very hot. They are easily seeded, and the seeds and veins are extremely hot. Available fresh or canned, the chiles are called chipotles when dried.*

Shrimp Dip

    2   (4-ounce) cans shrimp
 1/3   cup ketchup
    8   ounces cream cheese, softened
    1   tablespoon mayonnaise
    1   tablespoon French salad dressing
    2   teaspoons Worcestershire sauce
       Tabasco sauce to taste
1 1/2 teaspoons prepared horseradish sauce
    2 to 3 tablespoons grated onion

Drain, rinse and chop the shrimp. Combine the ketchup, cream cheese, mayonnaise, salad dressing, Worcestershire sauce, Tabasco sauce and horseradish sauce in a bowl and mix well. Stir in the shrimp and onion. Chill, covered, for 2 hours. Serve with chips or crackers.

Yield: 12 servings

SHRIMP *are sold according to size (number per pound). Generally, shrimp fall in the following size categories:*

Colossal—
    10 or fewer per pound

Jumbo—
    11 to 15 per pound

Extra-large—
    16 to 20 per pound

Large—
    21 to 30 per pound

Medium—
    31 to 35 per pound

Small—
    36 to 45 per pound

Miniature or baby—
    about 100 per pound

In general, 1 pound of shrimp yields 1/2 to 3/4 pound of cooked shrimp.

SHRIMP MOLD

16 ounces cream cheese, softened
1/4 cup mayonnaise
 2 teaspoons Worcestershire sauce
1/4 teaspoon Tabasco sauce
1/2 teaspoon lemon juice
1/2 cup finely chopped onion
 3 green onions, finely chopped
 1 tablespoon parsley flakes
 1 teaspoon curry powder
    Salt and pepper to taste
 1 pound miniature shrimp, cooked and peeled, or
        2 (4-ounce) cans shrimp

Blend the cream cheese and mayonnaise in a bowl. Add the Worcestershire sauce, Tabasco sauce, lemon juice, onion, green onions, parsley flakes, curry powder, salt and pepper and mix well. Add the shrimp and mix gently.

Spoon the mixture into an oiled ring mold. Chill, covered, for 8 to 12 hours. Unmold onto a bed of lettuce on a serving tray. Serve with crackers.

Yield: 16 servings

GRASSHOPPERS BY THE GALLON

 1 gallon vanilla ice cream
 8 ounces whipped topping
 1 cup crème de menthe
 1 cup crème de cacao

Soften the ice cream in a large bowl. Add the whipped topping, crème de menthe and crème de cacao and mix well. Spoon into a freezer container and store in the freezer. Serve in goblets.

You may add green food coloring to ice cream mixture to give dish desired shade of green.

Yield: 16 servings

RASPBERRY CHAMPAGNE APERITIF

Cassis is used in making crème de cassis and black currant syrup. It is produced from the European black currant.

> 1/4 cup frozen unsweetened whole raspberries, thawed
> 2 tablespoons Grand Marnier or other orange liqueur
> 2 teaspoons cassis
> 3/4 cup Champagne, chilled

Combine the raspberries, orange liqueur and cassis in a blender container and process until smooth. Strain the mixture into a small bowl. Fill 2 Champagne flutes half full with the raspberry mixture. Fill with Champagne; mix gently.

Yield: 2 servings

PLAIN GLASSWARE *can be given a new look. Mix the white of one egg with two tablespoons of water. Apply the mixture on the exterior of the glassware with a paintbrush in a decorative manner and dust with ultrafine sugar. Allow to dry completely before use.*

GRENADINE *is a red sweet syrup that is used to flavor beverages or desserts. It is made from pomegranates or other fruit juices. Users beware, as it may contain alcohol. Read the label.*

CANDLEHOLDERS *can be made from limes or other appropriate fruits or vegetables. Cut off the tops of the limes, shave off the bottoms so they stand straight, and hollow them out. Break used candles into a double boiler, reserving the wicks. Heat the candles over medium heat until melted. Secure the reserved wick with a small amount of hot wax, then while holding the wick erect totally fill the fruit with hot wax. Cool. Trim the wick.*

SUNRISE MIMOSA

1 fifth Champagne, chilled
14 ounces orange juice, chilled
14 ounces pineapple juice, chilled
   Grenadine

Combine the Champagne, orange juice and pineapple juice in a pitcher and mix gently. Pour into Champagne flutes. Pour a small amount of grenadine down the side of each filled glass.

Yield: 8 servings

MARGARITAS SUPREME

4 lime wedges
   Salt to taste
1 (6-ounce) can frozen limeade concentrate, thawed
6 ounces tequila
6 ounces Triple Sec
   Crushed ice

Coat the rims of 4 glasses by rubbing the rims with the lime wedges and rotating in salt in a saucer.

Combine the limeade concentrate, tequila and Triple Sec in a blender container and process until smooth. Add enough crushed ice to fill the blender container 3/4 full and process until slushy. Pour into the prepared glasses. Garnish with lime slices.

Yield: 4 servings

CELEBRATION PUNCH

1 (10-ounce) package frozen mixed fruit, thawed
2 quarts ginger ale, chilled
1 cup Southern Comfort
3 fifths Champagne, chilled

Combine the thawed fruit, ginger ale, Southern Comfort and Champagne in a punch bowl and mix gently. Serve immediately in punch cups.

Yield: 30 servings

HOLIDAY PUNCH

2 (16-ounce) cans jellied cranberry sauce
1 cup lemon juice
¼ cup almond extract
1 quart white wine
1 quart ginger ale, chilled

Combine the cranberry sauce, lemon juice and almond extract in a blender container and process until smooth. Add the wine and mix gently. Pour over ice in a punch bowl. Add the ginger ale at serving time and mix gently.

Yield: 30 servings

CHAMPAGNE PUNCH

1½ cups sugar
1 cup strong black tea
1½ cups orange juice
Thinly sliced zest of 2 lemons
½ cup lemon juice
1 cup light or dark rum
1 fifth Champagne, chilled

Dissolve the sugar in the tea in a pitcher. Add the orange juice, lemon zest, lemon juice and rum. Chill, covered, in the refrigerator. Pour rum mixture and Champagne over ice in a punch bowl at serving time. Garnish with fresh orange slices and mint sprigs.

Yield: 16 servings

POINSETTIA PUNCH

3 cups Champagne, chilled
3 cups cranberry juice cocktail, chilled
½ cup Grand Marnier

Combine the Champagne, cranberry juice cocktail and Grand Marnier in a 2-quart pitcher and mix gently. Pour into Champagne flutes. Garnish with fresh cranberries for a holiday touch, or with orange slices for other festive occasions.

Yield: 8 servings

COLORED SUGAR *can be made by placing granulated sugar in a sealable plastic bag; add a few drops of food coloring and shake to blend. Pour onto a plate and let dry. Use as a decorative embellishment.*

Timing Is Everything...

BREADS BREAKFAST & BRUNCH

This photograph is sponsored by:
Junean Witham

Timing Is Everything...

It's finally here—the dinner, brunch, or dining event that you've been planning for weeks. The house is ready, food well under way, and attire prepared. So now what? Let's walk through every step of the event from the arrival of your first guest until the last person leaves.

Start at the front door. It should look warm and welcoming. Once inside, check the closet area for adequate space and hangers for the coats of your guests.

Next, inspect the powder room. Check for tissues, soap, towels, and toilet tissue, and make certain it is clean. Flowers or scented candles are a nice touch that tells your guests that you want them to feel special.

Now on to the living room. It should be comfortable, clean, softly lit, and inviting. If beverages or food will be served in this space, there should be coasters to protect your table surface and space available for appetizers (if they are to be served outside the dining room).

The dining room is the ultimate destination. Check the table settings to make sure they are complete. The room should be picture perfect, yet comfortable and enticing for your guests. If you are using candles, make sure they are dripless and that matches or a lighter are accessible. The music should be loud enough to hear, but soft enough to talk over. The lighting should be indirect but substantial enough to see. Flowers should be inspected for wilting and water. Place cards should be in place, as should party favors.

Finally, the kitchen. All food should be prepared or, at the least, ready to place in the oven. Serving dishes and utensils should be set out, as well as beverage glasses, barware, and garnishes. It is also a great idea to have any last-minute ingredients for final recipes premeasured in small sauce bowls for quick preparation. Lastly, be prepared for accidental spills.

BUTTERSCOTCH PECAN ROLLS

Dough

- 1/2 envelope (1 1/8 teaspoons) dry yeast
- 1 1/2 teaspoons sugar
- 1/2 cup warm water
- 1/4 cup shortening, melted
- 1/2 cup sugar
- 3/4 teaspoon salt
- 1 cup warm water
- 1 egg, beaten
- 4 to 5 cups bread flour
- 1/4 cup butter, softened
- 1/2 cup packed brown sugar
- 2 teaspoons cinnamon

Butterscotch Pecan Topping

- 1/4 cup butter
- 3 tablespoons water
- 2 tablespoons white corn syrup
- 12 ounces (2 cups) butterscotch chips
- 1/2 cup chopped pecans

For the dough, dissolve the yeast and 1 1/2 teaspoons sugar in 1/2 cup warm water in a small bowl. Combine the shortening, 1/2 cup sugar, salt and 1 cup warm water in a large mixing bowl. Add the egg and mix well. Stir in the yeast mixture. Add half the flour and mix well.

Knead in enough of the remaining flour to form a soft dough on a floured surface, kneading for 10 minutes. Place in a large greased bowl, turning to coat the surface. Let rise, covered with plastic wrap, for 4 1/2 hours, punching down the dough every hour.

Reserve 1/3 of the dough for Dinner Rolls (this page). Roll the remaining dough into a 12×18-inch rectangle on a floured surface. Spread with 1/4 cup softened butter, leaving 1/2 inch along 1 long edge unbuttered.

Combine the brown sugar and cinnamon in a bowl. Sprinkle over the butter. Roll up the dough from the buttered long edge; press the edges to seal. Cut into 15 slices.

For the topping, combine the butter, water, corn syrup and butterscotch chips in a heavy saucepan. Cook over low heat just until the butter and butterscotch chips melt, stirring to mix well; do not boil. Pour into a buttered 10×15-inch baking pan. Sprinkle with the pecans.

Arrange the sliced dough in the prepared baking pan. Let rise, covered with plastic wrap, for 8 hours. Bake at 350 degrees for 25 to 30 minutes. Cool in the pan for 5 minutes; invert onto a serving plate to serve.

Yield: 15 servings

STICKY BUNS

For a variation on the Butterscotch Pecan Rolls (at left), prepare the dough in the same manner as for the butterscotch rolls. In place of the Butterscotch Pecan Topping, combine 6 tablespoons margarine, 1 cup vanilla ice cream and 1 cup packed brown sugar in a saucepan and cook until the brown sugar dissolves, stirring to blend well. Cool the mixture in the saucepan and pour it into the 10×15-inch baking pan. Proceed as for the Butterscotch Pecan Rolls.

DINNER ROLLS

To prepare the dough reserved from the Butterscotch Pecan Rolls recipe (at left), shape the reserved dough into 15 to 20 dinner rolls and arrange in a buttered 9×13-inch baking pan. Let rise in the same manner and bake at 350 degrees for 20 to 25 minutes or until light golden brown.

ALMOND COFFEE CAKES

ALMOND PASTE *is made of blanched ground almonds, sugar, and glycerin or another liquid. Almond extract is sometimes added to amplify the taste. The paste should be taut but yielding. If it is hard, it can be softened by heating for two or three seconds in a microwave oven. It should be wrapped tightly and refrigerated once opened.*

Coffee Cakes
  1   cup milk
  1/2 cup (1 stick) butter
  1   envelope dry yeast
  3   eggs
  1/2 cup sugar
  1/2 teaspoon salt
4 1/2 cups flour
  1/2 cup (1 stick) butter, softened
 14   to 16 ounces almond paste

Confectioners' Sugar Glaze
  1   tablespoon butter, softened
  1   cup confectioners' sugar
1 1/2 tablespoons milk
  1/4 teaspoon almond extract

For the coffee cakes, scald the milk in a large saucepan. Add 1/2 cup butter and stir until the butter melts. Pour into a bowl and cool to lukewarm. Sprinkle the yeast over the surface and stir to dissolve the yeast.

Beat the eggs lightly in a small bowl. Add the sugar and salt and mix well. Stir into the yeast mixture. Stir in the flour gradually to form a moist but stiff dough. Place in a greased large bowl, turning to coat the surface. Let rise, covered, in a warm place for 1 1/2 hours or until doubled in bulk.

Divide the dough into 2 equal portions. Knead each portion on a floured surface until smooth and elastic. Roll each into a 8×12-inch rectangle and spread each with 1/4 cup softened butter. Crumble the almond paste over the rectangles and roll from the long sides to enclose the filling.

Shape the rolls into rings, overlapping the ends and pressing to seal. Place in 2 greased 8- or 9-inch baking pans. Cut 2/3 of the way through the rings at 1-inch intervals with scissors. Twist each slice partially on its side so the top of each slice overlaps the bottom of another slice slightly.

Let rise, covered, for 35 to 45 minutes or until doubled in bulk. Bake at 350 degrees for 40 minutes or until the tops are golden brown. To bake 1 pan only, bake for 25 to 30 minutes or until the top is golden brown.

For the glaze, blend the butter, confectioners' sugar, milk and almond extract in a small bowl. Spread over the warm coffee cakes.

Note: *Almond extract is a flavoring resulting by consolidating bitter-almond oil with ethyl alcohol. The flavor is very extreme, so the extract should be used cautiously.*

Yield: 24 servings

KOLACHE BREAD

Apricot Filling

    1   pound dried apricots
    ½   cup sugar
         Cinnamon or nutmeg to taste

Dough

    1   envelope (2 teaspoons) dry yeast
    ½   cup sugar
    ¼   cup lukewarm water (may need up to ½ cup water)
    1   cup milk
    ½   cup (1 stick) butter, melted
    ½   teaspoon salt
    2   eggs, beaten
    4   cups (about) flour

Kolache Topping

    ½   cup sugar
    1   cup flour
    3   tablespoons butter, melted
    ½   teaspoon vanilla extract

For the filling, cook the apricots using the package directions. Drain, reserving 1 cup of the cooking liquid. Mash or grind the apricots and combine with the reserved liquid, sugar and cinnamon in a bowl; cool to room temperature.

For the dough, dissolve the yeast with 1 teaspoon of the sugar in the warm water in a bowl. Scald the milk in a saucepan. Pour into a bowl and cool to lukewarm. Stir in the butter, the remaining sugar and salt until dissolved. Add the yeast mixture, eggs and half the flour and beat until smooth. Add the remaining flour gradually, beating for 5 minutes to form a soft dough.

Place in a greased bowl, turning to coat the surface. Let rise, covered, in a warm place for 1 hour or until doubled in bulk. Punch the dough down and let rise again. Punch down and divide into 4 equal portions. Roll each portion into an 8×16-inch rectangle on a floured surface. Spread the filling down the centers of the rectangles and fold the sides over the filling; press the edges to seal.

For the topping, use a pastry blender to combine sugar, flour, butter and vanilla in a bowl and mix well until crumbly. Sprinkle over the loaves.

Place the loaves on 2 greased baking sheets. Let rise for 5 to 10 minutes. Bake at 375 degrees for 20 minutes or until golden brown.

Note: *This dough can be prepared in a bread machine. Let the dough rise a second time in the machine before dividing into 4 portions and proceeding with the recipe. The baked bread can be frozen. You may substitute one-half 12-ounce can of ready-to-use fruit filling for each loaf or use the Pineapple Filling or Poppy Seed Filling (at right) instead of the Apricot Filling.*

Yield: 32 servings

PINEAPPLE FILLING

Combine one 13-ounce can of crushed pineapple with ¼ cup water, ¼ cup sugar and 2 tablespoons corn syrup in a saucepan. Cook over low heat until thickened. Stir in 2 tablespoons butter. Cool to room temperature.

POPPY SEED FILLING

Combine 8 ounces ground poppy seeds and 1 cup water in a saucepan and cook over low heat until thickened. Stir in 1 cup milk and cook for 10 minutes longer, stirring and watching carefully. Stir in 1 tablespoon butter, 1 teaspoon vanilla extract and ½ teaspoon cinnamon. Add 1 cup sugar and cook for 5 minutes longer. Thicken the mixture with a few graham cracker crumbs if needed for the desired consistency.

YEAST *is a living entity that is used as a leavening agent primarily in baked goods. There are three types of yeast used in baking: active dry, compressed fresh, and yeast starters. Yeast requires moisture, food, and heat in order to grow. A liquid provides the moisture and requires a temperature from 105 to 115 degrees. Sugar or starch provides the necessary food, and heat (70 to 85 degrees) will activate its growth. Yeast should be stored in a cool, dark place and may be refrigerated or frozen, but it must be at room temperature before using. Yeast has an expiration date, which should be noted. Yeast requires a test to prove it's still living. Proofing works by dissolving it in warm liquid with a pinch of sugar. If the yeast rises or foams, it's active and good for use. If it doesn't, it should be discarded.*

FRENCH BREAD

1	envelope quick-rising dry yeast
1/4	cup warm water
3/4	cup flour
2	cups warm water
1 1/2	teaspoons salt
5	cups flour

Dissolve the yeast in 1/4 cup warm water in a bowl. Stir in 3/4 cup flour and knead until smooth and elastic. Shape into a ball. Place the ball of dough in 2 cups warm water in a bowl. Let rise, covered, for 15 minutes.

Add the salt and mix well. Add 5 cups flour 1 cup at a time, mixing well after each addition. Knead on a floured surface for 10 minutes. Place in a greased bowl and turn to coat the surface. Let rise, covered, in a warm place for 1 1/2 hours.

Punch the dough down and divide into 3 equal portions. Roll each portion into a rectangle on a floured surface. Roll up the rectangles to form loaves and place on baking sheets. Slash the tops at 1 1/2-inch intervals. Let rise until doubled in bulk.

Bake the loaves at 400 degrees for 30 minutes or until they sound hollow when tapped with a knife.

Yield: 36 servings

STREAMLINED WHITE BREAD

1	envelope (2 1/2 teaspoons) dry yeast
1 1/4	cups warm water
2	tablespoons shortening or margarine
2	tablespoons sugar
2	teaspoons salt
3	cups bread flour

Dissolve the yeast in the warm water in a bowl. Add the shortening, sugar and salt and mix well. Add 2 cups of the flour and mix well. Add the remaining 1 cup flour and beat for 300 strokes to form a sticky dough.

Let rise, covered, in a warm place until doubled in bulk, scraping down the side of the bowl and stirring. Place in a lightly greased loaf pan and smoooth the top with floured hands. Let rise until doubled in bulk. Bake at 375 degrees for 40 to 50 minutes or until golden brown.

Yield: 12 servings

APPLE BREAD

Apple Bread
- 1/2 cup (1 stick) butter or margarine, softened, or butter-flavor shortening
- 1 cup sugar
- 2 eggs
- 2 tablespoons sour milk
- 1 teaspoon vanilla extract
- 2 cups chopped peeled apples
- 2 cups flour
- 1 teaspoon baking soda
- 1 teaspoon salt
- 1 teaspoon cinnamon (optional)
- 1/2 teaspoon nutmeg (optional)
- 1/2 cup chopped nuts

Cinnamon Topping
- 1 1/2 tablespoons margarine, softened
- 2 tablespoons flour
- 1 tablespoon sugar
- 2 tablespoons brown sugar
- 1 teaspoon cinnamon

For the bread, cream the butter and sugar in a mixing bowl until light and fluffy. Beat in the eggs. Add the sour milk and vanilla and mix well. Stir in the apples.

Sift the flour, baking soda, salt, cinnamon and nutmeg together. Add to the apple mixture and mix well. Stir in the nuts. Spoon into a greased loaf pan or a loaf pan lined with greased waxed paper.

For the topping, combine the margarine, flour, sugar, brown sugar and cinnamon in a bowl and mix well. Sprinkle over the bread batter. Bake at 325 degrees for 1 hour. Cool in the pan for several minutes; remove to a wire rack to cool completely. You may glaze the cooled bread with Confectioners' Sugar Glaze (at right) if desired. You may also prepare it in 2 small loaf pans and bake for a shorter time.

Note: *To obtain sour milk add one tablespoon of distilled white vinegar to one cup of regular milk.*

Yield: 12 servings

CONFECTIONERS' SUGAR GLAZE

Combine 1/2 cup confectioners' sugar with 2 tablespoons milk and 1/4 teaspoon vanilla extract in a bowl and mix until smooth. Drizzle over cooled bread.

BANANA NUT BREAD

3½ cups flour
2 teaspoons baking soda
2½ cups sugar
1½ teaspoons each cinnamon and nutmeg
1½ teaspoons salt
1 cup vegetable oil
4 eggs
⅔ cup milk
4 to 6 bananas, mashed
1 cup raisins (optional)
1 cup chopped nuts (optional)

Sift the flour, baking soda, sugar, cinnamon, nutmeg and salt into a mixing bowl. Add the oil, eggs, milk and bananas and mix well. Stir in the raisins and nuts.

Spoon into 2 greased loaf pans. Bake at 350 degrees for 1 hour or until a wooden pick inserted in the center comes out clean. Cool in the pans for several minutes; remove to a wire rack to cool completely.

Yield: 24 servings

CRANBERRY ORANGE BREAD

2 cups flour
1½ teaspoons baking powder
1 teaspoon baking soda
1 cup sugar
½ teaspoon salt
1 egg
½ cup orange juice
Grated zest of 1 orange
2 tablespoons butter, melted
2 tablespoons hot water
1 cup cranberries, chopped
1 cup coarsely chopped walnuts

Mix the flour, baking powder, baking soda, sugar and salt together. Beat the egg in a mixing bowl. Add the orange juice, orange zest, butter and hot water and mix well. Fold in the flour mixture; do not overmix. Fold in the cranberries and walnuts.

Spoon into a greased 5x9-inch loaf pan. Bake at 325 degrees for 1 hour or until the bread tests done. Cool in the pan on a wire rack for 15 minutes; remove to the wire rack to cool completely.

Yield: 12 servings

FOLDING is a method of combining a lighter mixture with a heavier one by placing the lighter of the two on top in a large bowl and mixing the two together. Combine by placing a spatula on the back of the bowl and moving vertically down the center and up the side of the bowl until ingredients are well mixed. Turn the bowl one quarter turn each time.

Fruit Bread

    1/2 cup (1 stick) butter, softened
      1 cup sugar
      2 eggs
      2 cups flour
      1 teaspoon baking soda
      3 bananas, mashed, about 1 cup
    1/4 cup chopped maraschino cherries
    1/4 cup each chocolate chips and chopped nuts

Cream the butter and sugar in a mixing bowl until light and fluffy. Beat in the eggs. Sift the flour and baking soda together. Add to the creamed mixture alternately with the bananas, mixing well after each addition. Stir in the cherries, chocolate chips and nuts.

Spoon into a greased and floured loaf pan. Bake at 350 degrees for 1 hour, covering with foil if necessary to prevent overbrowning. Cool in the pan for several minutes; remove to a wire rack to cool completely.

Yield: 12 servings

Blueberry Muffins

       1 cup sugar
     1/3 cup vegetable shortening
       2 eggs
    1 3/4 cups flour
       2 teaspoons baking powder
     1/2 teaspoon salt
     1/4 teaspoon cinnamon
     2/3 cup milk or buttermilk
   1 1/2 to 1 3/4 cups fresh or frozen blueberries
       2 tablespoons sugar (optional)
     1/4 teaspoon cinnamon (optional)

Cream 1 cup sugar and shortening in a mixing bowl until light and fluffy. Add the eggs one at a time, beating well after each addition. Sift together the flour, baking powder, salt and 1/4 teaspoon cinnamon. Add the flour mixture and milk alternately to the creamed mixture, mixing just until blended. Fold in the blueberries. Do not overmix. Spoon into greased or paper-lined muffin cups, filling 2/3 full. Sprinkle with a mixture of 2 tablespoons sugar and 1/4 teaspoon cinnamon.

Bake at 400 degrees for 20 to 25 minutes or until golden brown. Remove from the pan immediately.

Yield: 18 servings

SIFTING *inserts air into dry ingredients by passing the dry ingredients through a sifter (a mesh utility), making the dry ingredients lighter.*

HONEY-GLAZED BRAN MUFFINS

Muffins
- 1 cup buttermilk
- 1 cup Bran Buds
- 1 cup flour
- 1 teaspoon baking powder
- 1 teaspoon baking soda
- 1 teaspoon cinnamon
- 1/2 teaspoon salt
- 1/3 cup butter, softened
- 1/2 cup packed brown sugar
- 1 egg
- 1/4 cup molasses
- 1/2 cup raisins
- 1/3 cup chopped dates

Honey Glaze
- 3/4 cup honey
- 1/3 cup corn syrup
- 1 tablespoon butter

For the muffins, pour the buttermilk over the cereal in a large mixing bowl and let stand for several minutes. Add the flour, baking powder, baking soda, cinnamon and salt and mix well.

Cream the butter and brown sugar in a medium mixing bowl until light and fluffy. Add to the cereal mixture and mix well. Add the egg, molasses, raisins and dates and mix well.

Spoon into nonstick muffin cups. Bake at 400 degrees for 20 to 25 minutes or until golden brown. Remove to a wire rack to cool slightly.

For the glaze, combine the honey, corn syrup and butter in a saucepan. Bring to a boil and reduce the heat. Simmer for 5 minutes. Spoon over the warm muffins.

Yield: 12 servings

BOUNTIFUL BREAKFAST MUFFINS

    2 cups flour
1 1/4 cups sugar
    2 teaspoons baking soda
    1 tablespoon cinnamon
  1/2 teaspoon salt
  1/2 cup each shredded coconut and raisins
    2 cups grated carrots
    1 Granny Smith apple, grated
    1 (8-ounce) can crushed pineapple, drained
  1/2 cup chopped pecans or walnuts
    3 eggs
    1 cup vegetable oil
    1 teaspoon vanilla extract

Sift the flour, sugar, baking soda, cinnamon and salt into a large bowl. Stir in the coconut, raisins, carrots, apple, pineapple and pecans.

Combine the eggs, oil and vanilla in a small bowl and mix well. Add to the fruit mixture and mix just until moistened. Spoon into greased muffin cups. Bake at 350 degrees for 25 to 30 minutes or until golden brown.

Yield: 12 servings

RHUBARB MUFFINS

1 1/2 cups flour
  3/4 cup packed brown sugar
  1/2 teaspoon each baking soda and salt
  1/3 cup vegetable oil
    1 egg, lightly beaten
  1/2 cup buttermilk
    1 teaspoon vanilla extract
    1 cup chopped fresh or thawed frozen rhubarb
  1/4 cup packed brown sugar
  1/2 teaspoon cinnamon

Mix the flour, 3/4 cup brown sugar, baking soda and salt in a large bowl. Combine the oil, egg, buttermilk and vanilla in a medium bowl and beat until smooth. Add to the dry ingredients and mix just until moistened. Fold in the rhubarb. Spoon into greased or paper-lined muffin cups.

Mix 1/4 cup brown sugar and cinnamon in a small bowl. Sprinkle over the muffin batter. Bake at 375 degrees for 20 minutes or until the muffins test done. Cool in the pan for 10 minutes; remove to a wire rack to cool completely.

You may add 1/4 to 1/2 cup chopped walnuts to the batter and 1/4 cup chopped walnuts to the topping if desired.

Yield: 10 servings

HANDLING BREAD *gracefully is an indicator of a well-educated diner. Break slices of bread, rolls, and muffins in half or in small pieces before eating and/or buttering them. Small muffins or biscuits do not have to be broken. Use your own butter knife and the butter on your plate. Butter bread on the plate or just above it. Place the butter knife somewhat to the right with the handle off the edge to keep it clean.*

GLAZED FRENCH TOAST

½ cup (1 stick) butter
1 cup packed brown sugar
1 teaspoon cinnamon
1 loaf French bread
5 eggs
1½ cups milk
¼ teaspoon salt

Melt the butter in a 9×13-inch baking pan. Add the brown sugar and cinnamon and mix well. Cut the French bread into double-thick slices. Arrange the slices in the prepared baking pan.

Combine the eggs, milk and salt in a bowl and mix well. Pour over the bread. Chill, covered, for 8 to 12 hours.

Bake, uncovered, at 350 degrees for 45 minutes. Cool for 5 minutes before serving. You may add pecans or walnuts with the brown sugar and cinnamon if desired.

Yield: 6 servings

CLASSIC BUTTERMILK PANCAKES

2 cups sifted flour
4 teaspoons sugar
1½ teaspoons baking powder
½ teaspoon salt
4 egg yolks, beaten
2½ cups buttermilk
1 teaspoon baking soda
¼ cup (½ stick) butter, softened
4 egg whites, stiffly beaten

Sift the flour, sugar, baking powder and salt together. Combine the egg yolks, buttermilk and baking soda in a bowl and beat with a rotary beater to mix well. Add the dry ingredients and butter and mix well. Fold in the stiffly beaten egg whites.

Ladle by spoonfuls onto a lightly greased heated griddle and cook until light brown on both sides.

Yield: 4 servings

ROTARY BEATERS *are manual kitchen utensils with two beaters connected to a gear-driven wheel with a handle, all of which is attached to a housing topped with a grip. Two hands are necessary for operation—one to hold the handle, the other to turn the wheel. As the wheel turns, the beaters rotate, providing aeration that can whip cream, eggs, or batters.*

DUTCH BABIES BAKED PANCAKE

  1 tablespoon unsalted butter
  1 egg
  ¹/₄ cup low-fat milk
  ¹/₄ cup flour
  ¹/₈ teaspoon baking powder
  ¹/₂ teaspoon grated lemon zest
  ¹/₄ teaspoon almond extract
    Sliced fruit, such as strawberries, apples or peaches
    Confectioners' sugar

Place the butter in a 4-inch individual ramekin or round baking dish and melt in the oven. Whisk the egg in a mixing bowl until light yellow and fluffy. Add the milk gradually, whisking constantly. Add the flour and baking powder and mix well. Stir in the lemon zest and almond extract.

  Spoon the batter into the heated butter in the ramekin. Bake at 475 degrees for 10 to 12 minutes or until puffed and golden brown. Remove to a serving dish and spoon the fruit into the center. Sprinkle with confectioners' sugar and serve with syrup. Garnish the plate with additional fruit.

  You may microwave ¹/₄ chopped peeled Jonathan apple, or other comparable apple, on High for 1 minute and spoon the apple and 1 tablespoon chopped pecans into the center of the batter before baking. You may also increase the recipe and prepare several Dutch Babies at once.

  Yield: 1 serving

RAMEKINS are 3- to 4-inch dishes used for baked or chilled dishes. Ramekins are generally made from earthenware or porcelain and look like small soufflé dishes.

ORANGE BUTTER

Beat ¹/₂ cup softened unsalted butter in a mixing bowl until smooth. Add 1 to 2 tablespoons confectioners' sugar, 2 teaspoons orange juice and the grated zest of 1 orange and mix well. Spoon into a serving bowl, shape into a log, and wrap in waxed paper or press ¹/₄ inch thick on waxed paper. Chill until firm; serve from the bowl, slice, or cut with a shaped cutter.

CREPES ICELAND

Mustard Sauce
- ¹/₂ cup (1 stick) butter, melted
- 2 cups milk
- ¹/₂ cup flour
- 1 cup chicken broth
- 1 teaspoon Dijon mustard
- 1 teaspoon French mustard
- ¹/₈ teaspoon cayenne pepper
- ¹/₂ teaspoon salt

Crepes
- 3 eggs
- 1 cup milk
- 1 cup flour
- ¹/₄ teaspoon salt
- Butter

Filling
- 3 cups cooked rice
- 1¹/₂ cups cottage cheese
- ³/₄ of the total Mustard Sauce
- 20 thin slices boiled ham
- 20 thin slices Swiss cheese

For the mustard sauce, combine the butter, milk, flour, chicken broth, Dijon mustard, French mustard, cayenne pepper and salt in a mixing bowl and mix until smooth.

For the crepes, combine the eggs, milk, flour and salt in a mixing bowl and mix until smooth. Melt ¹/₄ teaspoon butter at a time in a crepe pan. Spoon 2 tablespoons of the crepe batter into the pan at a time and tilt the pan to coat evenly. Cook each crepe until golden brown on both sides. Remove the crepes to a plate.

To fill the crepes, combine the rice and cottage cheese in a bowl and mix well. Add ¹/₂ to ³/₄ of the mustard sauce to the rice mixture. Layer 1 slice of ham and 1 slice of cheese on each crepe. Spread about ¹/₄ cup of the rice mixture over each layer. Roll or fold the crepes to enclose the filling. Arrange seam side down in a 9×12-inch microwave-safe dish.

To serve, pour the remaining mustard sauce over the crepes and microwave on High for 80 seconds.

You may prepare the crepes in advance and store in the refrigerator or freezer. Bake at 350 degrees for 35 minutes to serve.

Note: *Crepes may be made ahead and layered with waxed paper and refrigerated for up to one week or frozen for up to one month.*

Yield: 20 crepes

CREPES SYLVIA

Crepes
- 4 eggs
- 1 cup sifted flour
- 1 cup milk
- 2 tablespoons orange juice
- Grated zest of 1 orange
- 2 tablespoons butter, melted
- 1 tablespoon sugar
- 1/2 teaspoon salt

Orange Cream Cheese Filling
- 16 ounces cream cheese, softened
- 3 tablespoons sugar
- 3 tablespoons heavy cream
- Grated zest of 1 orange

Brandied Strawberry Sauce
- 1/2 cup (1 stick) butter
- 1/2 cup sugar
- Juice of 1 orange and 1/2 lemon
- 1/4 cup each brandy, orange liqueur and pear or peach brandy
- 1 pint strawberries, mashed
- 1 pint strawberries, cut into halves

For the crepes, combine the eggs, flour, milk, orange juice, orange zest, butter, sugar and salt in a blender container and process until smooth. Chill, covered, for 1 hour or longer.

Heat a 7- or 8-inch crepe pan and brush with butter. Spoon 2 to 3 table-spoons of the crepe batter into the pan for each crepe and tilt the pan to cover evenly. Cook over medium heat for 1 to 2 minutes or until golden brown. Stack the crepes on a plate or towel.

For the filling, combine the cream cheese, sugar, cream and orange zest in a bowl and mix well. Spoon about 1 tablespoon of the cream cheese mixture on 1 side of 16 of the crepes, reserving any remaining crepes for another use. Roll or fold the crepes blintz-style to enclose the filling. Arrange on a platter and chill, covered, for 1 hour or longer.

For the sauce, melt the butter in a large sauté pan. Blend in the sugar, orange juice, lemon juice, brandy, orange liqueur and pear brandy. Add the mashed strawberries and cook until bubbly. Stir in the strawberry halves.

To serve, add the crepes to the sauce. Cook just until the crepes are heated through, spooning the sauce over the tops; do not overcook. Arrange 2 crepes on each serving plate and top with the sauce.

Yield: 8 servings

FLAVORED BUTTERS *can be prepared using 1/2 cup softened unsalted butter. Prepare as for Orange Butter (page 56).*

For Cinnamon Butter, add 1 to 2 tablespoons confectioners' sugar and 1/2 teaspoon ground cinnamon.

For Honey Butter, add 1/4 cup honey.

For Maple Butter, add 1/4 cup maple syrup.

For Almond Butter, add 1/4 cup finely ground almonds.

For Savory Butter, add the herb of choice and season with salt and pepper.

$\mathcal{I}$OWA—It is spring. A time of rebirth. A time of awakening. How appropriate that the word Iowa comes from an Indian word meaning "beautiful land." We are a people who occupy land that transitions as does the great circle of life. We are witness to that circle every year, from season to season.

The land is abundant, fertile, and full. It is renewed each spring with lush beauty. The aromas that fill the dampened air vary from the pungent odor of rich black soil to the sweet fragrance of blossoms and flowering trees.

Spring replenishes the energy that is Iowa. A strong work ethic is obvious as it becomes a time for reworking the land. It is with great appreciation and admiration that we rejoice in the generous and abounding sense of hope that flows forth each year as the earth stirs.

The people that are Iowa are hardworking people who value faith and family. They are known to nurture the cyclical fiber that incorporates the vastness of nature with the necessity of agriculture. As stewards of the land, they place great importance on conservation, ecology, and the enduring quality of respect.

Photograph by:
David Cavagnaro

LAYERED MUSHROOM CREPES

Crepes

    1 egg
  $1/3$ cup milk
  $1/3$ cup flour
  $1/8$ teaspoon salt
      Butter

Filling

    8 ounces cream cheese, softened
    3 tablespoons chopped parsley
      Minced garlic to taste
  $1/4$ teaspoon pepper
    3 cups sliced button or shiitake mushrooms
  $1/2$ cup chopped onion
    2 tablespoons butter
    4 ounces thinly sliced prosciutto, chopped

For the crepes, combine the egg, milk, flour and salt in a mixing bowl and beat until well blended. Heat a 7- or 8-inch crepe pan and brush with butter. Spoon 2 to 3 tablespoons of the crepe batter into the pan for each crepe and tilt the pan to cover evenly. Cook over medium heat for 1 to 2 minutes or until golden brown. Stack the crepes on a plate or towel.

For the filling, combine the cream cheese, parsley, garlic and pepper in a bowl and mix well; set aside. Sauté the mushrooms and onion in the heated butter in a large skillet over medium-high heat until the vegetables are tender and most of the liquid has evaporated. Remove from the heat and stir in the prosciutto.

Layer the crepes in a 9-inch pie plate or baking dish, spreading each crepe with $1/5$ of the cream cheese mixture and $1/5$ of the mushroom mixture.

Bake, loosely covered with foil, at 350 degrees for 20 minutes or until heated through. Cut into wedges to serve.

Yield: 8 servings

EGG COOKERY *can take several forms. Eggs can be scrambled, fried, poached, baked, or boiled. They can be used in omelets, soufflés, meringues, crepes, and fu yung.*

QUICHE RANCHERO

    1   recipe (2-crust) pie pastry, or 2 refrigerator pie pastries
    2   cups shredded Cheddar, Colby-Jack or Monterey Jack cheese
    1   cup chopped onion
    1   tablespoon margarine or butter
    1   cup chopped tomato
    1   (4-ounce) can chopped green chiles, drained
  1/4   teaspoon each cumin, garlic powder and red pepper
    3   eggs
    3   tablespoons half-and-half

Line a glass pie plate with 1 of the pie pastries and sprinkle with half the cheese. Sauté the onion in the margarine in a skillet until tender. Add the tomato, green chiles, cumin, garlic powder and red pepper and mix well. Cook over low heat for 5 minutes. Spread over the cheese in the prepared pie plate and top with the remaining cheese.

Beat the eggs with the half-and-half in a mixing bowl. Reserve 1 tablespoon of the mixture and pour the remaining mixture over the layers. Top with the remaining pastry. Flute and trim the edge and cut vents; brush with the reserved egg mixture. Bake at 375 degrees for 50 minutes, covering the edge with foil after 15 minutes. Garnish with salsa, chopped tomatoes, jalapeño peppers and/or green onions.

Yield: 8 servings

SPINACH AND ASIAGO FRITTATA

    1   leek, thinly sliced
    2   garlic cloves, minced
    2   tablespoons olive oil or vegetable oil
    4   cups torn fresh spinach
    1   yellow or red bell pepper, cut into strips
 1 1/2 teaspoons chopped fresh thyme, or 1/4 teaspoon crushed dried thyme
  1/4   teaspoon salt
  1/8   teaspoon freshly ground pepper
  3/4   cup shredded asiago cheese
    6   eggs, lightly beaten

Sauté the leek and garlic in the heated olive oil in an ovenproof 10-inch skillet over medium heat for 2 minutes or until tender. Add the spinach and sauté for 1 minute or until the spinach wilts. Remove from the heat and stir in the bell pepper, thyme, salt, pepper and 1/2 cup of the cheese. Mix in the eggs.

Bake at 350 degrees for 13 to 15 minutes or until a knife inserted near the center comes out clean. Loosen the frittata from the pan with a flexible spatula and remove carefully to a plate. Sprinkle with 1/4 cup cheese. Cut into wedges.

Yield: 6 brunch servings or 12 appetizer servings

UNUSED EGGS *should be kept in a covered container as they will lose moisture. Because the shells are porous, they may absorb odors. Yolks keep best if covered in water, and whites are best kept in a tightly covered container.*

SAUSAGE AND EGG STRATA

- 10 slices white bread
- 1/4 cup (1/2 stick) butter, softened
- 1 pound pork sausage
- 1 (8-ounce) can sliced mushrooms, drained
- 1 medium onion, finely chopped
- 1/2 each green and red bell pepper, finely chopped
- 12 extra-large eggs
- 1 cup milk
- 1 teaspoon dry mustard
  Salt and pepper to taste
- 3 cups shredded sharp Cheddar cheese

Spray a 9×13-inch baking dish with nonstick cooking spray. Remove the crusts from the bread slices and spread 1 side of the bread with the butter. Arrange butter side down in the prepared baking dish.

Brown the sausage in a skillet, stirring until crumbly; drain. Sprinkle the sausage, mushrooms, onion and bell peppers evenly over the bread.

Beat the eggs in a bowl. Add the milk, dry mustard, salt and pepper and mix well. Pour over the layers and sprinkle with the cheese. Chill, covered, for 8 to 12 hours. Bake, uncovered, at 300 degrees for 1 hour. Serve hot.

Yield: 12 servings

ITALIAN ZUCCHINI CRESCENT PIE

- 4 cups thinly sliced zucchini
- 1 cup chopped onion
- 1/3 to 1/2 cup margarine or butter
- 1/2 cup chopped parsley, or 2 tablespoons parsley flakes
- 1/4 teaspoon each garlic powder, basil and oregano leaves
- 1/2 teaspoon each salt and pepper
- 2 eggs, beaten
- 2 cups shredded mozzarella cheese
- 1 (8-count) can refrigerator crescent rolls
- 2 teaspoons mustard

Sauté the zucchini and onion in the margarine in a large skillet for 10 minutes. Add the next 6 ingredients and mix well. Mix the eggs and cheese in a bowl. Stir in the zucchini mixture. Separate the crescent rolls into triangles and arrange in an ungreased 10-inch pie plate; press the edges to seal. Spread with the mustard. Spoon the vegetable mixture into the prepared pie plate.

Bake at 375 degrees for 18 to 20 minutes or until the center is set, covering with foil during the last 10 minutes of baking time if necessary to prevent overbrowning. Let stand for 10 minutes before serving.

Yield: 6 servings

APPLE LEMON CRESCENT BRAID

  1 (8-count) can refrigerator crescent rolls
  2 tablespoons sugar
  2 tablespoons sweetened lemonade drink mix
  3 tablespoons flour
1½ cups finely chopped peeled apples
  ¼ cup currants
  ¼ teaspoon grated lemon zest
  ½ cup confectioners' sugar
  1 to 2 tablespoons water

Unroll the crescent roll dough into 2 rectangles. Arrange the rectangles on an ungreased baking sheet with long sides overlapping to form an 8×14-inch rectangle; press the perforations and edges to seal.

Combine the sugar, drink mix and flour in a medium bowl. Add the apples, currants and lemon zest and mix well. Spread in a 2-inch strip lengthwise down the center of the dough.

Cut strips at 1-inch intervals, cutting from the long edges of the rectangles to the filling. Fold the strips over the filling, alternating the sides to create a braided look and overlapping the ends slightly; fold the ends under to seal.

Bake at 350 degrees for 20 to 25 minutes or until the braid is golden brown and the apples are tender. Remove to a wire rack and drizzle with a mixture of the confectioners' sugar and water while warm. Cool and slice to serve.

Yield: 8 servings

FRUIT COMPOTE

  ½ cup each orange marmalade and apricot jam
  4 teaspoons grated lemon zest
  ½ cup fresh lemon juice
2¼ cups packed brown sugar
  1 (16-ounce) can each cling peaches, pineapple chunks and pears
    Maraschino cherries
  1 cup wine
  ¼ cup brandy

Combine the orange marmalade, apricot jam, lemon zest, lemon juice and brown sugar in a saucepan and mix well. Simmer until blended, stirring constantly. Cool to room temperature.

Drain the peaches, pineapple, pears and cherries on paper towels and combine in a bowl. Add the wine to the cooled sauce and pour over the fruit and mix gently.

Add the brandy just before serving and ignite to serve flambé if desired.

Yield: 10 servings

TURNERS, *kitchen utensils made of stainless steel or nylon, are used to flip or turn food to enable both sides to cook. They come in many assortments for varying purposes. Slots allow liquid to pass through, and different shapes provide each form a unique purpose.*

SPATULAS *are kitchen utensils that are rather flat and may be constructed from wood, plastic, metal, or rubber. Spatulas vary in shapes and sizes. They may be used to scrape, fold, stir, or spread mixtures.*

RASPBERRY CREAM CHEESE COFFEE CAKE

CREAM CHEESE,
developed in 1872, has a
smooth, creamy texture. It is
a mildly tangy, spreadable
cheese. This unripened cheese
is produced from cow's milk,
and law dictates that it must
contain at least 33 percent
milk fat and not more than
55 percent moisture. Gum
Arabic is incorporated into
some cream cheese to increase
firmness and extend shelf life.
Tightly wrap cheese and
refrigerate to store.

2¼ cups flour
¾ cup sugar
¾ cup (1½ sticks) butter or margarine
½ teaspoon baking powder
½ teaspoon baking soda
½ teaspoon salt
¾ cup sour cream
1 egg, beaten
1½ teaspoons almond extract
8 ounces cream cheese, softened
½ cup sugar
1 egg
½ cup raspberry jam or other fruit jam
½ cup slivered almonds

Mix the flour and ¾ cup sugar in a large mixing bowl. Cut in the butter until crumbly. Reserve 1 cup of the crumbs for the topping.

Add the baking powder, baking soda, salt, sour cream, 1 egg and almond extract to the remaining crumb mixture and mix well with a fork to form a sticky dough. Press the mixture over the bottom and 2 inches up the side of a 9- or 10-inch springform pan sprayed with nonstick cooking spray.

Beat the cream cheese with ½ cup sugar and 1 egg in a small mixing bowl. Spread in the prepared springform pan. Dollop the raspberry jam over the cream cheese mixture and sprinkle with the almonds and reserved crumbs.

Bake at 350 degrees for 55 to 60 minutes or until the edges are golden brown. Cut into wedges to serve. Garnish with raspberries.

Yield: 16 servings

Apricot Orange Conserve

$3^{1}/_{2}$ cups chopped fresh apricots, drained canned apricots or
    cooked dried apricots
$1^{1}/_{2}$ cups orange juice
   2 tablespoons lemon juice
$3^{1}/_{2}$ cups sugar
   $^{1}/_{2}$ cup chopped pecans

Mix the apricots, orange juice, lemon juice and sugar in a large saucepan.
Cook for 35 minutes over medium heat or until thickened to the desired
consistency, stirring constantly and adding the pecans during the last 5 minutes.
    Remove from the heat and skim off the foam. Spoon into 5 to 6 hot
sterilized pint jars, leaving $^{1}/_{4}$ inch headspace; seal with 2-piece lids. Serve on
toasted bread or over ice cream. Store opened jars in the refrigerator.

    Yield: 96 (2-tablespoon) servings

Brunch Trifle

   1 pound cake
   1 (12-ounce) jar raspberry jam
   6 to 7 tablespoons white grape juice
   3 tablespoons sherry
   1 pint each fresh strawberries or a combination of strawberries,
       banana and kiwifruit, and fresh raspberries
   3 fresh peaches, peeled, sliced
   2 cups milk
   2 tablespoons confectioners' sugar
   4 egg yolks, beaten
   2 cups whipping cream
   3 to 4 tablespoons sugar
   1 teaspoon vanilla extract
   3 to 4 ounces sliced almonds, toasted

Cut the pound cake into halves horizontally. Spread the bottom half with the
raspberry jam and replace the top half. Cut the cake into small squares and
arrange in a trifle bowl. Sprinkle with the white grape juice and sherry.
    Reserve a few strawberries, raspberries and peach slices for the top and
spread the remaining fruit over the cake. Simmer the milk and confectioners'
sugar in a saucepan, stirring constantly. Stir a small amount of the milk into the
egg yolks; stir the egg yolks into the hot milk. Cook over medium heat until the
mixture coats the back of the spoon; do not boil. Pour over the fruit and cake.
Chill. Whip the cream with the sugar and vanilla in a mixing bowl until soft
peaks form. Spoon over the trifle. Top with the reserved fruit and almonds.

    Photograph for this recipe is on page 42.

    Yield: 12 servings

CONSERVES *are spreads
consisting of a mixture of
fruits, nuts, and sugar cooked
until thickened.*

JAM *is a spread or filling
made by combining fruit,
sugar and pectin to form a
thick, formless mixture.*

JELLY *is a spread or filling
made from fruit juice, sugar,
and pectin. Jelly is clear and
will maintain its consistency
when removed from
its container.*

MARMALADE *is similar to
a preserve with one exception;
marmalade contains fruit rind,
particularly citrus fruit.*

PRESERVES *are spreads
made from cooked fruit
combined with sugar and
pectin. Preserves contain
medium to large chunks
of fruit.*

In the Mood...

SALADS & DRESSINGS

This photograph is sponsored by:
Cathy Gallagher
Mary L. Lichty
Tom and Becky Poe

In the Mood...

The salad course is intended to entice your palate for the meal ahead. It indicates to the diner that the meal is under way and that the courses to follow will be as well-timed as the preparation for the culinary adventure.

By taking a little time to think through your dinner party, you can plan to do many tasks ahead of time so that you can be a relaxed and gracious hostess or host. This also allows you to give your guests that special attention that keeps them coming back for more with great anticipation.

Within a week or two of your gathering, it is time to take your theme and occasion one step further. The menu is perhaps the most pivotal aspect of your dining experience. It is both the foundation and the icing on the cake. Casual events lend themselves to a less formal menu where comfort foods are standard. Celebrations or more formal dining experiences require more tradition and generally more courses. It is well advised to look at the big picture and the meal as a whole, but note that it is far better to do a select few items that are very good rather than a large number of food items that are mediocre.

While you are planning your menu it is a great time to select and purchase your wines and beverages. Remember, you will need a clean glass for each different beverage served. This may require borrowing or renting additional glasses or stemware. All wines and beverages should complement the foods they accompany. Again, less is more. Take the time to know how flavors will blend, and do not hesitate to have your own taste test, particularly for exclusive celebrations.

Another task to consider in advance of your event is a meal preparation schedule. This tool provides you the time to evaluate all aspects of your adventure and to note the primary jobs and details that make planning and executing a vital aspect of success. Anything that can be done in advance greatly lightens the load the day of the event.

Evaluating your seating and serving arrangements is best done in advance. The need for additional tables, chairs, equipment, or serving pieces should be determined. What about tablecloths, napkins, place mats, napkin rings, etc.? And don't forget paper goods or flowers that may be needed.

BLUEBERRY SPINACH SALAD

Dijon Vinaigrette
  2 tablespoons blueberry or white wine vinegar
  1/2 cup vegetable oil
  1 teaspoon Dijon mustard
  2 teaspoons sugar
  Salt to taste

Salad
  1/2 cup pecans
  16 ounces fresh spinach or Bibb lettuce, torn
  1 cup fresh blueberries
  4 ounces bleu cheese, crumbled

For the dressing, combine the vinegar, oil, Dijon mustard, sugar and salt in a bowl and mix well. Chill, covered, in the refrigerator.

For the salad, spread the pecans on a baking sheet. Toast at 300 degrees for 8 to 10 minutes or until golden brown. Let cool. Combine with the spinach, blueberries and bleu cheese in a salad bowl. Add the salad dressing at serving time and toss to coat well. Garnish with fresh raspberries.

Yield: 8 servings

STRAWBERRY AND SPINACH SALAD

  3/4 cup sugar
  1/4 cup white or cider vinegar
  1/4 teaspoon salt
  1 cup vegetable oil, chilled
  1 teaspoon chopped green onions
  2 (10-ounce) packages spinach, torn
  1 pint strawberries, sliced
  1/3 cup sliced or slivered almonds

Combine the sugar, vinegar and salt in a small bowl and whisk until the sugar dissolves. Add the oil and green onions and mix well until thickened.

Combine the spinach, strawberries and almonds in a salad bowl just before serving. Add the desired amount of dressing and toss to coat.

Yield: 10 servings

SALAD GREENS are traditionally eaten with a fork. Greens that are too large should be cut with a knife into manageable pieces. If the salad is served at the same time as the entrée, it should not be placed on your dinner plate. If there is no salad plate, place the salad on your butter plate and position it next to your dinner plate. A roll or bread may be used to ease the salad onto the fork.

Arugula Salad with Pears and Beets

Arugula *is a salad green
with a biting mustard and
pepper taste. It is generally
sold in bunches. Arugula is
quite perishable and needs to
be refrigerated in a tightly
sealed plastic bag. It should be
used within two days. Wash
thoroughly prior to use.*

4 small beets
3 tablespoons raspberry vinegar
6 tablespoons olive oil
   Salt and pepper to taste
3 cups arugula
2 large firm pears, sliced
1/2 cup crumbled bleu cheese
1/4 cup coarsely chopped toasted walnuts (see sidebar, page 71)

Combine the beets with 1 inch of water in a baking dish. Bake, covered, at 400 degrees for 40 minutes or until tender. Remove the beets and cool to room temperature. Peel and cut into thin wedges.

Combine the vinegar, olive oil, salt and pepper in a bowl and whisk until smooth. Combine 3 tablespoons of the dressing with the arugula in a bowl and toss to coat well. Arrange on salad plates.

Toss the pears and beets with 3 tablespoons of the dressing in a bowl. Arrange over the arugula. Sprinkle with the bleu cheese and walnuts. Drizzle with the remaining dressing.

Yield: 4 servings

Spinach Salad with Garlic Vinaigrette

Garlic Vinaigrette
1/2 cup vegetable oil
1/4 cup vinegar
1 garlic clove, minced
3 tablespoons lemon juice
1 tablespoon sugar

Salad
1 large bunch spinach, torn
6 green onions, sliced
8 ounces fresh mushrooms, sliced
8 slices bacon, crisp-fried, crumbled
   Grated Parmesan cheese to taste
4 hard-cooked eggs, cut into wedges

For the vinaigrette, combine the oil, vinegar, garlic, lemon juice and sugar in a jar with a lid; cover and shake to mix well. Refrigerate.

For the salad, combine the spinach, green onions, mushrooms, bacon and Parmesan cheese in a salad bowl and mix well. Add the vinaigrette just before serving and toss to coat well. Top with the egg wedges.

Yield: 8 servings

Southwest Caesar Salad with Red Chile Dressing

Red Chile Dressing

- 6 anchovies
- 3 garlic cloves
- 2 tablespoons each Dijon mustard, Worcestershire sauce, cider vinegar and fresh lemon juice
- 1 tablespoon mild red chili powder
- 1 teaspoon paprika
- 1 cup olive oil

Salad

- 1 head romaine lettuce
- 1/2 cup croutons
- 1/2 cup freshly grated Parmesan cheese

For the dressing, combine the anchovies, garlic, Dijon mustard, Worcestershire sauce, vinegar, lemon juice, chili powder and paprika in a food processor container and process until smooth. Add the olive oil gradually, processing constantly to blend well.

For the salad, tear the lettuce into 2-inch pieces. Toss with the salad dressing in a bowl, coating well. Top with the croutons and Parmesan cheese.

Yield: 4 servings

Walnuts should be placed on a baking sheet in a single layer. In a 350-degree oven or 5 to 6 inches under a broiler, toast until lightly browned and aromatic. Stir periodically. Walnuts may also be toasted in an ungreased skillet over medium heat, stirring often.

Red Cabbage Salad

- 2 (3-ounce) packages ramen noodles, broken, discard seasoning packet
- 1 (2-ounce) package slivered almonds
- 1/2 cup salted sunflower kernels
- 1/3 cup butter
- 1 cup vegetable oil or olive oil
- 1/2 cup cider vinegar
- 3/4 cup sugar
- 1 tablespoon soy sauce
- 1 head red cabbage, grated
- 1 bunch green onions, sliced

Sauté the ramen noodles, almonds and sunflower kernels in the butter in a medium skillet until slightly browned.

Combine the oil, vinegar, sugar and soy sauce in a bowl and mix well. Toss the cabbage and green onions with the oil-vinegar dressing 20 minutes before serving. Add the ramen noodle mixture to the salad just before serving and toss well.

Yield: 12 servings

The cabbage family *includes brussels sprouts, broccoli, cauliflower, and kale. Cabbage comes in many forms—it may be flat, conical, or round; the heads compact or loose; and the leaves curly or plain. Choose a fresh cabbage with leaves that are tightly packed. It should be heavy for its size. Cabbage needs to be refrigerated, tightly wrapped, and used in about a week.*

Spinach and Orange Salad with Poppy Seed Dressing

Flavored vinegars,

such as raspberry or blueberry,
add zest to many dishes.
Vinegars should be stored in a
cool, dark location. Unopened,
they will store indefinitely.
Once opened, vinegars last
approximately six months.

Poppy Seed Dressing
- 1/3 cup raspberry vinegar
-   1 tablespoon grated onion
- 3/4 cup sugar
-   1 teaspoon dry mustard
-   1 teaspoon salt
-   1 cup vegetable oil
- 1 1/2 teaspoons poppy seeds

Salad
- 10 ounces fresh spinach
- 1/2 small red onion
-   1 (11-ounce) can mandarin oranges, drained
-   2 tablespoons roasted sunflower kernels

For the dressing, combine the vinegar, onion, sugar, dry mustard and salt in a food processor container and process for 15 seconds. Add the oil gradually, processing constantly until smooth. Add the poppy seeds and pulse 2 or 3 times. Chill, covered, until serving time.

For the salad, tear the spinach into bite-size pieces, discarding the stems. Cut the onion into halves crosswise and then cut into thin slices. Combine the spinach and onion with the oranges and sunflower kernels in a large salad bowl. Chill, covered, until serving time.

Add the salad dressing at serving time and toss to coat well.

Note: *If you soak onion in cold water for about an hour, it will taste milder in your salad.*

Yield: 8 servings

Cranberry and Apple Salad

- 1 1/2 cups coarsely chopped fresh cranberries
-   3 tablespoons sugar
-   2 tablespoons lime juice
-   2 teaspoons Dijon mustard
- 1/2 cup virgin olive oil
-   2 to 3 Granny Smith apples, chopped
- 1/4 cup sliced green onions
-   1 cup chopped walnuts

Mix the cranberries and sugar in a bowl. Chill, covered, for 8 to 12 hours.

Mix the lime juice, Dijon mustard and olive oil in a bowl. Add the cranberries, apples, green onions and walnuts and mix well. Chill, covered, for 1 hour before serving.

Yield: 6 to 8 servings

APPLE WALNUT SALAD WITH BACON VINAIGRETTE

    12 cups torn spinach
     2 red apples, thinly sliced
     1 cup crumbled bleu cheese or feta cheese
     1 cup coarsely chopped walnuts
        Bacon Vinaigrette (at right)

Rinse the spinach and spin dry. Arrange on serving plates. Arrange the apple slices over the spinach. Sprinkle with the cheese and walnuts. Drizzle with the Bacon Vinaigrette.

    Yield: 8 servings

BACON VINAIGRETTE

Combine 1 1/4 cups cider vinegar, 1 cup apple juice, 3/4 cup real bacon bits, 1/2 cup finely ground walnuts, 1/4 cup packed brown sugar, 2 teaspoons chopped fresh basil, 1/2 teaspoon pepper and 1 1/2 teaspoons salt in a bowl and mix well. Whisk in 1 cup vegetable oil and 1/4 cup walnut oil gradually. Store in an airtight container in the refrigerator.

BLACK BEAN AND BELL PEPPER SALAD

Sweet peppers vary greatly in color, with the color sometimes variegated. Colors include green, yellow, red, orange, purple, brown, or black. The size varies slightly, from 3 1/2 to 5 1/2 inches long and 2 1/2 to 4 inches wide. The skin may be thick or thin and flavors range from bland to very sweet. Bell peppers are well recognized by their bell shape. Peppers should be firm and heavy for their size. Store, refrigerated, for up to a week.

Lime and Date Dressing
- 1/2 cup water
- 16 pitted dates, finely chopped, about 4 ounces
- 1/2 cup lime juice
- 6 tablespoons extra-virgin olive oil
- 4 teaspoons honey
- 2 tablespoons dried oregano
- 4 teaspoons ground cumin
- 4 teaspoons ground coriander
- Salt and pepper to taste

Salad
- 4 (13-ounce) cans black beans, rinsed, drained
- 1/2 cup chopped red bell pepper
- 1/2 cup chopped yellow bell pepper
- 1/2 cup chopped green bell pepper
- 1/2 cup chopped red onion
- 1/2 cup chopped fresh parsley
- Salt and pepper to taste

For the dressing, combine the water and dates in a small saucepan and boil for 2 minutes. Remove from the heat and let stand, covered, for 1 hour.

Combine the undrained dates with the lime juice, olive oil, honey, oregano, cumin and coriander in a blender container. Process until puréed. Add salt and pepper. Store in the refrigerator for up to 24 hours; let stand at room temperature for 1 hour before serving.

For the salad, combine the black beans, bell peppers, onion and parsley in a large bowl. Add the dressing and toss to coat well. Season with salt and pepper. Chill, covered, for up to 6 hours if desired; bring to room temperature before serving.

Yield: 10 to 12 servings

Fresh Fruit Salad with Dates

Cooked Dressing

- 1/3 cup cornstarch
- 3 cups water
- 1 1/2 cups sugar
- 1/3 cup white vinegar
- 2 tablespoons butter
- 1 tablespoon vanilla extract

Salad

- 1 cup each chopped dates and chopped apples
- 1/2 to 1 cup finely chopped celery
- 1/2 to 1 cup chopped walnuts
- 1 cup red grape halves
- 1 cup pineapple chunks

For the dressing, blend the cornstarch with a small amount of the water. Bring the remaining water to a boil in a saucepan. Add the sugar, vinegar, butter and cornstarch mixture. Cook until the mixture is thickened and clear, stirring constantly. Remove from the heat and stir in the vanilla. Cool to room temperature. Store in the refrigerator.

For the salad, combine the dates, apples, celery, walnuts, grapes and pineapple chunks in a large salad bowl. Add 1 cup of the dressing and mix gently.

Yield: 6 servings

Broccoli and Almond Salad

- 8 slices bacon
- 1 cup mayonnaise
- 1/3 cup sugar
- 1 tablespoon vinegar
- 4 cups broccoli florets and sliced peeled stems
- 1 cup chopped celery
- 2/3 cup toasted slivered almonds
- 1 cup seedless green grape halves
- 1 cup seedless red grape halves
- 1/2 cup chopped green onions with tops

Fry the bacon in a skillet until crisp; drain and crumble the bacon. Mix the mayonnaise, sugar and vinegar in a bowl and set aside.

Combine the broccoli with the celery, almonds, grapes and green onions in a salad bowl. Add the mayonnaise mixture and mix well. Top with the crumbled bacon.

Yield: 8 servings

Toasted Almonds

Slivered almonds should be placed on a baking sheet in a single layer. Toast in a 350-degree oven or 5 to 6 inches under a broiler until light brown and aromatic, stirring occasionally. Almonds may also be toasted in a skillet over medium heat, stirring frequently.

TOMATO AND CUCUMBER BREAD SALAD

FLAT-LEAF PARSLEY *is commonly used as a flavoring or a garnish. There are numerous varieties of parsley, and the most strongly flavored is the Italian or flat-leaf variety. Italian parsley may be difficult to find and may be ordered through supermarkets or specialty markets. Sold in bunches, parsley should be selected for its green leaves with no sign of deterioration. Rinse parsley and shake off excess water, then wrap—first in paper towels, then in a plastic bag. Refrigerate for up to a week.*

¼ unsliced loaf crusty bread
3 tablespoons extra-virgin olive oil
  Sea salt and pepper to taste
6 small cucumbers, peeled, chopped
3 Roma tomatoes, coarsely chopped
1 small red onion, thinly sliced
¼ cup red wine vinegar
¼ cup extra-virgin olive oil
2 tablespoons flat-leaf parsley, chopped
¾ teaspoon salt
½ teaspoon pepper

Cut the bread into ½-inch cubes. Sauté in 3 tablespoons olive oil, sea salt and pepper in a heated large skillet over medium heat until crisp and golden brown on all sides.

Combine the cucumbers, tomatoes and onion in a bowl. Add the vinegar, ¼ cup olive oil, parsley, ¾ teaspoon salt and ½ teaspoon pepper and mix well. Chill, covered, for 30 minutes. Add the bread cubes at serving time and toss to coat well.

Yield: 6 servings

CREAMY POTATO SALAD

    6 large potatoes
    4 hard-cooked eggs, chopped
    6 green onions, chopped
    2 teaspoons salt
    1 cup whipping cream
    6 tablespoons mayonnaise
    2 hard-cooked eggs, sliced

Cook the potatoes in water to cover in a saucepan until tender; drain. Peel and chop the potatoes. Combine with the chopped eggs, green onions and salt in a bowl and mix well.

Beat the whipping cream in a mixing bowl until soft peaks form. Add the mayonnaise and mix well. Add to the potato mixture and mix gently. Top with the sliced eggs. Chill, covered, for 4 to 8 hours before serving.

Yield: 8 servings

PICNIC POTATO SALAD

    4 pounds red potatoes
    6 hard-cooked eggs, chopped
    1 cup chopped celery
  1/2 cup chopped yellow onion
    2 cups mayonnaise
    1 cup buttermilk
    1 teaspoon sugar
    2 tablespoons prepared yellow mustard
    2 tablespoons salt
    1 tablespoon white pepper

Cook the unpeeled potatoes in water to cover in a saucepan until tender; drain. Chill in the refrigerator. Cut the potatoes into bite-size pieces and combine with the eggs, celery and onion in a bowl.

Combine the mayonnaise, buttermilk, sugar, mustard, salt and white pepper in a small bowl and mix well. Add to the potato mixture and mix gently. Chill, covered, for 8 to 12 hours before serving.

Yield: 8 servings

HERB SALT *is produced by layering* 1/2 *inch noniodized salt with* 1/2 *inch fresh herbs in a sealed container that is free from light. It is ready for use two to three weeks after layering. The salt preserves the herb color while enhancing its flavor.*

MAYONNAISE

Combine 2 large eggs, 1/4 *cup apple cider vinegar, 1 teaspoon dry mustard and 1 tablespoon seasoned salt in a blender container and process until smooth. Add* 1 1/2 *cups vegetable oil very gradually, processing constantly until incorporated and stirring in the last of the oil if necessary. Store in the refrigerator.*

GRILLED VEGETABLE SALAD WITH PESTO VINAIGRETTE

Pesto Vinaigrette

   2   tablespoons balsamic vinegar
   1   tablespoon red wine vinegar
   1   tablespoon prepared pesto
   $1/2$ teaspoon salt
   $1/4$ teaspoon pepper
   $3/4$ cup extra-virgin olive oil

Salad

   1   medium eggplant, sliced $1/2$ inch thick
       Salt to taste
   2   medium zucchini, sliced diagonally $1/2$ inch thick
   2   medium yellow squash, sliced diagonally $1/2$ inch thick
   4   large tomatoes, thickly sliced
   4   cups mixed salad greens
   4   ounces goat cheese, crumbled (optional)

For the vinaigrette, combine the balsamic vinegar, red wine vinegar, pesto, salt and pepper in a bowl and mix well. Add the olive oil gradually, whisking constantly.

For the salad, sprinkle the eggplant with salt in a colander and let stand for 30 minutes; pat dry. Brush the eggplant, zucchini, yellow squash and tomatoes with $1/4$ cup of the vinaigrette. Grill the vegetables over hot coals just until tender, basting with $1/4$ cup of the vinaigrette.

Toss the salad greens with $1/4$ cup of the vinaigrette in a bowl. Spoon onto serving plates. Arrange the grilled vegetables over the greens. Drizzle with the remaining $1/4$ cup vinaigrette and sprinkle with the cheese.

Yield: 4 servings

Orzo with Everything

Orzo is a small (³⁄₈-inch), rice-shape pasta often substituted for rice or barley in soups or used as a rice replacement in a side dish.

1¹⁄₂ cups uncooked orzo
¹⁄₃ cup packed oil-pack sun-dried tomatoes, drained, chopped
5 tablespoons extra-virgin olive oil
¹⁄₄ cup red balsamic vinegar
¹⁄₄ cup packed chopped kalamata olives
1 cup finely chopped radicchio
¹⁄₂ cup pine nuts, lightly toasted
¹⁄₂ cup chopped fresh basil
¹⁄₂ cup freshly grated Parmesan cheese
1 cup crumbled feta cheese
2 large garlic cloves, crushed
Salt and pepper to taste

Cook the pasta al dente using the package directions; drain. Combine with the sun-dried tomatoes, olive oil, vinegar and olives in a large bowl and mix well. Let stand until the pasta cools.

Add the radicchio, pine nuts, basil, Parmesan cheese, feta cheese and garlic. Season with salt and pepper and toss to coat. Chill, covered, until serving time.

Yield: 6 servings

RADICCHIO is a salad green that is actually a red-leafed Italian chicory. There are a number of varieties, although Verona and Treviso are most common. The slightly bitter leaves are tender but firm, and the ribs may be white, pink, red, green, or variegated. Refrigerate in a sealable plastic bag for up to one week.

Rotini and Vegetable Salad

1 (16-ounce) can red kidney beans, drained
1 cup white vinegar
16 ounces uncooked rotini
1 (10-ounce) package frozen green peas, thawed
1 (16-ounce) can French-style green beans, drained
¹⁄₂ cup chopped green bell pepper
1 cup chopped celery
1 small onion, chopped
2 cups mayonnaise-type salad dressing
1 cup half-and-half
¹⁄₂ cup sugar

Combine the kidney beans with the vinegar in a small bowl and mix well. Let stand for 1 hour.

Cook the pasta using the package directions; drain. Combine with the peas, green beans, bell pepper, celery and onion in a bowl and toss to mix. Drain the kidney beans and add to the salad; mix gently.

Mix the salad dressing, half-and-half and sugar in a small bowl. Add to the salad and toss to coat well. Chill, covered, for 8 to 12 hours.

Yield: 8 servings

CHUTNEY *is a condiment containing fruit, vinegar, sugar, and spices. It can be chunky or smooth and vary in degree of spiciness from mild to hot. Chutney is often served as an accompaniment to curried recipes. The sweeter chutneys also make appealing spreads and are appetizing served with cheese.*

TROPICAL CHICKEN SALAD

2½ cups chopped cooked chicken
1 (11-ounce) can mandarin oranges, drained
2 (20-ounce) cans pineapple chunks, drained
¾ cup chopped celery
¾ cup mayonnaise-type salad dressing
2 tablespoons chopped chutney
1 teaspoon curry powder
⅓ cup peanuts
1 banana, sliced

Combine the chicken with the oranges, pineapple and celery in a bowl and mix well. Chill, covered, for several hours. Mix the salad dressing, chutney and curry powder in a small bowl. Chill, covered, for several hours.

Drain the chicken mixture well. Add the peanuts, banana and salad dressing mixture and toss gently. Serve on lettuce leaves and garnish with shredded coconut.

Yield: 8 servings

CHICKEN AND FRUIT SALAD

3½ cups chopped cooked chicken breast
1 cup seedless green grape halves
1½ cups drained crushed pineapple
1 cup chopped celery
Slivered almonds to taste
¾ cup mayonnaise
½ cup mayonnaise-type salad dressing
1 teaspoon curry powder

Combine the chicken, grapes, pineapple, celery and almonds in a bowl. Mix the mayonnaise, mayonnaise-type salad dressing and curry powder in a small bowl. Add to the chicken mixture and toss gently. Chill, covered, for several hours. Serve in lettuce cups.

Yield: 6 servings

GRILLED CHICKEN CAESAR SALAD

Salad

- 4 boneless skinless chicken breasts
  Garlic salt and freshly ground pepper to taste
- 2 tablespoons olive oil
- 1 head romaine, chopped or torn

Caesar Dressing

- 1 egg
- 3 tablespoons lemon juice
  Tabasco sauce to taste
  Salt and freshly ground pepper to taste
- $1/2$ cup extra-virgin olive oil
- $1/2$ cup freshly grated Parmesan cheese

For the salad, sprinkle the chicken with garlic salt and pepper and brush with olive oil. Grill over hot coals for 4 minutes on each side, brushing with olive oil. Cut diagonally into $1/4$-inch slices. Place the lettuce in a large bowl.

For the dressing, place the egg in boiling water for 20 seconds. Remove the egg with a slotted spoon, crack it and scoop it into a medium bowl. Whisk in the lemon juice 1 tablespoon at a time. Whisk in the Tabasco sauce, salt and pepper. Add the olive oil gradually, whisking constantly. Mix in the cheese and adjust the seasonings.

To assemble the salad, add most of the dressing to the lettuce and toss to coat well. Spoon onto serving plates. Fan the chicken slices over the lettuce and drizzle with the remaining dressing. Garnish with additional Parmesan cheese.

Note: *If you choose not to use a coddled egg, you can use the following method to prepare Cooked Caesar Dressing. It will have a creamier consistency. Combine the egg, olive oil, lemon juice, Tabasco sauce, salt and pepper in a food processor or blender container and process until smooth. Pour into a small saucepan and cook over low heat for 8 to 10 minutes or just until thickened, stirring constantly; do not boil. Spoon into a small bowl and place a sheet of plastic wrap directly on the surface. Chill for 2 to 24 hours. Add the Parmesan cheese at serving time.*

Photograph for this recipe is on page 66.

Yield: 4 servings

CODDLING *is a slow-cooking method in which an egg (or other food) is placed in a small covered container and simmered slowly in a hot water bath in the oven or on the stove. It may also be accomplished by lowering the food item into water that has already boiled and has been removed from the heat source.*

Baby greens are harvested while young and tender. Varieties of lettuce, greens, and cabbage include: Iceberg, Bibb, Red Leaf, Green Leaf, Spinach, Romaine, Red Oakleaf, Mizuna, Sorrel, Red Mustard, Frisée, Tatsoi, Kale, Collards, Curly Endive, Leaf Endive, Escarole, Swiss Chard, Arugula, Watercress, Dandelion, Anise, Red Cabbage, Green Cabbage, Savoy Cabbage, Chinese Cabbage, Mustard Greens, Beet Greens, Chicory, and Butterhead Lettuce.

SHRIMP AND FENNEL SPINACH SALAD WITH BACON BALSAMIC VINAIGRETTE

Salad

- 1³/₄ pounds uncooked large shrimp, peeled, deveined
- 6 tablespoons olive oil
- 1 tablespoon fennel seeds, crushed
- 1 teaspoon dried red pepper, crushed
  Salt and black pepper to taste
- 2 (6-ounce) fennel bulbs, cut into ¹/₂-inch wedges
- 2 tablespoons olive oil
- 12 ounces baby spinach leaves
- 2 cups chopped seeded peeled tomatoes

Bacon Balsamic Vinaigrette

- 5 thick slices bacon, cut into ¹/₂-inch pieces
- 5 tablespoons olive oil
- ¹/₄ cup balsamic vinegar
- 3 tablespoons minced shallot
- 1 tablespoon minced garlic
- 1 tablespoon brown sugar
  Salt and pepper to taste

For the salad, soak 12 bamboo skewers in water in a shallow bowl for 30 minutes; drain. Thread the shrimp onto the skewers and place on a baking sheet with sides. Mix 6 tablespoons olive oil, fennel seeds and crushed red pepper in a small bowl. Pour over the shrimp, turning to coat well. Season with salt and black pepper. Marinate, covered, in the refrigerator for 30 minutes.

Brush the fennel bulb wedges with 2 tablespoons olive oil and sprinkle with salt and black pepper. Place on a rack over medium-hot coals. Grill for 3 minutes on each side or until golden brown. Remove to a large bowl. Add the spinach and tomatoes and mix well.

Drain the shrimp and place on the grill. Grill for 2 minutes on each side or until opaque. Remove to a plate and tent with foil to keep warm.

For the vinaigrette, fry the bacon in a heavy large skillet over medium heat until crisp; remove with a slotted spoon and drain on paper towels. Drain all but 3 tablespoons of the drippings from the skillet. Stir the olive oil into the skillet. Whisk the vinegar, shallot, garlic and brown sugar in a small bowl. Add to the reserved drippings and olive oil in the skillet. Cook over medium-low heat just until warm. Season with salt and pepper.

To serve, pour the warm vinaigrette over the salad and toss to coat well. Spoon onto plates and sprinkle with the bacon. Arrange the shrimp around the salad. Garnish with chopped fennel tops.

Yield: 8 servings

CREAMY HOT BACON DRESSING

 ½ cup chopped bacon
 ½ cup chopped onion
 ¾ cup mayonnaise-type salad dressing
 ⅓ cup cider vinegar
 ⅓ cup sugar

Sauté the bacon in a skillet until nearly crisp. Add the onion and sauté until the bacon is crisp; drain. Add the mayonnaise-type salad dressing, vinegar and sugar and mix well. Cook until heated through. Serve warm over a salad of spinach or other fresh greens, fresh mushrooms, tomatoes, red onions and hard-cooked eggs. Store unused portions in the refrigerator for up to 7 days.

Yield: 32 tablespoons

BLEU CHEESE DRESSING

 2 cups mayonnaise
 6 tablespoons half-and-half
 2 teaspoons white vinegar
 2 teaspoons fresh lemon juice
 1 teaspoon Worcestershire sauce
 2 teaspoons sugar
 2 teaspoons finely chopped onion
 2 teaspoons parsley flakes
 1 teaspoon horseradish
 ½ teaspoon garlic salt
   White pepper to taste
 4 ounces bleu cheese, crumbled

Combine the mayonnaise, half-and-half, vinegar, lemon juice and Worcestershire sauce in a bowl and whisk until smooth. Whisk in the sugar, onion, parsley flakes, horseradish, garlic salt and white pepper. Add the cheese and mix well. Chill, covered, for several hours before serving.

Yield: 48 tablespoons

HOT BRIE DRESSING

Remove the rind from 10 ounces of Brie cheese and cut the cheese into 1-inch pieces. Heat ½ cup olive oil in a saucepan over low heat. Add 5 teaspoons minced shallots and 2 teaspoons minced garlic and cook until translucent. Add ½ cup sherry wine vinegar, 2 tablespoons fresh lemon juice and 4 teaspoons Dijon mustard and mix well. Stir in the cheese and cook until the cheese melts. Season with salt and pepper to taste. Toss with greens.

FETA CHEESE SALAD DRESSING

2 cups each crumbled feta cheese and mayonnaise
2 tablespoons olive oil
6 tablespoons red wine vinegar
1 tablespoon Worcestershire sauce
2 garlic cloves, minced
1 teaspoon mixed equal parts dried herbs such as marjoram,
  thyme and basil
1 teaspoon dried oregano leaves

Combine the cheese, mayonnaise, olive oil, vinegar, Worcestershire sauce,
garlic, mixed herbs and oregano in a blender container. Process until smooth.
Serve on a salad of mixed greens or store in the refrigerator for several weeks.

Yield: 72 tablespoons

HONEY SALAD DRESSING

3/4 cup vegetable oil
1/4 cup fresh lemon juice
1/3 cup honey
1/3 cup sugar
1 teaspoon mustard
  Several drops of onion juice or garlic juice
1 teaspoon each celery seeds and salt
1/4 teaspoon pepper

Combine the oil, lemon juice, honey, sugar, mustard, onion juice, celery
seeds, salt and pepper in a bowl or covered jar. Beat or shake to mix well. Store
in the refrigerator. Serve over a fruit salad or green salad.

Yield: 27 tablespoons

MAPLE DIJON VINAIGRETTE

1 cup olive oil
1 cup apple cider vinegar
1 cup pure maple syrup
1/2 cup Dijon mustard
1/2 cup coarsely ground Dijon mustard in white wine
1/4 cup minced fresh garlic

Combine the olive oil, vinegar, maple syrup, Dijon mustards and garlic in a
food processor container and process until smooth. Serve over a salad of
greens and mixed vegetables.

Yield: 64 tablespoons

PEPPERCORN PARMESAN DRESSING

   ½ cup mayonnaise
   ¾ cup sour cream
   1 teaspoon fresh lemon juice
   ½ cup freshly grated Parmesan cheese
   ½ teaspoon garlic salt
   ¼ teaspoon each onion salt and paprika
   ¾ teaspoon cracked pepper
   ¼ cup buttermilk

Mix the mayonnaise, sour cream, lemon juice, Parmesan cheese, garlic salt, onion salt, paprika and pepper in a bowl. Add enough buttermilk gradually to make of the desired consistency, mixing until smooth. Store in the refrigerator.

Yield: 32 tablespoons

PEPPERCREAM DRESSING

   2 cups mayonnaise
   2 tablespoons each lemon juice and liquid Maggi seasoning
   ½ tablespoon each Worcestershire sauce and A.1. steak sauce
      Tabasco sauce to taste
   ¼ teaspoon salt
   ½ teaspoon cracked peppercorns
   1 tablespoon grated Parmesan cheese

Combine the mayonnaise, lemon juice, Maggi seasoning, Worcestershire sauce, A.1. sauce, Tabasco sauce, salt and peppercorns in a bowl and mix well. Fold in the Parmesan cheese. Store, covered, in the refrigerator.

Yield: 40 tablespoons

POPPY SEED DRESSING

   5 tablespoons sugar
   3 tablespoons white wine vinegar
   ½ cup vegetable oil
   1 teaspoon minced onion
   ¼ teaspoon dry mustard
   ½ teaspoon salt
   ½ to ¾ teaspoon poppy seeds

Combine the sugar and vinegar in a blender container and blend for 1 minute. Add the oil, onion, dry mustard and salt and process for 1 minute. Stir in the poppy seeds. Store, covered, in an airtight container in the refrigerator.

Yield: 16 tablespoons

BASIC HERB OILS OR VINEGARS *may be made by taking fresh herbs that have been bruised, placing them in a jar, then adding oil or vinegar that has been heated to a simmer. The jar should be filled within two inches of the top and sealed with a non-metal lid. Shake the mixture every few days. After ten days, taste and add any additional herbs to enhance the flavor. When the correct flavor has been infused, strain, add decorative fresh herbs, and seal.*

Elementary My Dear...

SOUPS
SANDWICHES
& CONDIMENTS

This photograph is sponsored by:
Terri Jackson

Elementary My Dear...

A key component to successful entertaining is creating the mood. Many of the decisions made regarding the mood of the occasion can be done well in advance (one to two weeks.)

It is important to consider all five senses when determining the ambiance for the affair. Sight, smell, taste, hearing, and touch are all vital elements. By satisfying the senses, guests recognize the difference between the mundane and a truly memorable occasion.

Given that the home and table will be featured, it is critical to remember that your visual sense is at the top of the list. Lighting is an ingredient that makes an understated statement when done correctly or a glaring error when ignored. A balance between moody and gloomy can be achieved by soft lights such as wall lights, spotlights, firelight, or candlelight. Candles are by far the most flattering. Direct, bright lights should be avoided.

A wonderful sense of smell can be accomplished in a number of ways. Your menu, of course, is the most obvious. Delicious food can't help but embellish the entire experience. The aroma of a great meal speaks for itself. Richly scented flowers or candles also add an irresistible element. Candles and flowers can give heights of grandeur for formality, but lower arrangements lend themselves to elegance and visibility for guests.

Music is a fabulous mood enhancer. The selection of music sets the tone for the entire evening. Music should be loud enough to fill silences, but not so loud as to compete with conversation. Recorded music is perfect for most occasions. It is desirable to have enough music available so that it does not pull the hostess or host away from guests to facilitate its consistency. Live music can be an excellent choice for a less intimate affair such as a cocktail party. Live music should be appropriate for the function, well balanced, and well performed.

Touch is facilitated by a comfortable room temperature for starters. A room that is too hot or cold will definitely impair the success of the festivities. Remember that a large group of guests will raise the room temperature, so adjust accordingly. Crisp linens, velvet runners, satin trims, silky tassels, lacy tablecloths, or metallic finishes are all contributors to a well-balanced mood. Comfortable chairs and table size and height are also considerations.

Last, but certainly not least, are the flavors that your menu provides. A menu that has symmetry between dishes and beverages is critical to a distinguished happening. Diversity should also be an integral ingredient in the menu.

Iced Parsley Soup

    3 leeks, finely chopped
    2 onions, finely chopped
    2 tablespoons butter, melted
    3 cups chicken broth
    5 medium potatoes, peeled, sliced
    1 bay leaf
    1 tablespoon salt
    3 cups heavy cream
    1 tablespoon Worcestershire sauce
       Salt and pepper to taste
    2 cups chopped fresh parsley
    1 cup chicken broth

Sauté the leeks and onions in the butter in a 3- to 4-quart saucepan until translucent. Add 3 cups chicken broth, potatoes, bay leaf and 1 tablespoon salt. Simmer, covered, for 35 to 40 minutes or until the potatoes are tender. Discard the bay leaf.

Pour into a food processor container and process until smooth. Chill in the refrigerator. Combine with the cream and Worcestershire sauce in a bowl. Season with salt and pepper to taste.

Purée the parsley and 1 cup chicken broth in a blender. Add to the soup and mix well. Chill until serving time.

Photograph for this recipe is on page 86.

Yield: 8 servings

Strawberry Cantaloupe Soup

Purée 8 cups strawberries in a food processor. Pour into a bowl. Cut 1 cantaloupe in half. Remove and discard the seeds and peel. Cut into chunks and purée in a food processor. Add to the strawberries. Add 1 cup sugar, 4 teaspoons fresh lemon juice, 2 cups 2% milk and 1 cup plain yogurt and mix well. Chill until serving time. Serve with a dollop of whipped cream and garnish with a mint leaf. You may serve this soup in hollowed-out cantaloupe shells for an interesting presentation.

Photograph for this recipe is on page 86 and at left.

CREAM OF BRIE SOUP

      8 large leek bulbs, chopped
    1/4 cup (1/2 stick) butter, melted
      4 cups lightly salted chicken broth
    1/4 cup (1/2 stick) butter
    1/3 cup flour
      4 cups half-and-half
     16 ounces Brie cheese, rind removed, cut into chunks
         Lemon juice, salt and pepper to taste

Sauté the leeks in 1/4 cup butter in a heavy saucepan for 10 minutes. Add the chicken broth and bring to a boil. Reduce the heat and simmer, covered, for 30 minutes. Process the mixture in batches in a blender until smooth. Press through a fine sieve into a bowl.

Melt 1/4 cup butter in a heavy saucepan and stir in the flour. Cook for several minutes, stirring constantly. Add the strained soup and half-and-half. Bring to a boil, stirring constantly. Add the cheese and cook just until the cheese melts. Season with lemon juice, salt and pepper. Garnish servings with chopped chives.

Yield: 10 servings

CREAM OF FENNEL SOUP

      3 pounds fennel with leafy tops, about 5 medium bulbs
    3/4 cup chopped onion
    1/2 cup (1 stick) butter, melted
      3 tablespoons each Pernod and dry vermouth
   7 1/2 cups homemade chicken stock or canned chicken stock
   3 1/2 cups milk
      5 tablespoons butter
    1/4 cup flour
      1 cup heavy cream
         Lemon juice, salt and pepper to taste

Remove the fennel tops and reserve some for garnish. Core and quarter the bulbs, discarding the outer layer. Sauté the fennel and onion in 1/2 cup butter in a heavy saucepan for 20 to 30 minutes or until tender, stirring frequently.

Add the Pernod and vermouth. Cook for 1 minute. Add the chicken stock and milk and simmer for 30 minutes. Purée the soup in batches in a blender and press through a sieve into the saucepan. Bring to a boil.

Melt 5 tablespoons butter in a small saucepan. Add the flour and cook for several minutes, stirring constantly. Add to the hot soup gradually. Cook until thickened, stirring constantly. Add the cream and cook just until heated through. Season with lemon juice, salt and pepper. Garnish with fennel leaves.

Yield: 10 servings

BRIE CHEESE *is a cheese with a white rind and a creamy, buttery interior that should ooze at the peak of ripeness. Several countries make the cheese, but Brie from France is considered the best. Pick a cheese that is elastic to the touch; it may have a pale brown edge. Ripe Brie has a short shelf life and should be used within a few days.*

PERNOD *is a yellowish, licorice-/anise-flavored liqueur similar to absinthe.*

VERMOUTH *is a white wine that has been enhanced and fortified with herbs and spices. There are three primary varieties: white dry vermouth, sweet vermouth, and Bianco b'Italians. Vermouths are often served as aperitifs or used in cocktails such as the Martini and Manhattan.*

ROASTED GARLIC SOUP WITH PROSCIUTTO AND GRUYÈRE

40 garlic cloves, peeled
1/4 cup extra-virgin olive oil
6 cups chicken broth
1 cup dry white wine
2 large russet potatoes, peeled, chopped
12 ounces Gruyère cheese, shredded
1/2 cup heavy cream
2 tablespoons dry sherry
2 tablespoons Cognac
1 cup finely chopped onion
1 cup finely chopped prosciutto
Salt and white pepper to taste

Toss the garlic with the olive oil in a baking dish. Bake, covered with foil, at 350 degrees for 45 minutes or until tender. Remove the garlic to a heavy large saucepan, reserving the oil.

Add the chicken broth, white wine and potatoes to the saucepan. Simmer until the potatoes are tender. Remove from the heat and let stand for 5 minutes.

Purée the soup in batches in a blender and strain into a large saucepan. Add the cheese and cook until melted, stirring constantly. Add the cream, sherry and Cognac. Cook until heated through.

Heat the reserved oil in a skillet and add the onion. Sauté until golden brown. Add the prosciutto and sauté for 2 minutes longer. Stir into the soup and season with salt and white pepper. Garnish servings with edible flowers and chopped parsley.

You may omit the prosciutto to serve as a first course.

Yield: 6 servings

COGNAC is considered the finest of all brandies. It originates in Cognac, France. It is double-distilled right after fermentation. Cognacs are rated as follows:

One star—aged three years
Two star—aged four years
Three star—aged five years
V.S.—very superior
V.S.O.P.—very superior old pale
V.V.S.O.P.—very, very superior old pale
X.O.—oldest produced
"Extra"—oldest produced
"Reserve"—oldest produced

Soup may be served either in a soup plate or in a cup, depending on the type of soup and the formality of the meal. Clear soups are often served in small, doubled-handled consommé cups. You can check the heat of the soup with a spoon, then lift the cup to drink it. Any vegetables or noodles left at the bottom can be eaten with a spoon. A two-handled cream-soup bowl is larger than a consommé cup. You can drink the soup or use a spoon. In both cases, when you are finished, place the spoon on the plate underneath and to the right of the cup. Do not leave it standing in the cup. When using a soup plate, always spoon away from the table's edge. When you reach the plate's bottom, tilt the plate slightly away from you. When using a soup spoon, always sip from the side and never put the entire bowl of the spoon into your mouth. Always drink soup quietly.

POTATO SOUP

6   slices bacon, chopped
1   (14-ounce) can chicken broth
3   cups chopped peeled potatoes
1   small carrot, chopped
1/2 cup chopped onion
1   tablespoon parsley flakes
1/2 teaspoon each celery seeds, salt and pepper
3   tablespoons flour
3   cups milk
8   ounces process American cheese, cubed
2   green onions, thinly sliced (optional)

Cook the bacon in a large saucepan until crisp; remove and drain the bacon, discarding the drippings. Add the chicken broth, potatoes, carrot, onion, parsley flakes, celery seeds, salt and pepper. Simmer, covered, for 15 minutes or until the vegetables are tender.

Blend the flour into the milk in a bowl. Add to the soup. Bring to a boil and cook for 2 minutes, stirring constantly. Add the cheese and cook until melted, stirring to mix well. Sprinkle servings with the bacon and green onions.

Yield: 8 servings

CREAMY SWEET POTATO SOUP

1   large sweet potato, peeled, chopped
2   medium carrots, chopped
1   small yellow or red onion, chopped
1   small russet potato, chopped
2   tablespoons finely chopped gingerroot
1/2 cup skim milk
1/4 cup low-fat sour cream
    Salt to taste
1/4 teaspoon pepper

Combine the sweet potato, carrots, onion, potato and gingerroot with water to cover in a 4-quart saucepan. Bring to a boil over high heat and reduce the heat. Simmer, covered, for 30 minutes or just until the vegetables are tender; drain half the water.

Process the mixture in batches in a blender or food processor container until smooth. Combine with the skim milk, sour cream, salt and pepper in a saucepan. Cook until heated through, stirring occasionally. Garnish servings with a dollop of sour cream and a sprinkle of nutmeg.

You may increase or decrease the amount of skim milk added to the soup to produce the desired consistency.

Yield: 10 servings

TUSCAN SOUP

    1 pound bulk pork sausage or Italian sausage
  1/4 teaspoon crushed red pepper
    8 ounces yellow onions, chopped
    2 ounces bacon, chopped
    1 tablespoon garlic purée
   10 cups hot water
  1/4 cup chicken stock base
 2 1/2 pounds potatoes, peeled, chopped
    4 ounces fresh kale, cut into 3/4-inch strips
    1 cup heavy cream

Cook the sausage with the red pepper in a skillet over low heat, stirring until crumbly; remove with a slotted spoon and drain.

Sauté the onions with the bacon in a skillet until the onions are transparent and the bacon is very crisp. Add the garlic purée. Sauté for 1 minute.

Add the water and chicken base. Bring to a boil, stirring to dissolve the chicken base. Add the potatoes. Cook for 15 to 20 minutes or until the potatoes are tender. Reduce the heat to medium and add the kale, sausage and cream. Simmer for 5 minutes.

Yield: 12 servings

PROVOLONE SPINACH SOUP

    1 (10-ounce) package frozen chopped spinach, thawed
  1/4 cup finely chopped onion
  1/4 cup (1/2 stick) butter, melted
  1/4 cup flour
    4 cups milk
 1 1/2 teaspoons salt, or to taste
       Pepper to taste
  3/4 cup shredded provolone cheese

Process the undrained spinach in a food processor until puréed. Sauté the onion in the butter in a saucepan. Add the flour and cook for 2 minutes, stirring constantly. Stir in the milk and cook until slightly thickened, stirring constantly. Stir in the spinach, salt and pepper. Cook until heated through. Top servings with shredded cheese and garnish with crumbled crisp-fried bacon.

Yield: 6 servings.

PURÉE *refers to any food (usually a fruit or vegetable) that is finely mashed to a smooth, thick consistency. This can be accomplished by using a food processor or a blender or by forcing the food through a sieve. Purées can be used as a garnish, a side dish, or added as a thickener to sauces or soups.*

*I*OWA is known by its residents and visitors as a plethora of recreational options. It is the only state to be bordered by two navigable rivers—the Missouri and the Mighty Mississippi. Both provide breathtaking beauty, with winding water reflecting limestone bluffs covered with abundant foliage. Water activities abound, with riverboating, sailing, fishing, and waterskiing, while the land provides hiking and scenic drives.

The rolling hills and natural prairies make state and county parks a desired destination, as do the many lakes and rivers. A quiet nap under a large oak tree or sunning on a beach may be the choices for some. For others there is fishing, canoeing, swimming, and water sports. Those desiring a more solid foundation enjoy camping, picnicking, and hiking. Iowa also takes great pride in offering mile after mile of groomed bicycle paths and trails. Each summer thousands of bicyclists from every state and many foreign countries take part in the *Des Moines Register*'s Annual Great Bicycle Ride Across Iowa (RAGBRAI).

Festivals, fairs, and celebrations multiply during the summer and fall. Practically every community has its own offering, including such affairs as the Iowa State Fair, Corn Carnival, Field of Dreams, Covered Bridges of Madison County, or the Dvořák Music Festival. These, among countless other opportunities, promote a strong sense of family, friendship, and community. The combination of great natural beauty and strong personal values makes Iowa the state of choice for its citizens.

Photograph by:
Larsh Bristol

WILD RICE

To prepare 3 to 4 cups of wild rice, rinse 1 cup wild rice in a strainer under running water and drain. Combine with 1 teaspoon salt and 4 cups water in a heavy saucepan. Bring to a boil. Simmer, covered, for 45 to 55 minutes or just until tender; drain excess liquid.

WILD RICE ARITHMETIC

One pound of uncooked wild rice measures $2^2/3$ to $2^3/4$ cups. One pound of cooked wild rice will yield 20 to 25 servings. One cup of uncooked wild rice will yield 3 to 4 cups cooked.

WILD RICE SOUP

Wild rice is a long-grain marsh grass native to the northern Great Lakes area and is now commercially produced in California and in the Midwest.

   1 tablespoon minced onion
   6 tablespoons butter, melted
   $1/2$ cup flour
   3 cups chicken broth
   2 cups cooked wild rice
   $1/3$ cup minced cooked ham
   $1/2$ cup finely grated carrot
   3 tablespoons chopped slivered almonds
   $1/2$ teaspoon salt (optional)
   1 cup half-and-half
   2 tablespoons dry sherry (optional)
      Pepper to taste

Sauté the onion in the butter in a saucepan until tender. Stir in the flour and cook for several minutes. Add the chicken broth gradually. Bring to a boil and boil for 1 minute, stirring constantly.

   Add the wild rice, ham, carrot, almonds and salt. Simmer for 5 minutes. Add the half-and-half and sherry. Cook just until heated through. Season with pepper. Garnish servings with minced parsley or chives.

   Note: *It's important to clean wild rice completely before cooking it. Depending on the technique utilized, wild rice can take up to an hour to cook. Do not overcook as rice will become too starchy.*

   Yield: 6 servings

ACORN SQUASH SOUP

> 4 acorn squash
> 1 onion, sliced
> 3 carrots, sliced
> 1/3 cup water
> 2 tablespoons butter
> 1 tablespoon flour
> 1 teaspoon salt
> 1/2 to 1 teaspoon freshly ground pepper
> 2 (14-ounce) cans chicken broth
> 1/2 cup sherry
> 1/2 teaspoon nutmeg
> 1/8 teaspoon paprika
> Ground allspice and red pepper to taste
> 1 cup half-and-half
> 1 1/2 tablespoons sherry (optional)

Cut the squash into halves lengthwise and discard the seeds. Place cut side down in a baking pan and add 1 inch hot water. Bake at 350 degrees for 30 minutes. Spoon the tender pulp into a food processor or blender container, reserving the shells. Cool the shells, cover and store in the refrigerator.

Combine the onion and carrots with water to cover in a saucepan. Bring to a boil and reduce the heat. Simmer, covered, for 15 minutes or until tender; drain. Add the onion mixture and 1/3 cup water to the squash pulp in the food processor container and process for 30 seconds or until smooth.

Melt the butter in a heavy large saucepan. Add the flour, salt and pepper and cook for 1 minute, stirring constantly. Add the puréed squash mixture gradually. Stir in the chicken broth, 1/2 cup sherry, nutmeg, paprika, allspice and red pepper. Bring to a boil and reduce the heat. Simmer, covered, for 1 hour, stirring occasionally. Stir in the half-and-half and 1 1/2 tablespoons sherry. Cook just until heated through.

Reheat the squash shells at 350 degrees for 15 to 20 minutes. Serve the soup in the shells on a bed of kale leaves. Garnish with paprika.

Yield: 8 servings

AUTUMN TABLECLOTHS can be assembled in just a few minutes. This effect requires a solid color tablecloth, fall leaves, and a sheer fabric such as tulle, chiffon, or georgette cut the same size as the tablecloth. First, place the tablecloth on the table. Next, arrange fall leaves in a complementary manner. Finally, lay the sheer fabric on top, taking care to accent place settings or centerpieces.

Chicken Stock

Cut 2 pounds chicken wings into 1½-inch pieces and place in a heavy roasting pan. Roast at 400 degrees for 1 hour or until brown. Chop 4 celery ribs, 2 carrots and 2 onions and add to the roasting pan. Roast for 1 hour or until the vegetables begin to brown. Combine the chicken and vegetables with 4 quarts water, 4 bay leaves, 4 parsley sprigs, 4 thyme sprigs and 8 black peppercorns in a large saucepan. Simmer for 6 hours or until the liquid is reduced to 4 cups. Strain into a medium saucepan and simmer for 40 minutes or until reduced to 1½ cups. Store in the refrigerator.

TORTELLINI SOUP

Tortellini is a small pasta stuffed with various fillings such as cheese, mushrooms or pesto. The filled pasta is folded over and shaped into a ring. A larger version is called tortelloni.

5	cups chicken stock
1	(28-ounce) can chopped tomatoes
1	medium onion, chopped
1	cup chopped celery
1	cup chopped carrots
¼	cup chopped fresh parsley
¼	teaspoon garlic powder
1½	teaspoons Italian seasoning
1	teaspoon dried basil
½	teaspoon dried chives
¼	teaspoon dried oregano
1	teaspoon salt
½	teaspoon pepper
9	ounces uncooked cheese tortellini
1	cup chopped cooked chicken

Combine the chicken stock, tomatoes, onion, celery, carrots, parsley, garlic powder, Italian seasoning, basil, chives, oregano, salt and pepper in a large saucepan. Cook for 45 to 60 minutes or until the vegetables are tender.

Add the tortellini and cook using the package directions, adding the chicken during the last 5 to 10 minutes of cooking time. Top each serving with Parmesan cheese.

You may use several colors of tortellini if desired, or add instant chicken bouillon to the stock for enhanced flavor.

Yield: 6 servings

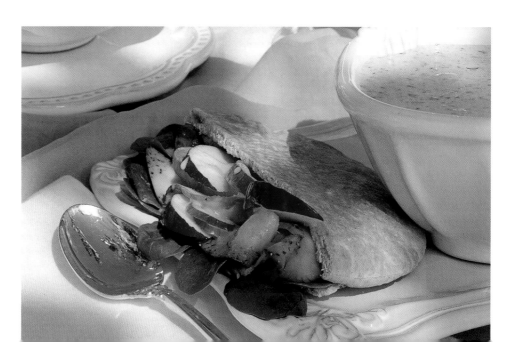

CHILI BLANCO

    1 pound dried white beans
    6 cups chicken broth
    1 teaspoon chicken stock base
    2 onions, chopped
    1 tablespoon vegetable oil
    6 to 8 garlic cloves, minced
    1 (7-ounce) can chopped green chiles
    2 to 3 teaspoons ground cumin
    2 teaspoons dried oregano leaves
    1 teaspoon cayenne pepper
    4 cups chopped cooked chicken
    8 ounces (1 cup) sour cream
    3 cups shredded Monterey Jack cheese

Rinse and sort the beans. Combine with the chicken broth and chicken stock base in a large saucepan. Simmer, covered, for 2 hours.

Sauté the onions in the oil in a skillet until golden brown. Add to the bean mixture with the garlic, green chiles, cumin, oregano, cayenne pepper and chicken. Simmer for 30 minutes longer or until the beans are tender.

Add the sour cream and cheese and heat until the cheese melts. Serve with sour cream, green onions, cilantro and chopped tomatoes.

Yield: 6 servings

TURKEY AND APPLE PITAS

    2 large whole wheat pita rounds
    2 cups fresh spinach leaves
    1 red onion, sliced, separated into rings
   12 thin slices cooked turkey breast
    1 small apple, thinly sliced
    2 tablespoons nonfat plain yogurt
    1 tablespoon honey
  1 1/2 teaspoons Dijon mustard

Cut the pita rounds into halves and open to form pockets. Fill with the spinach, onion rings, turkey and apple slices.

Mix the yogurt, honey and mustard in a bowl. Spoon some of the mixture over the sandwich filling and serve the remaining mixture with the sandwiches.

Photograph for this recipe is on page 86 and opposite.

Yield: 4 servings

PITA BREAD is a round Middle Eastern flat bread. When slit horizontally, it forms a pocket. This bread is great to stuff with a variety of ingredients to make an out-of-the-ordinary sandwich. Pita bread can be toasted and cut into wedges and used with dips and spreads. It is available at most supermarkets in white or whole wheat.

Runza Bread

Dissolve 1 package (2½ teaspoons) active dry yeast in 1¼ cups warm water. Add 2 tablespoons shortening, 2 tablespoons sugar and 2 teaspoons salt and mix well. Add 2 cups flour and mix well. Add an additional 1 cup flour and mix until stiff. Turn onto a well floured surface and knead 4 to 5 minutes or until smooth and elastic. Cover and let rise for 15 minutes. Roll dough out and use with Kraut Runza recipe.

Kraut Runza

- 1 head cabbage, cored, chopped
- 1 medium-large onion, chopped
- 2 medium garlic cloves, crushed
- 3 tablespoons vegetable oil
- 1 pound lean ground beef
- 1 tablespoon (or more) salt
  Pepper to taste
- 1 recipe Runza Bread (at left)

Sauté the cabbage, onion and garlic in the heated oil in a heavy large saucepan over medium-high heat until the cabbage is translucent. Add the ground beef and mix well. Stir in the salt and pepper. More salt may be needed.

Roll the bread dough ¼ inch thick on a lightly floured surface. Cut into squares measuring 3×3 inches or more. Place a scoop of the cabbage mixture in the center of each square and bring the corners up to enclose the filling; pinch to seal.

Place on a baking sheet. Bake at 400 degrees for 20 minutes or until golden brown.

It is important to use a generous amount of salt in this recipe.

Yield: 15 servings

Hot Italian Sandwiches

- ¼ cup sour cream
- 2 tablespoons chopped onion
- ½ teaspoon dried oregano
- ¼ teaspoon seasoned salt
- 8 slices Italian bread
- 8 slices bacon, cut into halves, crisp-fried
- 8 tomato slices
- 4 slices mozzarella cheese
- 3 tablespoons butter or margarine

Combine the sour cream, onion, oregano and seasoned salt in a bowl and mix well. Spread the mixture over half the bread slices. Layer each with 4 bacon pieces, 2 tomato slices and 1 slice of cheese. Top with the remaining bread.

Melt 2 tablespoons of the butter in a skillet over medium heat. Add the sandwiches and cook until the bread is golden brown on both sides and the cheese melts, adding remaining 1 tablespoon butter if needed.

Yield: 4 servings

Pressed Picnic Sandwiches

Tapenade is a black olive paste.

Dijon Vinaigrette
- 1½ teaspoons Dijon mustard
- 1 tablespoon balsamic vinegar
- ¼ cup extra-virgin olive oil
- 2 tablespoons warm water
- Salt and pepper to taste

Sandwich
- 1 flat loaf Italian ciabatta or paisan bread
- ½ cup black olive tapenade
- 3 medium roasted red bell peppers
- 8 ounces goat cheese, crumbled
- 1 (8-ounce) jar marinated artichoke hearts, drained
- 6 ounces thinly sliced prosciutto
- 4 ounces thinly sliced salami
- 2¼ cups loosely packed fresh herbs, such as basil, cilantro and/or parsley

For the vinaigrette, mix the mustard and vinegar in a small bowl. Whisk in the olive oil and warm water gradually. Season with salt and pepper and mix well.

For the sandwich, slice the bread into halves horizontally. Spread the tapenade on the bottom half. Cut the roasted peppers into 1-inch strips and arrange over the tapenade. Layer the goat cheese and artichoke hearts over the top and drizzle with half the vinaigrette.

Add layers of prosciutto and salami, sprinkle with the herbs and drizzle with the remaining vinaigrette. Place the top of the bread on the sandwich and wrap tightly with plastic wrap.

Place a heavy weight on the sandwich and let stand for 1 hour or longer. Cut into 10 pieces to serve.

Yield: 10 servings

Hot Ground Ham Sandwiches

Place 1 pound cooked ham, 2 chopped green bell peppers, 1 chopped onion, 1 drained 3-ounce bottle stuffed olives and 1 pound chopped American cheese separately in a meat grinder and grind to mix well. Combine with one 6-ounce can tomato paste and ½ cup softened unsalted butter in a bowl and mix well. Store, covered, in the refrigerator for 24 hours or longer. Spread the ham mixture on each of 18 bakery luncheon or regular sandwich buns. Wrap the sandwiches individually in foil. Bake at 350 degrees for 20 minutes.

BAKED CHEESY HAM SANDWICHES

Mix ¹/₄ cup softened margarine with 1 teaspoon each horseradish, mustard, minced onion and poppy seeds in a bowl. Split 12 whole wheat cocktail buns and spread with poppy seed butter. Cut 6 slices baby Swiss cheese into halves and fold 1 slice of thinly sliced honey ham around each slice of cheese. Place in the buns and wrap individually with foil. Bake at 350 degrees for 20 minutes.

GRILLED ASPARAGUS PÂTÉ SANDWICHES

  1 (3-ounce) package dry-pack sun-dried tomatoes
  2 (10-ounce) packages frozen asparagus, thawed, drained
12 ounces cream cheese, softened
  1 cup freshly grated Parmesan cheese
  1 teaspoon each salt and white pepper
30 slices sourdough bread
¹/₄ cup (¹/₂ stick) butter, softened
¹/₂ cup grated Parmesan cheese

Combine the sun-dried tomatoes with water to cover in a bowl and let stand to rehydrate; drain well and chop.

Combine the asparagus, cream cheese, 1 cup Parmesan cheese, salt and white pepper in a food processor container and process until smooth. Spread the mixture evenly over half the bread slices. Sprinkle with the sun-dried tomatoes and top with the remaining bread slices.

Spread both sides of the sandwiches with the butter and sprinkle evenly with ¹/₂ cup Parmesan cheese. Grill the sandwiches on a heated griddle for 3 minutes on each side or until golden brown.

Yield: 15 servings

CRANBERRY CHUTNEY

¹/₄ cup minced onion
  1 garlic clove, minced
¹/₂ cup sugar
  2 tablespoons vinegar
¹/₂ cup water
¹/₄ teaspoon ground cloves
¹/₂ teaspoon ground cinnamon
¹/₂ teaspoon ground cardamom
¹/₈ teaspoon ground ginger
¹/₄ teaspoon salt
1¹/₂ cups fresh cranberries
2¹/₂ tablespoons brown sugar

Combine the onion, garlic, sugar, vinegar, water, cloves, cinnamon, cardamom, ginger and salt in a saucepan and mix well. Simmer for 5 minutes. Add the cranberries and brown sugar. Simmer for 15 minutes or until thickened.

Cool the mixture to room temperature and store in the refrigerator. Serve as an accompaniment to pork and poultry.

You may also spoon the chutney over molded cream cheese and serve as an appetizer.

Yield: 14 servings

Cornichons au Vinaigre

3½ pounds tiny (gherkin) pickling cucumbers
8 ounces pearl or boiling onions, peeled
1 cup kosher or pickling salt
1 quart cold water
2 tablespoons white wine or rice vinegar
5 grape leaves
5 garlic cloves
5 sprigs of thyme
5 sprigs of tarragon
30 black peppercorns
15 white peppercorns
5 whole cloves
5 (¼-inch) pieces of hot dried red pepper
Coriander seeds to taste
8 cups white wine vinegar or rice vinegar

Rinse and well drain the cucumbers in cold water. Dry gently with a towel, rubbing to remove any spines. Combine with the onions in an earthenware or enamel bowl and sprinkle with the salt. Let stand for 24 hours, turning frequently.

Drain the cucumbers and onions and rinse with a mixture of the cold water and 2 tablespoons vinegar. Drain and dry with a towel.

Place 1 grape leaf, 1 garlic clove, 1 sprig of thyme, 1 sprig of tarragon, 6 black peppercorns, 3 white peppercorns, 1 whole clove, 1 piece of red pepper and 1 pinch of coriander seeds in each of 5 hot sterilized 1-pint jars. Fill the jars with the cucumber mixture.

Bring 8 cups of vinegar to a boil in a saucepan and pour into the prepared jars, leaving ½ inch headspace. Wipe the rims with a damp cloth and seal with 2-piece lids. Process in a boiling water bath for 10 minutes. Cool on a rack away from drafts. Store in a cool dark place for 1 month or longer before serving.

Yield: 80 (2-tablespoon) servings

CORNICHON *is a French word for gherkin. If you love cornichons, the tiny, sour pickles that you get as an accompaniment when you order pâté in a fancy restaurant, you can make your own. Imported cornichons are jarringly expensive, probably why you generally get only one or two when you order pâté.*

Some seed catalogs now offer the special variety of cucumber that the French grow for these tiny pickles. Or, you can use very tiny pickling cucumbers. The secret is to pick them when they are no more than 2 inches in length. Or, lacking a cucumber patch of your own, buy the smallest pickling cucumbers you can find at the farmers market.

Use only freshly picked pickling cucumbers. The outside should be a healthy green, without any soft spots or discoloration. And use only white wine or rice vinegar, which lacks the harsh taste of the distilled white vinegar.

Forget Me Not...

SIDE DISHES

This photograph is sponsored by:
Carol, Kate, Grace, and Frances Williams

Forget Me Not...

Throughout the previous chapters we've discussed various entertaining, food, and serving ideas. Now we continue to look at organizational skills and their importance within the big picture. The following is a working timetable set up as a checklist.

Timing	Mission
2–4 weeks in advance	Set a date.
	Prepare the guest list.
	Send out the invitations.
	Reserve the rented items.
	Develop a theme.
1–2 weeks in advance	Plan the menu.
	Prepare the order of preparation list.
	Note special equipment, furniture, or serving pieces necessary.
	Purchase beverages and paper goods.
	Order special foods/flowers/favors.
3–5 days in advance	Clean and press tablecloths and napkins.
	Choose your attire and make sure it is clean and pressed.
	Pick up the rented/borrowed items.
	Prepare the grocery list from recipes.
	Purchase the groceries.
	Wrap the favors.
	Design the place cards.
3 days in advance	Clean the house.
	Clean the serving pieces.
	Prepare recipes that may be made and stored ahead.
	Plan for additional storage.

Timing	Mission
1–3 days in advance	Set up the beverage area.
	Pick out the music.
	Arrange the decorations.
	Set the table.
	Set out serving dishes/utensils.
1 day in advance	Prepare additional recipes.
	Add the finishing touches.
	Pick up the ice, flowers, and other perishables.
	Check the house for final needs, fresh towels, etc.
	Make a schedule of things to be done tomorrow, with a timetable for cooking dishes.
Day of the event	Compile a list of things you need to remember.
	Make a list for cleanup.
	Prepare the remaining food items according to timetable so everything will finish at the same time.
	Wash the dishes as you go to save cleanup later.
	Make sure that everything that needs to be chilled is well chilled by party time.
	Allow time to relax, breathe, and dress.

By utilizing lists and reminders one insures a relaxed and well organized event.
Take a deep breath and enjoy the fruits of your labor.

Green Beans with Bacon

   1   teaspoon butter
  2 or 3 slices lean bacon, chopped
  1/2 small onion, finely chopped
1 1/2 pounds fresh green beans, whole or cut
   2 tablespoons white vinegar
  1/4 cup water
   2 teaspoons sugar
     Salt and pepper to taste

Heat a pressure cooker and add the butter, bacon and onion. Sauté, uncovered, until the bacon and onion are brown. Add the beans, vinegar, water, sugar, salt and pepper.

Seal the pressure cooker and allow the steam to vent to remove the air from the cooker. Cook using the manufacturer's instructions for 3 to 4 minutes or for the time recommended by the manufacturer; do not overcook. Cool the pressure cooker immediately to stop the cooking process.

Photograph for this recipe is on page 105.

Yield: 6 servings

Scalloped Broccoli

   1 (10-ounce) package frozen broccoli
  1/4 cup toasted almonds
   1 tablespoon butter
   1 tablespoon flour
   1 cup milk
  1/3 cup shredded sharp Cheddar cheese
  1/2 teaspoon salt
   2 slices lean bacon, crisp-fried, crumbled
  1/4 cup bread crumbs
   1 teaspoon butter, melted

Cook the broccoli using the package directions; drain. Arrange in an oiled baking dish. Sprinkle with almonds.

Melt 1 tablespoon butter in a saucepan and stir in the flour. Cook for several minutes, stirring constantly. Add the milk and cook until thickened, stirring constantly. Add the cheese and cook until melted. Season with the salt.

Pour the sauce over the broccoli and almonds and sprinkle with the bacon. Toss the bread crumbs with 1 teaspoon butter in a bowl. Sprinkle over the top. Bake at 350 degrees for 30 to 35 minutes or until bubbly.

Note: *Seeds and nuts, both shelled and unshelled, keep best and longest when stored in the freezer. Nuts in the shells crack more easily when frozen.*

Yield: 4 servings

PRESSURE COOKERS *are cooking devices that utilize steam, high heat, and pressure to cook food while maintaining its nutritional value and moistness. The pressure created by steam at high temperatures may cut cooking time by as much as two-thirds. The greater the pressure, the shorter the cooking time. New models have built-in valves and indicator rods that monitor the pressure. Old models have a detached pressure regulator. All models have safety valves to vent steam as needed. Most pressure cookers are designed for the stove, with a few models catering to the microwave.*

PORT WINES *consist of many types and labels. This chart should simplify the options.*

Label	Vintage	Aged
Vintage	Single	2 to 50 years
Late Bottled	Single	6 years
Single Vintage	Single	7 years
Tawny	Blend	up to 40 years
Vintage Character	Several	2 to 10 years
Ruby	Several	2 to 10 years

All are aged in wood and ready to drink when bottled.

SWEET-AND-SOUR CABBAGE

2 cups coarsely chopped cabbage
1 cup sauerkraut
1 1/2 cups coarsely chopped onions
2 (14-ounce) cans stewed or chopped tomatoes
2 large garlic cloves, minced
6 cups beef stock
1 1/2 teaspoons lemon juice
3/4 cup packed brown sugar
2 teaspoons paprika
1 1/2 teaspoons parsley
1/2 teaspoon thyme
1/4 teaspoon sour salt or citric salt
3/4 teaspoon salt
1/2 teaspoon pepper
1 cup (1/4-inch) carrot slices

Combine the cabbage, sauerkraut, onions, tomatoes and garlic in a large saucepan. Add the beef stock, lemon juice, brown sugar, paprika, parsley, thyme, sour salt, salt and pepper and mix well. Bring to a boil and reduce the heat. Simmer for 30 minutes.

Add the carrots. Simmer for 45 minutes longer or until the vegetables are tender.

Note: *Sour salt or citric salt can be found in the kosher section at your favorite grocery.*

Yield: 10 servings

CARROTS IN PORT SAUCE

1 onion, sliced 1/4 inch thick
2 medium garlic cloves, minced
1/4 cup olive oil
1 1/2 pounds baby carrots, cut into quarters lengthwise
Salt and pepper to taste
1/4 cup strong beef broth
1/4 cup port

Sauté the onion and garlic in the heated olive oil in a skillet over low heat for 5 minutes. Add the carrots, salt and pepper and mix well.

Bring the beef broth and wine to a boil in a small saucepan. Pour over the carrots. Cook, covered, over medium heat for 5 minutes or until the carrots are tender-crisp. Cook, uncovered, over high heat until the liquid evaporates, stirring constantly. Garnish with fresh parsley to serve. Serve with pork.

Yield: 6 servings

HONEY-GLAZED CARROTS

2 pounds carrots
1/2 cup (1 stick) butter
1/4 cup honey
1/4 teaspoon pumpkin pie spice, or a mixture of
   cinnamon and nutmeg

Peel the carrots and cut into 1/2-inch pieces. Steam in a steamer until partially cooked. Combine the butter, honey and pumpkin pie spice in a saucepan. Add the carrots and cook, uncovered, over medium-low heat until the sauce thickens and the carrots are tender.

Photograph for this recipe is on page 104.

Yield: 12 servings

SCALLOPED CARROTS

12 medium carrots, peeled, sliced
 8 ounces sliced sharp American cheese
 1 small onion, minced
1/4 cup (1/2 stick) butter
1/4 cup flour
1/4 teaspoon dry mustard
 1 teaspoon salt
 2 cups milk
1/4 teaspoon celery salt
1/8 teaspoon pepper
 2 cups fresh bread crumbs
 2 tablespoons butter, melted

Cook the carrots in water to cover in a saucepan until tender; drain. Alternate layers of the carrots and cheese in a 2-quart baking dish until both ingredients are used, beginning and ending with the carrots.

Sauté the onion in 1/4 cup butter in a saucepan for 2 to 3 minutes. Stir in the flour, dry mustard and salt. Cook over low heat until the flour is well mixed, stirring constantly. Stir in the milk gradually. Bring to a boil and cook for 1 minute or until thickened, stirring constantly. Add the celery salt and pepper.

Pour the sauce over the layers in the baking dish. Top with a mixture of the bread crumbs and 2 tablespoons butter. Bake, uncovered, at 350 degrees for 25 minutes or until golden brown and bubbly.

You may prepare this in advance and chill until serving time. Allow 10 to 15 minutes longer to bake.

Yield: 8 servings

MUSTARD *comes in two primary varieties: (1) white (yellow) and (2) brown (Asian). White seeds are larger, less intense in flavor, and are used in American and English mustards. Brown seeds are smaller, more pungent, and are used in European and Chinese mustards. Mustard seeds are packaged whole or ground, or can be used in prepared mustards. Whole seeds keep up to one year, while ground seeeds keep for six months. Store in a dry, dark place.*

Iowa and corn just naturally go together, for Iowa is a primary producer of corn in the United States. The top two varieties are white and yellow. White is smaller and sweeter, while yellow is larger and full-flavored. Because the picking of corn converts sugar into starch, it's important to eat corn soon after picking. Husks should be green and tight and silks golden brown. Kernels should be full and well rounded.

Scalloped Corn

1/4	cup chopped onion
2	tablespoons butter or margarine
2	tablespoons flour
1/2	teaspoon paprika
1/4	teaspoon dry mustard
1	teaspoon salt
3/4	cup milk
2	cups fresh, frozen or drained canned corn
1	egg, lightly beaten
1	cup bread crumbs
1	tablespoon butter, melted

Sauté the onion in 2 tablespoons butter in a saucepan until golden brown. Stir in the flour, paprika, dry mustard and salt. Cook until bubbly; remove from the heat. Stir in the milk gradually. Bring to a boil and cook for 1 minute or until thickened, stirring constantly; remove from the heat. Add the corn and then the egg and mix well. Spoon into a 1-quart baking dish. Top with a mixture of bread crumbs and 1 tablespoon butter. Bake at 350 degrees for 30 minutes.

Yield: 6 servings

Elegant Eggplant

1	large eggplant, peeled, chopped
1/2	teaspoon ground marjoram
	Salt to taste
1/3	cup chopped parsley
1/4	cup chopped onion
2	tablespoons butter or margarine
2	cups soft bread crumbs
2	tablespoons butter or margarine, melted
1	large tomato, peeled, chopped
1/2	cup half-and-half
1/4	cup grated Parmesan cheese

Combine the eggplant with the marjoram, salt and a small amount of water in a saucepan. Cook, covered, for 8 to 10 minutes or until tender; drain. Combine with the parsley in a bowl.

Sauté the onion in 2 tablespoons butter in a small skillet until tender but not brown. Combine with the eggplant and mix well.

Toss the bread crumbs with 2 tablespoons butter in a bowl. Layer the eggplant mixture, tomato and bread crumb mixture 1/2 at a time in a greased 9×9-inch baking dish. Pour the half-and-half over the layers and sprinkle with the cheese. Bake at 375 degrees for 45 minutes or until brown and bubbly.

Yield: 6 servings

Onion Casserole

   3 large onions, thinly sliced
   1/4 cup (1/2 stick) butter or margarine
   1 sleeve of butter crackers, crushed
   1 tablespoon butter or margarine, melted
   1 cup shredded sharp Cheddar cheese
   3 tablespoons milk

Sauté the onions in 1/4 cup butter in a skillet until tender but not brown. Toss the cracker crumbs with 1 tablespoon melted butter in a bowl.

Layer half the crumb mixture in a 1 1/2- to 2-quart baking dish. Layer the onions, cheese and remaining crumb mixture in the prepared dish. Drizzle with the milk. Bake at 350 degrees for 20 to 30 minutes or until heated through.

Note: *To crush is to reduce a food to its finest form, such as crumbs, paste or powder. Crushing is often accomplished with a mortar and pestle or a rolling pin.*

Yield: 6 servings

Potatoes with Leeks and Gruyère Cheese

   1 pound leeks
   2 tablespoons butter
   8 ounces cream cheese, softened
   1/4 teaspoon ground nutmeg
   1 1/2 teaspoons salt
   1 teaspoon freshly ground pepper
   1 cup milk
   3 large eggs
   2 pounds large white-skinned potatoes, peeled, shredded
   3 cups shredded Gruyère cheese

Thinly slice the white and light green portions only of the leeks. Sauté in the butter in a large skillet over medium heat for 10 minutes or until tender. Remove to a large bowl.

Combine the cream cheese, nutmeg, salt and pepper in a food processor container and process until smooth. Add the milk and eggs and process just until blended. Add to the sautéed leeks. Stir in the potatoes and cheese.

Spoon into a buttered 9×13-inch baking dish. Bake at 350 degrees for 55 minutes or until the potatoes are tender and the top is brown. Serve immediately or cool and store, covered, in the refrigerator. Reheat for 25 minutes to serve.

Yield: 8 servings

CORN ON THE COB *will generally be served at informal meals. It may be broken into halves to make it easier to handle. It tends to be rather messy to eat, so limit the amount of butter and seasoning. Eating across the cob or around it is a matter of individual preference. Eat only a few rows or a section at a time. Adding butter and salt to each section as you eat limits the mess.*

VEGETABLES *that grow under the ground (potatoes, carrots, turnips, etc.) should be placed in cold water to cook. Vegetables that grow above the ground (beans, peas, tomatoes, etc.) should be placed in boiling water to cook.*

MURPHY'S POTATOES

    9 large baking potatoes
    3 cups shredded Cheddar cheese
 1/2 cup (1 stick) butter
    1 teaspoon salt or seasoned salt
    2 cups half-and-half

Cook the unpeeled potatoes in water to cover in a saucepan until tender; drain. Cool to room temperature and chill in the refrigerator for 8 hours or longer. Peel and grate the potatoes.

Layer the potatoes and cheese 1/2 at a time in a greased baking dish. Melt the butter with the salt and half-and-half in a saucepan. Pour over the layers. Bake at 350 degrees for 30 to 35 minutes or until the cheese is golden brown.

Yield: 10 servings

POTATO AND CARROT BAKE

      6 to 8 large potatoes
 1 1/2 cups shredded carrots
   1/2 cup finely chopped onion
      2 garlic cloves, minced
   1/2 cup shredded Swiss cheese
      2 cups half-and-half
 1 1/2 teaspoons salt
   1/8 teaspoon white pepper
      1 tablespoon butter or margarine
   1/2 cup soft bread crumbs
      2 tablespoons chopped fresh parsley

Peel the potatoes and shred into a bowl of cold water to prevent discoloring; potatoes should measure about 6 cups.

Combine the carrots, onion, garlic, cheese, half-and-half, salt and white pepper in a bowl and mix well. Drain the potatoes and pat dry. Add to the carrot mixture and mix well. Spoon into a lightly greased 8×12-inch baking dish.

Melt the butter in a small saucepan over low heat. Add the bread crumbs and parsley and toss to mix well. Sprinkle over the potato mixture. Bake at 325 degrees for 1 hour and 10 minutes or until the potatoes are tender. Let stand for 5 minutes before serving.

Yield: 8 servings

GARLIC MASHED POTATOES

1¼ pounds russet potatoes
¼ cup milk
6 large garlic cloves, crushed
¼ cup heavy cream
¼ cup (½ stick) butter, softened
Salt and pepper to taste

Peel the potatoes and cut into ½-inch pieces. Combine with the milk, garlic and cold water to cover in a medium saucepan. Bring to a boil and reduce the heat. Simmer, covered, for 25 minutes or until the potatoes are very tender.

Drain, reserving ¼ cup cooking liquid. Return the potatoes and garlic to the saucepan and add the cream and butter. Mash until smooth, adding a small amount of the reserved liquid if necessary for the desired consistency. Season with salt and pepper.

Yield: 4 servings

SWEET POTATO PUFF

3 cups mashed cooked sweet potatoes, chilled
½ cup sugar
½ cup (1 stick) butter, melted
2 eggs, beaten
⅓ cup milk
1 teaspoon vanilla extract
½ cup packed brown sugar
2 tablespoons butter
¼ cup flour
½ cup chopped pecans

Combine the sweet potatoes, sugar, melted butter, eggs, milk and vanilla in a bowl and beat until smooth. Spoon into a greased 2½-quart baking dish.

Mix the brown sugar, 2 tablespoons butter, flour and pecans in a small bowl. Sprinkle over the sweet potato mixture. Bake, uncovered, at 350 degrees for 35 to 40 minutes or until golden brown.

You may prepare this in advance and chill or freeze until needed; allow a slightly longer baking time.

Note: *Submerge peeled sweet potatoes in lightly salted water to prevent darkening.*

Yield: 10 servings

SWEET POTATOES *come in two primary varieties: a pale sweet potato and the darker skinned sweet potato, often mistakenly referred to as a yam. The lighter skinned sweet potato is not sweet when cooked, but is more like a regular white baking potato. The darker skinned sweet potato has a thick orange skin and an orange sweet pulp. Store sweet potatoes in a cool, dry place for 5 to 7 days.*

SQUASH *fall into two primary types: summer squash and winter squash. Summer squash is thin skinned with a mild flavor, high water content, and soft seeds. Three major varieties are Crookneck, Pattypan, and Zucchini. Look for blemish-free, bright-colored, small summer squash. Winter squash have a hard skin and seeds in addition to a firm pulp. Winter varieties include Acorn, Buttercup, Butternut, Hubbard, Spaghetti, and Turban. They require a longer cooking time due to the density of the pulp. Select winter squash with a hard skin and deep color free from bruises or mold. Winter squash require no refrigeration and may be stored for several months.*

BAKED ACORN SQUASH WITH PEARS AND APPLES

- 2 medium acorn squash
- 2 large apples, peeled, chopped
- 2 large pears, peeled, chopped
- 1/4 cup raisins
- 2 tablespoons dark brown sugar
  Grated zest of 1 small orange
- 1/4 teaspoon cinnamon
- 1/8 teaspoon nutmeg
- 2 tablespoons butter
- 1/4 cup apple cider or orange juice
- 1 tablespoon bourbon or dark rum

Cut the squash into halves, discarding the seeds. Place cut side down in a buttered baking pan. Add 1/4 inch hot water. Bake at 325 degrees for 45 minutes.

Combine the apples, pears, raisins, brown sugar, orange zest, cinnamon and nutmeg in a bowl and toss to mix well. Sauté the fruit mixture in the butter in a large skillet for 5 minutes. Stir in the apple cider and bourbon. Simmer for 8 minutes or until the fruit is tender.

Pour the water from the baking pan with the squash and turn the squash cut side up. Fill the centers with the fruit mixture. Bake, uncovered, for 15 minutes longer.

Yield: 4 servings

CIDER-ROASTED SQUASH

- 6 1/2 cups (1-inch) winter squash cubes
- 1 medium onion, cut into wedges
- 1/4 cup apple cider
- 2 tablespoons olive oil
- 1 tablespoon brown sugar
- 1/4 teaspoon ground nutmeg
- 1/2 teaspoon salt
- 1/4 teaspoon pepper

Combine the squash and onion in a greased rectangular 3-quart baking dish. Combine the cider, olive oil, brown sugar, nutmeg, salt and pepper in a bowl and mix well. Pour over the squash mixture. Bake, uncovered, at 450 degrees for 35 minutes or until the squash is tender, stirring frequently.

You may substitute yams for the winter squash if preferred.

Yield: 8 servings

Orange-Glazed Squash

 2 acorn squash, cut into 1-inch pieces
 $1/3$ cup orange juice
 $1/2$ cup packed brown sugar
 $1/4$ cup light corn syrup
 $1/4$ cup ($1/2$ stick) butter or margarine
 2 teaspoons grated lemon zest
 $1/8$ teaspoon salt

Arrange the squash in a baking dish. Pour the orange juice over the squash. Bake, covered, at 350 degrees for 40 minutes. Combine the brown sugar, corn syrup, butter, lemon zest and salt in a saucepan. Bring to a simmer over medium heat, stirring occasionally. Pour over the squash. Bake, uncovered, for 15 minutes.

Yield: 4 servings

Tomato Pie

 5 medium tomatoes
 $1/2$ to 1 medium onion, chopped
 $1/2$ garlic clove, minced
 1 tablespoon brown sugar
 2 tablespoons chopped fresh basil
   Salt and pepper to taste
 1 baked (10-inch) pie shell, cooled
 $3/4$ cup mayonnaise
 1 cup shredded Cheddar cheese
 1 cup shredded Swiss cheese

Peel, seed and chop the tomatoes; drain well. Combine with the onion, garlic, brown sugar, basil, salt and pepper in a bowl and mix well. Spoon into the pie shell.

Mix the mayonnaise, Cheddar cheese and Swiss cheese in a bowl. Spread over the tomato mixture. Bake at 400 degrees for 20 minutes. Let stand for several minutes before slicing to serve.

Note: *You can make your own piecrust using the recipe at right or on page 29.*

Yield: 8 servings

Basic Piecrust

Combine $2^2/3$ cups flour, 2 tablespoons sugar and $1/2$ teaspoon salt in a food processor container. Add $1/2$ cup each chilled and chopped shortening and unsalted butter and pulse until the mixture resembles coarse cornmeal. Add a mixture of 1 egg beaten with 3 tablespoons ice water and process until the mixture begins to clump. Add additional water 1 teaspoon at a time, processing until the mixture forms a ball. Shape into 2 disks and wrap with plastic wrap. Chill for 1 to 24 hours. Let stand at room temperature for several minutes before rolling. Makes 2 pie shells or enough pastry for a 2-crust pie.

Roasted Corn on the Cob

Remove the outer husks from the ears of corn, leaving 1 or 2 layers of the inner husks. Fold the inner husks back and remove the silks and bad kernels; wash and dry the ears. Spread the kernels with butter and sprinkle with salt and pepper. Bring the husks up to cover the ears. Roast at 400 degrees for 10 to 12 minutes or until tender. Remove the husks and serve immediately.

Tomatoes Parmesan

  6 tomatoes
  1 cup seasoned bread crumbs
  1 cup grated Parmesan cheese
$^1\!/_2$ cup (1 stick) butter, sliced into 24 pieces

Cut each tomato into four $^1\!/_2$-inch slices and arrange in a baking pan. Mix the bread crumbs and cheese in a bowl and sprinkle on the tomatoes. Top each with butter. Broil for 5 minutes or until golden brown. Serve immediately.

Yield: 12 servings

Garlic Tomatoes

$^1\!/_3$ cup olive oil
  2 tablespoons red wine vinegar
  2 tablespoons chopped onion
  1 garlic clove, minced
  1 tablespoon chopped fresh basil, or 1 teaspoon dried basil
  1 teaspoon salt
  3 tomatoes, cut into wedges

Combine the olive oil, vinegar, onion, garlic, basil and salt in a bowl and mix well. Pour over the tomatoes in a shallow dish. Marinate, covered, in the refrigerator for several hours before serving.

Yield: 6 servings

COUSCOUS WITH DRIED FRUITS AND PECANS

- ¼ cup minced onion
- 2 tablespoons unsalted butter
- ¼ cup golden raisins
- ¼ cup dried cranberries
- ½ cup chopped dried apricots
- 2½ cups water
- ¼ teaspoon cinnamon
- ¼ teaspoon allspice
- ¾ teaspoon salt
- Pepper to taste
- 1¼ cups uncooked couscous
- ½ cup toasted pecans, chopped

Sauté the onion in the butter in a large saucepan over medium heat until golden brown. Add the raisins, cranberries, apricots, water, cinnamon, allspice, salt and pepper and mix well. Bring to a boil.

Remove the saucepan from the heat and stir in the couscous. Let stand, covered, for 10 minutes; fluff with a fork. Add the pecans and toss gently to mix. Serve immediately.

Yield: 8 servings

Couscous should be rinsed in a strainer under cool water until the water runs clear. Combine with fresh water to cover in a bowl and let stand for 30 minutes; drain well. Press any lumps to break them up and place in a colander lined with cheesecloth. Place the colander over boiling water and steam, uncovered, for 30 minutes or until tender.

QUICK-COOKING COUSCOUS

- Boiling water
- Couscous
- Boiling stock
- 2 tablespoons butter
- Salt and pepper to taste

Pour boiling water over the couscous in a bowl and let stand for 20 to 30 minutes; drain.

Add the couscous gradually to a mixture of the boiling stock and butter in a saucepan. Return to a boil and remove from the heat. Let stand, covered, for 10 minutes. Fluff with a fork and season to taste.

Yield: variable

BEEF STOCK

Cut 4 pounds of beef shank, knuckle, leg and neck bones into 2¹/2-inch pieces and place in a roasting pan. Roast at 450 degrees for 30 minutes or until brown, turning occasionally. Chop 2 carrots, 2 celery ribs with leaves and 2 tomatoes; quarter 2 onions. Add to the pan and baste with the pan drippings. Roast for 30 minutes, stirring occasionally. Remove to a stockpot. Defat the drippings and add a small amount of water, stirring to deglaze the pan. Add to the stockpot. Add 4¹/2 quarts water and bring to a boil; skim. Add ¹/2 cup parsley stems, ³/4 teaspoon dried thyme, 2 bay leaves, 10 peppercorns, 1 tablespoon kosher salt and 2 halved garlic cloves. Simmer, loosely covered, for 4 to 6 hours, adding water as needed to cover completely; strain and skim. Store in the refrigerator for up to 5 days or freeze for up to 6 months.

RISOTTO

```
1   medium onion, chopped
1   cup uncooked rice
¹/4 cup (¹/2 stick) butter
1   beef bouillon cube
2   cups boiling water
¹/4 cup dry white wine
2   tablespoons dried lentils (optional)
2   tablespoons grated Parmesan cheese
```

Sauté the onion and rice in the butter in a heavy skillet until golden brown. Dissolve the bouillon in the water in a saucepan. Stir in the rice mixture.

Add the wine and lentils and mix well. Simmer, covered, for 20 to 30 minutes or until the rice is tender. Stir in the cheese.

The flavor improves if prepared the day before and reheated to serve.

Yield: 4 servings

SPINACH AND WILD RICE CASSEROLE

```
 1   (6-ounce) package white and wild rice mix
 1   (10-ounce) can beef stock
 2   (10-ounce) packages frozen chopped spinach
 8   ounces cream cheese, softened
16   ounces fresh mushrooms, thinly sliced
 3   tablespoons butter
```

Cook the rice using the package directions and substituting the beef stock for an equivalent amount of the water.

Cook the spinach using the package directions; drain and press to remove the excess moisture. Combine with the cream cheese in a bowl and mix well. Add the rice.

Sauté the mushrooms in the butter in a skillet just until golden brown. Add to the rice mixture and mix well. Spoon into a buttered 2-quart baking dish. Bake, covered, at 350 degrees for 50 minutes or until heated through.

Note: *Instead of using canned beef stock, make your own using the recipe to the left.*

Yield: 8 servings

HERBED WILD RICE AND CRANBERRY STUFFING

1 cup chopped onion
1 cup chopped celery
1/2 teaspoon minced garlic, or to taste
3 tablespoons butter
3 tablespoons dry white vermouth or other dry white wine
1 tablespoon maple syrup or honey, or to taste
3/4 teaspoon dried tarragon
3/4 teaspoon poultry seasoning
1/2 teaspoon rubbed sage
   Dried thyme to taste
2 to 3 teaspoons chicken stock base, or salt to taste
8 cups dry bread cubes
3/4 cup cooked wild rice
1/2 cup dried cranberries (craisins)
1/2 to 3/4 cup (or more) chicken stock or turkey stock
2 to 3 tablespoons chopped parsley (optional)
   Freshly ground pepper to taste

Sauté the onion, celery and garlic in the butter in a heavy skillet or saucepan over medium heat until the onion is translucent. Add the wine and bring to a boil. Cook for 1 minute. Add the maple syrup, tarragon, poultry seasoning, sage, thyme and chicken stock base and mix well. The mixture should taste salty.

Combine the bread cubes, wild rice and cranberries in a large bowl and toss to mix. Add the vegetable mixture and enough chicken stock to make of the desired consistency; mix gently. Stir in the parsley and pepper.

Spoon into a buttered shallow baking dish. Bake, uncovered, at 350 degrees for 25 to 35 minutes or until heated through and slightly crusty on the top.

You may also use this mixture to stuff poultry.

Yield: 8 serving

TASTE FOOD for salt before you add it at the table. It is an insult to the cook to season food before trying it.

Fine Tuning...

PASTA

This photograph is sponsored by:
The Bernhard Family—
Rudy, Jan, Christine, and Kim

Fine Tuning...

There are quite a number of elements that make up a dynamic table setting. The theme or occasion will assist you in determining the menu and ultimately the service necessary to support the dining experience. The theme and menu may foster a rustic, casual, informal, intimate, celebratory, or formal table. There are service items necessary to further the theme and menu. Have you given thought to how to integrate your ideas? Let's walk through the process.

First, determine the formality of the event. Your invitation may have already set the tone. Casual themes may include pottery, stoneware, or even paper products. Informal may also include the more day-to-day dishware. Formal situations call for china, crystal, silver, and fine linens.

The table covering is the next consideration. Placemats are appropriate, particularly if the table has a lovely surface. Runners may also complement a pretty dining table. Tablecloths and napkins are traditionally white, especially in formal settings. Colored cloths and napkins are now readily used in less than formal meals or to define a distinct theme.

Cutlery correlates with the theme and formality. Flatware varies from plastic-handled casual ware to ornate silver or gold services. Cutlery should be placed on either side of the plate so that the utensils for the first course are on the outside and work in course by course. Knives are placed on the right and forks on the left. Dessert implements are placed above the plate or on either side, and a butter knife may be placed on the butter plate.

Glassware may be arranged from left to right or right to left, but should always be placed above the primary knife (meat knife). All glasses may be placed when the table is set unless the table becomes crowded. Dessert glasses, such as liqueur or port glasses, may be brought with their corresponding course. Glassware should be the best quality possible and should be spotless.

Plates and soup bowls are brought to the table in the order they are served. The bread plate goes to the left of the place setting. If the first course is cold, it may be placed on the table prior to seating.

Servers or condiments should be placed well within the reach of the guests, which may mean that multiple sets are necessary.

Seating guests should alternate male and female, paying particular attention to relationships, conversation, and spacing. A left-handed guest may be best seated at an end or corner. Eliminate the query of who sits where by using place cards. These may include first name and last name in extremely formal situations.

Serving is always done from the left. This allows the right hand to be free to assist. Clearing of everything, including condiments, is done prior to dessert.

The menu will determine the essential dishes, glasses, and flatware. The more formal the affair, the more stringent the rules. Casual or informal dining allows for more flexibility and creativity.

SHRIMP AND TORTELLINI CASSEROLE

- 1/4 cup (1/2 stick) butter
- 3 tablespoons lemon juice
- 2 garlic cloves, chopped
- 3 cups uncooked medium shrimp, peeled, deveined, or 1 1/2 pounds cooked shrimp
- 3 cups fresh cheese tortellini, cooked
- 2 tablespoons white wine
- 3/4 cup low-fat sour cream
- 1/2 cup low-fat plain yogurt
- 1 teaspoon ground oregano
- 1/2 teaspoon salt
- 1/2 teaspoon pepper
- 6 green onions, sliced
- 1/2 cup grated Parmesan cheese

Melt the butter in a skillet and add the lemon juice and garlic. Cook for 2 minutes over medium heat, stirring constantly. Add the shrimp and sauté for 3 to 5 minutes or until the shrimp are opaque; remove from the skillet.

Combine the shrimp, tortellini, wine, sour cream, yogurt, oregano, salt and pepper in a bowl and mix lightly.

Spoon into a greased 2-quart baking dish. Top with the green onions and cheese. Bake at 400 degrees for 20 minutes or until bubbly. Garnish with lemon twists and sprigs of fresh oregano.

Yield: 4 servings

CHINESE VERMICELLI

- 1/4 cup dark sesame oil
- 1 to 2 tablespoons hot chile oil, or to taste
- 2 tablespoons balsamic vinegar
- 1/4 cup black soy sauce
- 2 tablespoons sugar
- 18 ounces uncooked fresh vermicelli
- 1/2 cup sesame seeds, toasted
- 1 cup diagonally sliced green onions

Whisk the sesame oil, chile oil, vinegar, soy sauce and sugar in a large bowl.

Cook the vermicelli in water to cover in a saucepan for 1 minute or just until tender. Drain the pasta, rinse and drain again.

Add the pasta to the oil mixture and toss to coat well. Add the sesame seeds and fold in evenly. Spoon onto a shallow platter and top with the green onions. Serve warm or at room temperature.

Yield: 6 servings

PASTA *comes in a variety of shapes and sizes:*

Ravioli	Raviolinni
Spaghetti	Tripolini
Angel Hair	Ditalini
Bow Tie	Fusilla
Egg Noodles	Ziti
Vermicelli	Penne
Lasagna	Orzo
Manicotti	Wagon Wheels
Spaghettini	Rotini
Shells	Macaroni
Fettuccini	Gemelli
Linguini	Rigatoni
Cavatappi	Gnocchi
Pastina	Radiatore

SOY SAUCE *comes in several types and varieties. It is a dark, salty Asian condiment ranging from dark to light, thin to thick, and salty to mild. China and Japan are responsible for producing most soy sauces, which are made from soy beans and wheat or barley. It may be stored in a cool, dark location for many months.*

CHICKEN AND PECAN FETTUCCINI

Uncooked pasta of similar shapes and sizes may be substituted for one another. They should be measured by weight, not volume. Cooked pasta should be substituted cup for cup. One to two ounces of pasta equals one-half to one cup cooked pasta.

Linguini, Spaghetti, or
   Vermicelli
4 oz. dry = 2 to 3 cups cooked
8 oz. dry = 4 to 5 cups cooked
16 oz. dry = 8 to 9 cups cooked

Macaroni, Penne, Rotini,
   or Shells
4 oz. dry = 2½ cups cooked
8 oz. dry = 4½ cups cooked
16 oz. dry = 9 cups cooked

Fine or Medium Egg Noodles
4 oz. dry = 2 to 3 cups cooked
8 oz. dry = 4 to 5 cups cooked

1	pound boneless skinless chicken breasts
¼	cup (½ stick) butter, melted
3	cups sliced fresh mushrooms
1	cup sliced green onions with tops
¼	teaspoon garlic powder
½	teaspoon salt
¼	teaspoon freshly ground pepper
10	ounces fettuccini
½	cup (1 stick) butter
1	egg yolk
⅔	cup half-and-half
2	tablespoons chopped fresh parsley
¼	teaspoon garlic powder
¼	teaspoon salt
¼	teaspoon freshly ground pepper
½	cup freshly grated Parmesan cheese
1	cup toasted chopped pecans

Cut the chicken into ¾-inch pieces. Sauté in ¼ cup butter in a large skillet until light brown; remove with a slotted spoon and set aside. Add the mushrooms, green onions, ¼ teaspoon garlic powder, ½ teaspoon salt and ¼ teaspoon pepper to the drippings in the skillet. Sauté until the vegetables are tender. Return the chicken to the skillet and simmer for 20 minutes. Prepare the fettuccini according to the package directions; drain and keep warm.

Melt ½ cup butter in a 12-inch skillet over low heat. Combine the egg yolk, half-and-half, parsley, ¼ teaspoon garlic powder, ¼ teaspoon salt and ¼ teaspoon pepper in a bowl and mix well. Add to the skillet and cook until thickened, stirring constantly. Remove from the heat and stir in the cheese.

Pour over the fettuccini in a bowl. Add the chicken mixture and toss to mix well. Spoon onto a warm serving platter and sprinkle with the pecans.

Note: *It is much easier to trim and cube boneless chicken breasts if done while chicken is partially frozen.*

Yield: 6 servings

Ham and Asparagus Fettuccini

  8 ounces fresh asparagus, cut into 1-inch pieces
  2 cups low-fat cottage cheese
  3 tablespoons grated Parmesan cheese
$\frac{1}{2}$ teaspoon instant chicken bouillon
  2 tablespoons butter-flavor granules
$\frac{1}{2}$ teaspoon dried basil
$\frac{1}{2}$ teaspoon ground red pepper
  2 cups cubed cooked ham
  1 (2-ounce) jar chopped pimentos, drained
12 ounces uncooked fettuccini, cooked

Cook the asparagus, covered, in a small amount of water in a saucepan for 4 to 6 minutes or until tender-crisp; drain and keep warm.

Combine the cottage cheese, Parmesan cheese, chicken bouillon, butter-flavor granules, basil and red pepper in a blender container and process until smooth, scraping the side of the blender once. Spoon into a saucepan and cook over low heat until heated through, stirring constantly. Stir in the ham, asparagus and pimentos. Spoon over the pasta.

Photograph for this recipe is on page 121.

Yield: 4 servings

Fettuccini with Shrimp and Garlic

12 ounces medium shrimp, peeled, deveined, about 20 shrimp
     Salt and freshly ground black pepper to taste
$\frac{1}{4}$ cup olive oil
  4 teaspoons minced garlic
  1 teaspoon dried red pepper flakes, or to taste
$\frac{1}{4}$ cup dry white wine
  2 teaspoons fresh lemon juice
  6 tablespoons butter, softened
  6 ounces uncooked fettuccini or tagliarini, cooked

Season the shrimp with salt and black pepper. Heat half the olive oil in a large skillet over high heat. Add the shrimp and sauté for 1 minute on each side; remove with a slotted spoon.

Heat the remaining olive oil in the skillet over medium heat and add the garlic and red pepper flakes. Sauté for 1 minute. Add the wine, stirring to deglaze the skillet. Cook over high heat until reduced by $\frac{1}{2}$, stirring constantly.

Add the shrimp, lemon juice and butter to the skillet. Cook until the butter melts and the sauce thickens, stirring constantly. Season to taste. Toss with the pasta in a bowl. Serve hot.

Yield: 2 servings

PIMENTOS *are heart-shape red sweet peppers that provide a sweet, zesty version of a red bell pepper. They are 3 to 4 inches long and 2 to 3 inches wide. They are marketed fresh, canned, and bottled. Pimentos are primarily used to make paprika.*

SPINACH-FILLED LASAGNA ROLLS

12 uncooked lasagna noodles
1/2 cup finely chopped shallots
1 teaspoon finely chopped garlic
1/4 cup (1/2 stick) butter, melted
1 pound fresh spinach, or 2 (10-ounce) packages thawed frozen spinach, cooked, drained, chopped
8 ounces mushrooms, coarsely chopped
2 tablespoons butter, melted
2 eggs
1/4 cup freshly grated Parmesan cheese
4 ounces mozzarella cheese, chopped
2 ounces prosciutto or smoked ham, coarsely chopped
1/2 teaspoon salt
   Freshly ground pepper to taste
   Balsamella Sauce (page 127)
   Marinara Sauce (page 127)

Cook the noodles using the package directions; drain and pat dry on cotton towels.

Sauté the shallots and garlic in 1/4 cup butter in a saucepan for 5 minutes. Add the spinach and increase the heat. Cook until the moisture evaporates. Remove to a large bowl.

Sauté the mushrooms in 2 tablespoons butter in the saucepan over medium heat for 2 to 3 minutes or until tender. Add to the spinach mixture and stir to mix. Let cool. Add the eggs and mix well. Stir in the Parmesan cheese, mozzarella cheese, prosciutto, salt and pepper.

Spoon 3 tablespoons of the spinach mixture onto each noodle and roll as tightly as possible to enclose the filling.

Spread a thin layer of the Balsamella Sauce in a 9×13-inch baking dish. Arrange the lasagna rolls seam side down in the prepared dish. Pour the Marinara Sauce over the rolls and pour the remaining Balsamella Sauce over the top. Garnish with additional Parmesan cheese.

Bake, loosely covered with foil, at 350 degrees for 25 to 30 minutes or until bubbly, removing the foil during the last 10 minutes to brown.

Yield: 6 servings

MARINARA SAUCE

      2 tablespoons butter
      2 tablespoons olive oil
      1 cup finely chopped onion
   1/2 cup finely chopped carrot
      2 teaspoons crumbled dried basil
      2 tablespoons finely chopped flat-leaf parsley
      1 medium bay leaf
      1 (16-ounce) can tomatoes
      1 tablespoon tomato paste
         Salt and freshly ground black pepper to taste
   1/2 teaspoon hot red pepper

Melt the butter with the olive oil in a saucepan over very low heat. Add the onion and sauté for 10 minutes or until tender. Stir in the carrot. Sauté for 4 minutes.

Add the basil, parsley and bay leaf. Simmer for 1 minute, stirring constantly. Add the undrained tomatoes. Increase the heat and bring the mixture to a boil, mashing the tomatoes with a spoon to break them up. Stir in the tomato paste, salt, black pepper and red pepper. Cook over medium heat for 30 to 45 minutes or until thickened to the desired consistency.

Remove the bay leaf. Purée the mixture in a food mill. Return the purée to the saucepan and bring to a simmer over low heat, stirring frequently.

Yield: 6 servings

BALSAMELLA SAUCE

      3 tablespoons butter
      3 tablespoons flour
   1/2 cup milk
   1/2 cup heavy cream
   1/2 teaspoon salt
         White pepper and nutmeg to taste

Melt the butter in a saucepan over medium heat; do not brown. Remove from the heat and blend in the flour. Whisk in the milk and cream. Bring to a boil over medium heat, whisking constantly. Cook until thickened and smooth. Simmer for 2 to 3 minutes longer. Stir in the salt, white pepper and nutmeg.

Yield: 6 servings

PARMESAN is a hard, dry cheese made from skimmed or partially skimmed cow's milk. It has a rigid, sallow-golden rind and a straw-colored interior with a sumptuous, sharp flavor. Most domestic cheeses are aged fourteen months. Parmigiano-Reggianos (Italian) are usually aged two years, while those labeled stravecchio have been aged three years and stravecchiones are four years old. The complexity of the flavor and exceptionally granular texture are a consequence of the long aging.

CLASSIC LASAGNA

FRESH PASTA cooks faster than dried because of its high water content. Fresh or refrigerated pasta is pushed through a commercial pasta machine and is then cut, cooled, and packaged. It is not dried, as is dry packaged pasta.

Add fresh pasta to boiling, salted water and return to a boil. Start checking for doneness immediately. Pasta may cook in as fast as 2 to 3 minutes. Fettuccini or linguini may take slightly longer.

- 12 ounces ground sweet or hot Italian sausage
- 8 ounces ground round
- 1 small onion, chopped
- 7 or 8 fresh mushrooms, sliced
- 1/2 cup chopped green bell pepper
- 2 or 3 garlic cloves, minced
- 1 cup red table wine
- 1 (16-ounce) can stewed tomatoes
- 1 (15-ounce) can tomato sauce
- 1 teaspoon dried basil
- 1 teaspoon oregano
- 1/2 teaspoon fennel seeds
  Salt and pepper to taste
- 2 cups ricotta cheese
- 1 egg
- 3 tablespoons chopped fresh parsley
- 1/2 cup freshly grated Parmesan cheese
- 8 ounces uncooked lasagna noodles
- 2 tablespoons olive oil
- 8 ounces freshly shredded mozzarella cheese
  Chopped parsley

Remove the sausage from its casing. Brown the ground round and sausage with the onion, mushrooms, bell pepper and garlic in a saucepan, stirring until the ground round and sausage are crumbly; drain. Add the wine, tomatoes, tomato sauce, basil, oregano, fennel seeds, salt and pepper; mix well. Simmer, uncovered, for 2 to 3 hours.

Mix the ricotta cheese, egg, 3 tablespoons parsley and Parmesan cheese in a bowl. Cook the noodles al dente using the package directions and adding the olive oil to the cooking water; drain.

Spread a small amount of the sauce over the bottom of a 9×13-inch baking dish. Layer the noodles, ricotta cheese mixture, mozzarella cheese and remaining sauce 1/2 at a time in the prepared dish. Sprinkle with additional parsley. Bake, uncovered, at 350 degrees for 1 hour.

Yield: 8 servings

White Lasagna

   8 ounces fresh mushrooms, sliced
   2 tablespoons butter, melted
 1/2 cup dry white wine
 1/2 teaspoon dried tarragon
 1/4 cup (1/2 stick) butter
 1/4 cup flour
 1/4 teaspoon nutmeg
      Salt to taste
 1/4 teaspoon white pepper
   2 cups half-and-half
   2 cups chicken broth
   8 ounces uncooked lasagna noodles
   5 cups shredded cooked chicken breasts
  12 ounces Swiss cheese, shredded

Sauté the mushrooms in 2 tablespoons butter in a large skillet until light brown. Add the wine and tarragon and cook over medium heat until the liquid evaporates.

Melt 1/4 cup butter in a small saucepan. Whisk in the flour, nutmeg, salt and white pepper. Cook for 1 to 2 minutes, stirring constantly. Remove from the heat and stir in the half-and-half and chicken broth gradually. Cook until thickened and smooth, stirring constantly. Stir in the mushrooms.

Cook the noodles using the package directions; rinse with cold water and drain.

Spread a thin layer of the sauce in a greased 9×13-inch baking dish. Layer the noodles, chicken, sauce and cheese 1/3 at a time in the prepared dish.

Bake, uncovered, at 350 degrees for 40 to 50 minutes or until bubbly. Let stand for 5 minutes before serving.

Note: *To save leftover wine, freeze it in ice cube trays. The cubes can then be dropped into soups, stews, or any dish infused with wine.*

Yield: 8 servings

NUTMEG *is the product of a tree with a taupe one-inch seed that is hard and oval. It provides a sweet spice and spicy essence. It is sold whole or ground. Fresh is best, and whole nutmeg can be grated or ground with the assistance of a hand grater, electric grinder, or food processor.*

PENNE WITH YELLOW PEPPERS AND TOMATOES

Penne is large, straight tubes of macaroni cut diagonally.

- 2 garlic cloves, minced
- 2 tablespoons extra-virgin olive oil
- 2 large yellow bell peppers, thinly sliced
- 1 (28-ounce) can peeled Italian tomatoes, drained, chopped
  Salt and pepper to taste
- 16 ounces uncooked penne

Sauté the garlic in the olive oil in a large skillet for 2 minutes or until golden brown. Add the bell peppers. Sauté for 10 minutes or until the peppers are tender. Add the tomatoes. Cook over medium heat for 5 minutes or until thickened. Season with salt and pepper and keep warm.

Cook the penne al dente in salted water using the package directions; drain the pasta and return it to the saucepan. Add the pepper mixture and toss lightly to mix. Adjust the seasoning. Spoon the pasta onto a warm serving platter. Garnish with freshly grated Parmesan and Romano cheeses.

Photograph for this recipe is on page 120.

Yield: 6 servings

PENNE WITH ASIAGO CREAM SAUCE

ASIAGO *is a thick Italian cheese with a nutty, sumptuous taste, a glossy rind, and a yellow interior with numerous small holes. It is produced from skim cow's milk. Asiago under one year of age is used as table cheese; that aged over a year is used for grating.*

- 3 ounces pancetta or prosciutto
- 1 (14-ounce) can crushed tomatoes
- 1/2 cup (1 stick) butter
- 3 tablespoons brandy
- 1 cup heavy cream
- 1/2 teaspoon each oregano and pepper
- 1 cup coarsely chopped mixture of red onion and green onions
- 8 ounces uncooked penne
- 1/3 cup freshly grated asiago or Parmesan cheese

Cut the pancetta into 1/2-inch pieces. Brown lightly in a large skillet. Add the undrained tomatoes. Cook until the liquid is reduced by 1/2. Add the butter, brandy, cream, oregano and pepper and mix well. Cook over medium-high heat for 3 minutes or just until the mixture begins to thicken. Blanch the onion and green onions in water to cover in a saucepan; drain. Add to the sauce.

Cook the pasta partially in salted water in a saucepan. Drain and add to the sauce; mix gently. Cook until the pasta is tender. Stir in the cheese.

Note: *Pancetta, an unsmoked Italian bacon, cured with salt and spices, comes in a roll, similar to sausage. Tightly wrapped it will keep chilled for 3 weeks and frozen up to 6 months.*

Yield: 8 servings

Spaghetti with Shiitake and Tomato Cream Sauce

    16 ounces fresh shiitake mushrooms, stemmed, sliced
     3 tablespoons butter, melted
     1 (14-ounce) can crushed Italian plum tomatoes
     1 cup chicken broth
     1 cup heavy cream
    ½ cup freshly grated Parmesan cheese
     8 ounces uncooked spaghetti

Sauté the mushrooms in the butter in a large skillet over medium heat for
5 minutes or until tender. Add the undrained tomatoes, chicken broth and
cream. Simmer for 15 to 20 minutes or until reduced by ⅓, stirring constantly.
Remove from the heat and stir in the cheese.

Cook the spaghetti al dente using the package directions; drain. Add to
the sauce and toss lightly to mix well. Garnish servings with additional
Parmesan cheese.

You may also serve the sauce over the spaghetti if preferred.

Yield: 4 servings

Pesto Spaghetti

     3 cups fresh basil leaves
     1 garlic clove
    ¼ cup pine nuts
    ¼ cup (½ stick) butter, softened
    ¼ cup olive oil
    ½ cup freshly grated Parmesan or asiago cheese
        Salt to taste
     2 pounds uncooked spaghetti

Combine the basil, garlic, pine nuts, butter, olive oil, cheese and salt in a
food processor container and process until smooth and the consistency of a
thick purée.

Cook the spaghetti using the package directions; drain. Spoon into a
heated serving dish. Add the pesto and toss lightly. Serve with additional grated
Parmesan or asiago cheese.

Yield: 8 servings

MUSHROOMS *come in
thousands of varieties. They
vary from white to black and
small to large with a wide
range of textures and flavors.
Those most commonly
available include Cèpe,
Chanterelle, Enoki, Morel,
Puffball, Shiitake, and
Wood Ear.*

SENSATIONAL SPAGHETTI

AL DENTE *is Italian for "to the tooth." This phrase denotes pasta that has been cooked until it is tender but not mushy or overcooked. This terminology also applies to other foods.*

1 medium onion, chopped
2 garlic cloves, minced
1/4 cup (1/2 stick) butter, melted
1 tablespoon olive oil
12 ounces lean ground beef
12 ounces lean ground pork or Italian sausage
1/2 green bell pepper, chopped
8 ounces fresh mushrooms, chopped
1 (28-ounce) can stewed Italian tomatoes
2 (6-ounce) cans tomato paste
1 1/2 teaspoons Worcestershire sauce
1 cup dry red wine
1 tablespoon sugar
2 bay leaves
1/2 teaspoon salt
1/2 teaspoon celery salt
1/4 teaspoon freshly ground black pepper
   Cayenne pepper to taste
16 ounces uncooked spaghetti

Sauté the onion and garlic in the butter and olive oil in a heavy large saucepan until translucent. Add the ground beef and ground pork and cook over medium heat until brown and crumbly; drain.

Add the bell pepper, mushrooms, tomatoes, tomato paste, Worcestershire sauce, wine, sugar, bay leaves, salt, celery salt, black pepper and cayenne pepper and mix well. Simmer for 3 hours. Discard the bay leaves.

Cook the spaghetti al dente using the package directions; drain. Spoon onto warmed serving plates and top with the sauce. You may sprinkle with freshly grated Parmesan cheese. Serve immediately.

Yield: 8 servings

ANGEL HAIR PASTA WITH TOMATOES AND RICOTTA CHEESE

     1   pound Roma tomatoes, cored
    12   ounces fresh ricotta cheese, crumbled
     4   medium garlic cloves, minced
    1/3 cup packed finely shredded fresh basil
     6   tablespoons lemon juice
    1/4 cup olive oil
     1   teaspoon sugar
     2   teaspoons each salt and freshly ground white pepper
    16   ounces uncooked angel hair pasta or capellini

Score the tomato skin lightly into 4 segments. Place the tomatoes in boiling water to cover and boil for 30 seconds. Remove and cool slightly. Peel and cut into halves horizontally. Discard the seeds; coarsely chop the tomatoes.

Combine the tomatoes with the ricotta cheese, garlic, basil, lemon juice and olive oil in a bowl. Add the sugar, salt and white pepper and mix gently.

Cook the pasta using the package directions; drain. Add to the tomato and cheese mixture and toss gently to mix well. Serve hot or cold.

Yield: 10 servings

SHRIMP AND FARFALLE TOSS

     1   cup sliced mushrooms
    1/2 cup chopped onion
     2   garlic cloves, minced
     1   tablespoon chopped fresh basil, or 1 teaspoon dried basil leaves
     2   tablespoons each olive oil and lemon juice
    1/2 cup water
     2   teaspoons instant chicken bouillon
     1   pound uncooked medium shrimp, peeled, deveined
     1   cup chopped green bell pepper
     1   large tomato, seeded, chopped
     2   tablespoons grated Parmesan cheese
     6   ounces farfalle, cooked

Sauté the mushrooms, onion, garlic and basil in the olive oil in a large skillet until tender. Add the lemon juice, water and chicken bouillon and bring to a boil. Reduce the heat and add the shrimp and bell pepper. Simmer, uncovered, for 5 to 8 minutes or just until the shrimp are pink. Stir in the tomato.

Combine the shrimp mixture and cheese with the hot pasta in a large bowl and toss to mix well. Serve with additional cheese if desired.

Photograph for this recipe is on page 120 and opposite.

Yield: 2 servings

RICOTTA is a somewhat grainy, light, white milk product. Moist, rich, and rather sweet in flavor, it is generally a combination of whey and skim or whole milk. Because the product is a cheese by-product, it was named ricotta, which is Italian for "recooked." It is often used in manicotti and lasagna.

VEGETABLE TERRINE ON LINGUINI

Terrine

  6 cups loosely packed spinach
    Salt to taste
  2 red bell peppers, thinly sliced
  8 teaspoons olive oil
  4 garlic cloves, minced
  3/4 cup each thinly sliced leeks and grated peeled parsnips
  1/2 cup shredded Jarlsberg cheese
  5 eggs
  3/4 cup half-and-half
  1 tablespoon tomato paste
  1 teaspoon each salt and white pepper
1 1/2 cups grated carrots

Linguini

 16 ounces uncooked linguini
  2 tablespoons olive oil
  1 garlic clove, minced
    Salt and freshly ground pepper to taste

For the terrine, steam the spinach until tender. Chop the spinach, sprinkle lightly with salt to taste and drain in a colander, pressing to remove as much moisture as possible.

Sauté the bell peppers lightly in 2 teaspoons of the olive oil in a skillet. Drain well and remove to a bowl to cool. Repeat the process with the garlic, leeks and parsnips, adding 2 teaspoons of the olive oil to the skillet for each vegetable and removing each to a separate bowl. Combine the leeks, parsnips and cheese in 1 bowl and mix well.

Combine the eggs, half-and-half, tomato paste, garlic, 1 teaspoon salt and white pepper in a blender container and process until smooth.

Butter a 5x9-inch loaf pan and line it with waxed paper or parchment. Brush generously with melted butter or oil. Spread the spinach evenly over the bottom of the pan. Pour in just enough of the egg mixture to barely cover the spinach and spread evenly. Layer the carrots, parsnip mixture and bell peppers over the spinach, spreading each vegetable with a thin layer of the egg mixture.

Cover with foil and place in a larger pan with enough hot water to reach halfway up the sides of the loaf pan. Bake at 375 degrees for 1 hour and 25 minutes, removing the foil for the last 15 minutes. Let stand in the pan of water for 20 minutes. Run a knife around the sides of the loaf pan to loosen the waxed paper; invert onto a platter and remove the waxed paper.

For the pasta, cook the linguini using the package directions; drain. Combine with the olive oil, garlic, salt and pepper in a bowl and toss.

To serve, spoon the pasta onto serving plates. Slice the terrine and arrange on the pasta. Serve with a salad and whole wheat French bread.

Yield: 6 servings

BASIC PASTA DOUGH

    2 cups (or more) unbleached flour
    3 large eggs
    1 teaspoon olive oil
    1 teaspoon water
    1 teaspoon salt

Combine 2 cups flour, eggs, olive oil, water and salt in a food processor container or mixing bowl. Process or mix by hand just until the mixture begins to form a ball. Knead on a lightly floured surface for 8 minutes or until smooth and elastic, kneading in additional flour as needed. Roll immediately for best results or store, wrapped in plastic wrap, in the refrigerator for 8 to 24 hours.

Cut the dough into 4 equal pieces and wrap 3 of the pieces individually in plastic wrap. Set the smooth rollers of the pasta machine on the widest setting. Flatten the remaining dough into a rectangle and feed through the rollers. Fold in half and repeat the process 8 or 9 more times, dusting with flour as necessary to prevent sticking.

Reduce the rollers to the next setting and feed the dough through 8 or 9 times without folding. Repeat the process, continuing to reduce the setting until the thinnest setting is reached.

Cut the dough into halves crosswise and place on a dry towel, allowing the dough to hang over the edge of the work surface. Roll the remaining dough in the same manner. Cut the dough while it is still soft.

Yield: 4 servings (1 pound pasta)

For *Green Pasta*, blanch 12 ounces of spinach, Swiss chard or other greens. Drain well, squeeze to remove excess moisture and purée or mince. Add with the eggs.

For *Fresh Herb Pasta*, mince 1 cup loosely packed fresh herbs, such as basil, flat-leaf parsley or cilantro, and add with the eggs.

For *Tomato Pasta*, add $1\frac{1}{2}$ tablespoons tomato paste with the eggs.

For *Lemon Pasta*, add $1\frac{1}{2}$ tablespoons grated lemon zest with the eggs.

For *Garlic and Herb Pasta*, add $\frac{1}{4}$ cup minced fresh parsley and oregano or marjoram and 1 or 2 minced garlic cloves with the eggs.

For *Saffron Pasta*, add $\frac{1}{2}$ teaspoon ground saffron to the flour and salt or soak $\frac{1}{2}$ teaspoon saffron threads in 1 tablespoon very hot water and strain in with the eggs.

For *Whole Wheat Pasta*, substitute $\frac{1}{2}$ to 2 cups whole wheat flour for the same amount of unbleached flour.

THICK PASTAS *such as macaroni, lasagna, or cannelloni may be cut for eating with a fork if necessary. Remaining sauce may be absorbed by small pieces of bread and eaten with a fork. Spaghetti is eaten by picking up a few strands of pasta and twirling them to an edible size. A spoon or piece of bread can be used to assist in twirling the pasta. The spoon should never leave the plate. Never cut long pasta such as spaghetti or fettuccini. Sauce and grated cheese may be gently tossed into the pasta.*

The Main Event...

MEAT POULTRY & SEAFOOD

This photograph is sponsored by:
Peg McGarvey
Anne Gallagher Nass

The Main Event...

A fabulous menu will define a memorable culinary experience. Guests will greatly anticipate the event and will appreciate all the planning it takes. It is significant to note, however, that if the menu falls short, the impact of the event will falter.

It is always wise to know your audience. Likes and dislikes, food allergies, or alcohol issues may pose problems for guests. The last thing a hostess or host wants to do is serve an undesirable dish or beverage.

A menu that includes seasonal ingredients while at their best insures an element of seasonal savvy. The success of the menu is based on several fundamentals. Among those fundamentals are color, diversity, texture, and flavor.

Menus may consist of the following courses: Appetizer, Salad, Soup, Pasta, Fish, Meat, Side Dishes, and Dessert or Cheese. Beverages such as Aperitifs, Cocktails, Wines, and Cordials are also included. Choosing a palatable menu is an art to be mastered by every entertainer.

Prepare a menu that you would enjoy having served to you. If it calls for food items or tastes that you dislike, chances are your guests may also dislike them. Try to limit reinforcing the same basic flavor. Foods with strong overtones of salt, garlic, sweetness, or spiciness are wonderful, but not if every course has the same intense flavor.

Balance is critical. If the salad is substantial, perhaps the soup should be lighter, avoiding heavy cream. Or reverse the concept—if the salad is light and fresh, the soup may be heavier, thick, or rich.

Think color. After the entrée and side dishes are prepared, analyze how they look on the plate together. Color should further the desirability of the recipes. The menu should not contain a dish that is watery and may take over the plate. An individual vegetable bowl can control such an item. If the menu calls for a sauce, determine how it will be served. Think about consistency, shape, and texture. Menu items should vary in uniformity, density, and richness. Harmony is of critical importance, but so is diversity.

Take time to consider the wines you will be serving. Plan for symmetry between the food and wine. When in question, ask your local wine merchant. An intensely flavored food can hold up to a red wine with rich tannin overtones. "Red with meat, white with fish" is the old rule of thumb. That maxim has gained flexibility. Poultry, veal, pork, salmon, or lobster are capable of entertaining a light red wine or a robust white. Sauces also alter the varietal of wine. One way of insuring continuity between a sauce and wine is to use the wine called for in the sauce as your accompaniment. Wine should be poured as the first course is brought to the table. Fill the glass no more than half full so that there will be space for the bouquet.

Once a decision has been made regarding the menu, it is time to compile a grocery list, order hard-to-find items, and compose an "Order of Preparation" list. These organizational tools allow freedom from the unknown and the ability to avoid catastrophe by changing one's menu in a timely manner.

BEEF TENDERLOIN WITH BORDELAISE SAUCE

1 (3-pound) beef tenderloin
1 tablespoon minced onion
3 tablespoons butter
3 tablespoons flour
1 cup beef broth
2 tablespoons burgundy
1 tablespoon lemon juice
1 cup sliced mushrooms (optional)
1 teaspoon chopped parsley
1/2 teaspoon dried tarragon

Place the beef on a rack in a shallow roasting pan. Roast at 450 degrees for 45 minutes or until done to taste. Let stand for several minutes.

Sauté the onion in the butter in a saucepan until tender. Stir in the flour and cook for several minutes, stirring constantly. Stir in the beef broth, wine, lemon juice, mushrooms, parsley and tarragon. Cook over medium-high heat until thickened, stirring constantly. Serve with the sliced beef.

Yield: 6 servings

COOK BEEF *using a meat thermometer to determine when it is done to taste.*

Rare . . . . 125° to 130°
Medium-rare . . . . 135°
Medium . . . . . 140° to 145°
Well done . . . . 160°

PEPPER STEAK

1 (2 1/2-pound) beef tenderloin
4 green bell peppers
2 Spanish onions
2 tablespoons butter
16 ounces fresh mushrooms, sliced
2 garlic cloves, minced
1/2 ounce cracked pepper
1 tablespoon B-V sauce
3/4 cup burgundy
2 tablespoons soy sauce
2 tablespoons cornstarch
1/2 cup water
Salt to taste

Slice the beef or cut into cubes. Cut the bell peppers and onions into thin slices. Sauté the beef in the butter in a skillet until brown. Add the bell peppers, onions, mushrooms, garlic and pepper. Cook over medium heat until the vegetables are tender.

Add the B-V sauce, wine and soy sauce. Simmer for several minutes. Blend the cornstarch into the water. Add to the beef mixture and cook until slightly thickened, stirring constantly. Season with salt to taste. Serve over rice or rice pilaf.

Yield: 8 servings

ONIONS *consist of two primary types: green onions (scallions) and dry onions. Dry onions include the white or yellow Bermuda and the yellow Spanish. Dry onions should be heavy with a dry, paperlike skin and no moist spots. They may be stored in a cool, dry place for several months. Freezing an onion for twenty minutes helps eliminate tears while cutting.*

FILLET OF BEEF

1 (4¹/₂-pound) beef tenderloin
1 garlic clove, slivered
  Salt and freshly ground pepper to taste

Cut slits in the beef with the tip of a sharp knife and insert the slivers of garlic into the slits. Season generously with salt and pepper and place in a shallow roasting pan. Insert a meat thermometer into the thickest portion.

Roast at 425 degrees for 10 minutes. Reduce the oven temperature to 350 degrees and roast for 25 minutes longer or to 120 degrees on the meat thermometer for rare; roast to 130 degrees for medium.

Let stand for 10 minutes or until room temperature if preferred. Slice to serve.

Yield: 10 servings

FILLET OF BEEF DIJONNAISE

1 garlic clove
6 slices bacon
3 tablespoons Dijon mustard
¹/₂ teaspoon salt
¹/₂ teaspoon lemon pepper
1 (4-pound) beef tenderloin

Mince the garlic in a food processor. Add the bacon, Dijon mustard, salt and lemon pepper and process until smooth.

Pat the beef dry and spread half the mustard mixture over the top; place on a rack in a shallow roasting pan. Broil for 7 minutes. Turn the beef and spread with the remaining mustard sauce. Broil for 7 minutes longer.

Roast the beef at 350 degrees for 15 minutes or until done to taste. Roast to 135 degrees on a meat thermometer for medium-rare or 145 degrees on a meat thermometer for medium. Let stand for 5 minutes before slicing.

Photograph for this recipe is on page 136 and opposite.

Yield: 8 servings

Fillets are expensive, boneless cuts of beef that come from the small end of the tenderloin. The fillet of beef is generally 1 to 2 inches thick and 1¹/₂ to 3 inches in diameter. It is exceptionally tender and lean.

OVEN-BARBECUED BRISKET

    1 teaspoon minced garlic
1 1/2 teaspoons paprika
    1 teaspoon garlic powder
    1 teaspoon sugar
 1/4 teaspoon cumin
 1/4 teaspoon celery salt
    1 teaspoon salt
    1 teaspoon red pepper
    1 (4-pound) beef brisket
 1/2 onion, sliced
    3 tablespoons Worcestershire sauce
 1/2 cup water
    1 (20-ounce) bottle barbecue sauce

Combine the garlic, paprika, garlic powder, sugar, cumin, celery salt, salt and red pepper in a small bowl and mix well. Place the brisket on a large piece of heavy-duty foil and rub on all sides with the seasoning mixture. Top with the onion slices and pull up the sides of the foil; place in a roasting pan.

Sprinkle with the Worcestershire sauce and pour in the water; seal the foil. Roast at 325 degrees for 3 to 4 hours or until done to taste, opening the foil and basting once or twice with the pan juices, resealing foil each time.

Slice the brisket across the grain. Combine the slices with the barbecue sauce in a skillet and cook until heated through.

Yield: 6 servings

BEEF BRISKET *is a cut of beef taken from the breast section under the first five ribs. Brisket is principally sold boneless and is divided into two portions—the flat cut and the more flavorful point cut, which has a higher fat content. Brisket requires long, slow cooking.*

Consommé

Cut the meat from 2 pounds of beef shanks and 2 pounds of veal shanks; crush the bones. Combine the meat and crushed bones with 3 quarts water in a saucepan. Add 1 bay leaf, 1 tablespoon chopped parsley, 1 clove, 2 teaspoons salt and 2 teaspoons pepper. Simmer, covered, for 2½ to 3 hours, skimming the surface frequently. Add 1 quart chicken stock. Sauté ¼ cup chopped carrot, ¼ cup chopped celery and 2 tablespoons minced onion in 2 tablespoons butter or margarine in a skillet and add to the saucepan. Season with salt and pepper to taste. Simmer, covered, for 2 hours. Strain into a bowl. Serve at once or store in the refrigerator.

BARBECUED BEEF BRISKET

1 (4- to 5-pound) beef brisket
1 (10-ounce) can beef consommé
1 (5-ounce) bottle soy sauce
¼ cup fresh lemon juice
1 tablespoon liquid smoke
   Garlic powder to taste
½ cup barbecue sauce

Place the beef brisket in a shallow baking dish. Combine the beef consommé, soy sauce, lemon juice, liquid smoke and garlic powder in a bowl and mix well. Pour over the beef, turning to coat well. Marinate, covered, in the refrigerator for 8 to 12 hours.

Remove the brisket and marinade to a roasting pan. Cover and place in a 300-degree oven. Roast a 4-pound brisket for 2½ to 3 hours or a 5-pound brisket for 3½ to 4 hours, basting occasionally.

Increase the oven temperature to 350 degrees. Pour the barbecue sauce over the brisket and roast, uncovered, for 1 hour longer. Carve the brisket into thin slices and serve with the cooking liquids.

Note: *Instead of using canned consommé, make your own using the recipe at left.*

Yield: 12 servings

BEEF ROAST

1 (2- to 3-pound) beef tenderloin or other boneless beef roast
1 tablespoon vegetable oil
1 medium onion, minced
3 hot banana peppers
1 bay leaf
   Salt and pepper to taste
2 tablespoons water

Brown the roast on all sides in the heated oil in a pressure cooker. Add the onion, banana peppers, bay leaf, salt, pepper and water. Seal the pressure cooker and allow the steam to be released from the vent. Cook the roast using the manufacturer's instructions. Discard the bay leaf to serve.

Note: *See page 107 for information on pressure cookers.*

Yield: 6 servings

GRILLED MARINATED POT ROAST

    1½ cups vegetable oil
     2 garlic cloves, crushed
    ¾ cup soy sauce
    ¼ cup Worcestershire sauce
    ⅓ cup fresh lemon juice
    ½ cup sauterne
     2 tablespoons dry mustard
    ½ teaspoon each parsley flakes, rosemary and marjoram
     2 teaspoons salt
     1 tablespoon freshly ground pepper
     1 (1- to 2-pound) beef roast

Heat the oil in a saucepan. Remove from the heat and stir in the garlic, soy sauce, Worcestershire sauce, lemon juice, wine, dry mustard, parsley flakes, rosemary, marjoram, salt and pepper; mix well. Pour into a shallow dish or sealable plastic bag.

Add the beef and turn to coat well. Marinate, covered, in the refrigerator for 8 to 12 hours.

Remove from the marinade and place on a rack over hot coals. Grill until done to taste.

    Yield: 4 servings

LONDON BROIL

     1 tablespoon white vinegar
    ⅓ cup vegetable oil
    ¼ cup soy sauce
     1 small onion, chopped
     1 tablespoon brown sugar
    ¾ teaspoon ground ginger
    ¾ teaspoon garlic powder
     1 (1½- to 2-pound) flank steak

Combine the vinegar, oil, soy sauce, onion, brown sugar, ginger and garlic powder in a shallow dish or sealable plastic bag. Score the steak lightly on both sides and place in the marinade. Marinate, covered, in the refrigerator for up to 12 hours.

Remove the steak from the marinade and place on a rack in a broiler pan. Broil for 3 minutes on each side for medium-rare or until done to taste. Carve diagonally across the grain into thin slices.

    Yield: 4 servings

GRILLING TIMES *vary for different meats. For medium doneness cook:*

¾-inch beef patty
5 minutes per side

¾-inch turkey patty
6 minutes per side

1½-inch pork chop
14 to 18 minutes per side

¾-inch pork chop
6 to 7 minutes per side

1¼-inch fish fillet
5 to 6 minutes per side

1-inch fish
3 to 5 minutes per side

½-inch fish fillet
1½ to 2½ minutes per side

2-inch steak
10 to 12 minutes per side

1½-inch steak
7 to 8 minutes per side

1-inch steak
5 to 6 minutes per side

CLASSIC BEEF STROGANOFF

Noodles *vary from pastas such as spaghetti or lasagna because eggs or egg yolks have been added to the recipe. They are offered in various widths and lengths and may even be square (ravioli). Noodles may be tinted with beet juice, tomato paste, or spinach. Fresh noodles should be refrigerated for no more than three days, while dried will keep for up to six months in a cool, dark place.*

- 3 pounds top sirloin
- 3 large onions, chopped
- 8 ounces fresh mushrooms, sliced
- 2 tablespoons butter
- 1 teaspoon Worcestershire sauce
- 1/2 cup water
- 2 bay leaves
- 1 teaspoon salt
- 1/4 teaspoon pepper
- 1/2 to 1 cup sherry
- 2 cups sour cream

Cut the sirloin into 1x2-inch thin strips. Brown the sirloin and onions in the butter in a heavy medium saucepan. Add the mushrooms. Sauté until the mushrooms are browned. Add the Worcestershire sauce, water, bay leaves, salt and pepper and stir to combine. Bring to a boil and reduce the heat. Simmer, covered, for 1 hour. Let stand until cool.

Add the sherry 1/2 cup at a time and taste for the desired flavor. Cook for 30 minutes longer or until the beef is tender. Cool to room temperature. Discard the bay leaves. Stir in the sour cream and cook just until heated through; do not boil. Serve over hot cooked medium noodles.

Yield: 8 servings

LEG OF LAMB WITH PARSLEY AND CRUMB CRUST

1 (6- to 9-pound) leg of lamb
6 tablespoons butter, melted
1 cup fresh white bread crumbs
1/2 cup chopped fresh parsley
1 shallot, finely chopped
   Bulb and 1 inch of the pale green portion of 1 leek, chopped
3 tablespoons Dijon mustard

Place the leg of lamb in a roasting pan. Roast at 350 degrees for 1 hour, basting frequently with the melted butter.

Mix the bread crumbs, parsley, shallot and leek in a bowl. Remove the lamb from the oven. Spread with the Dijon mustard and press the crumb mixture over the mustard. Roast for 30 minutes longer or until the crust is golden brown.

You may also prepare this recipe with boneless lamb, adjusting the roasting time.

Yield: 8 servings

COOK LAMB *using a meat thermometer to determine when it is done to taste.*

Rare . . . . 130° to 135°
Medium . . . . . 140° to 145°
Well done . . . . 160°

SERVING ALLOWANCES *vary for boneless and bone-in meat. Allow 5 to 7 ounces per serving for boneless meat and 8 ounces per serving for bone-in meat. A roast with a bone will cook faster that a roast without a bone that weighs the same amount. The bone conducts heat and cooks the meat faster.*

Toasted Pecans

Pecans should be placed on a baking sheet in a single layer. Toast in a 350-degree oven or 5 to 6 inches under a broiler until light brown and aromatic, stirring occasionally. Pecans may also be toasted in a skillet over medium heat, stirring frequently.

Rack of Lamb with Honey Mustard and Pecan Crust

1/4 cup Dijon mustard
  1 tablespoon honey
  1 tablespoon light unsulfured molasses
  2 small garlic cloves, minced
1/2 cup pecans, toasted
  3 tablespoons fresh bread crumbs
  1 teaspoon minced fresh rosemary, or 1/4 teaspoon crumbled dried rosemary
  2 (1 1/4-pound) racks of lamb, trimmed
  2 tablespoons olive oil

Mix the Dijon mustard, honey, molasses and garlic in a small bowl. Combine the pecans, bread crumbs and rosemary in a food processor container and process until the mixture resembles fine meal.

Sear the racks of lamb one at a time in the heated olive oil in a heavy large skillet over high heat for 5 minutes or until brown on all sides. Pat the racks dry and spread with the mustard mixture.

Place the racks rounded side up in a roasting pan and sprinkle with the pecan mixture. Roast at 375 degrees for 25 minutes for medium-rare. Carve into chops between the ribs.

Note: *See instructions at left for toasting pecans.*

Yield: 4 servings

ROAST LAMB WITH POTATO AND TOMATO GRATIN

1 garlic clove, cut into halves
2 pounds potatoes, peeled, thinly sliced
  Salt and pepper to taste
1 tablespoon chopped fresh thyme
5 garlic cloves, chopped
2 large onions, thinly sliced
5 medium tomatoes, cored, thinly sliced
2/3 cup dry white wine
1/3 cup extra-virgin olive oil
1 (6- to 7-pound) leg of lamb

Rub an oval 10×16-inch porcelain gratin dish with the garlic halves. Arrange the potatoes in a single layer in the prepared dish. Sprinkle with salt, pepper and 1/3 of the thyme and chopped garlic.

Arrange the onions in the dish and season with salt and 1/3 of the remaining thyme and chopped garlic. Arrange the tomatoes over the onions and season with salt and the remaining thyme and chopped garlic. Drizzle with the wine and olive oil. Place a rack over the top of the dish.

Trim the fat from the lamb. Season the lamb with salt and pepper and place on the rack. Roast at 400 degrees for 1¼ hours for rare, turning the lamb and basting with juices from the gratin dish every 15 minutes.

Remove the lamb to a cutting board and let stand for 20 minutes. Carve into thin slices and serve with the gratin.

Yield: 10 servings

WIDE-RIM PLATES *allow more options for designs in the center and on the edge of the plates. Wide-rim plates are larger.*

Rack of Lamb with Spicy Pepper Crust

1 teaspoon each cumin seeds, coriander seeds and green peppercorns
2 garlic cloves, chopped
1 tablespoon each grated orange zest and olive oil
1 (1¼- to 1½-pound) rack of lamb, trimmed
   Salt and pepper to taste

Combine the cumin seeds, coriander seeds and peppercorns in a plastic bag and crush with a mallet. Add the garlic, orange zest and olive oil and mash to a coarse paste.

Sprinkle the lamb with salt and pepper. Rub the spice paste over the lamb and place paste side up in a roasting pan; insert a meat thermometer into the thickest portion.

Roast at 450 degrees for 10 minutes. Reduce the oven temperature to 400 degrees. Roast for 15 minutes longer or to 135 degrees on the meat thermometer. Carve into chops between the ribs.

Note: *Trim fat from lamb before cooking to avoid a slightly musky flavor. Rub meat with your favorite oil to prevent drying.*

Yield: 2 servings

Fillet of Pork Amandine

2 to 2½ pounds pork tenderloins, in 2 pieces
1 cup crushed roasted almonds
   Salt and pepper to taste
½ cup flour
¼ cup lard or shortening
½ cup sherry
2 tablespoons chopped scallions or shallots
1 cup chicken broth
3 tablespoons heavy cream

Cut a lengthwise slit down both pork tenderloins. Fill the slits with the almonds and sprinkle with salt and pepper; tie the tenderloins together. Roll in the flour, coating well. Brown on all sides in the lard in a heavy saucepan.

Reduce the heat and add the sherry. Bring to a boil and cook for several minutes. Stir in the scallions and cook for several minutes. Add the chicken broth. Cook, covered, over medium-low heat for 1 hour, turning the pork once.

Remove the pork to a platter and degrease the drippings in the saucepan. Whisk in the cream gradually. Carve the pork into slices. Serve with the sauce and Garlic Mashed Potatoes (page 113).

Yield: 6 servings

CORIANDER *provides seeds and leaves used in cooking. It is a member of the parsley family. The seeds and leaves are very different from one another, although they have an odor combining lemon, caraway, and sage.*

CUMIN *is a member of the parsley family. The fragrant, nutty seeds vary in taste according to their color. White and amber are very similar, but black has a more peppery taste. Cumin is available ground or in seed form.*

BARBECUED PORK RIBS

    4 to 6 pounds lean country-style pork ribs, trimmed
       Salt to taste
    1 (16-ounce) bottle hickory or mesquite barbecue sauce
    1 (32-ounce) bottle ketchup
  ½ (6-ounce) bottle chili sauce
    2 tablespoons (or more) black molasses
  ¼ cup (or more) liquid smoke
  ¼ cup balsamic vinegar or white vinegar
       Tabasco sauce or cayenne pepper to taste
    1 tablespoon Worcestershire sauce
    1 tablespoon soy sauce
    2 tablespoons bottled lemon juice
  ¼ cup packed brown sugar
  ½ tablespoon chili powder
    1 tablespoon horseradish
    1 tablespoon onion flakes, or 2 tablespoons chopped onion
    1 teaspoon basil
  ½ teaspoon (or more) dried orange peel (optional)
  ¼ teaspoon garlic powder

Boil the ribs in salted water in a large saucepan for 15 to 20 minutes; drain and rinse under hot water.

Combine the barbecue sauce, ketchup, chili sauce, molasses, liquid smoke, vinegar, Tabasco sauce, Worcestershire sauce, soy sauce, lemon juice, brown sugar, chili powder, horseradish, onion flakes, basil, orange peel and garlic powder in a saucepan and mix well. Adjust the seasonings. Bring to a boil and reduce the heat. Simmer for 15 to 20 minutes or to the desired consistency.

Spread a layer of the sauce in a slow cooker. Layer the ribs and remaining sauce in the slow cooker until all the ingredients are used, ending with enough sauce to cover the ribs. Cook, covered, on High for 1 hour. Cook, covered, on Low for 4 hours or more; uncover and cook for 30 minutes longer.

You may use baby back ribs and eliminate the preliminary boiling step. You may also cook the ribs in the oven or on the grill if preferred.

Yield: 6 servings

MOLASSES *is the dark syrup that remains after sugar has been refined. Light molasses is the result of the first boiling. It is lighter in color and taste and is commonly used in flavored syrups. The second boiling yields dark molasses and is thicker and less sweet.*

$\mathscr{A}$UTUMN is a season of abundance in Iowa. This season creates a palette of colors within its patchwork quilt that makes up the countryside. The various pigments and textures that are provided by our agricultural industry create a background of natural beauty that is incomprehensible to those who have failed to experience it.

Agriculture or agriculturally affiliated businesses utilize 93 percent of Iowa's bountiful land. It is with great pride that we lead the nation in pork, beef, corn, soybean, and grain production. Just one family farm grows enough food to feed 279 people throughout the world. The land is valued for what it can provide agriculturally and scenically.

Autumn is also a time of united effort toward quality education for our children. Iowa-raised residents have led the nation in both ACT and SAT scores for the past twenty years. Education is a priority that has kept Iowa in the top five states for academic success for many years. This accomplishment provides Iowa and the remainder of the nation with well-educated and well-rounded citizens. We are proud to share them and claim them as our own.

Photograph by:
Larsh Bristol

NORMANDY-STYLE PORK LOIN

CALVADOS *is an apple*
brandy made in Calvados,
France. It's often used for
cooking, particularly in
chicken, pork, and veal dishes.

1   (3- to 4-pound) boneless pork loin
1   tablespoon butter
1   tablespoon vegetable oil or butter
5   tablespoons Calvados, peach or apricot brandy
3   medium onions, sliced
3   yellow Delicious apples, peeled, sliced
2   tablespoons flour
1 1/2 cups chicken stock
    Rosemary, salt and pepper to taste
1/4 cup heavy cream (optional)

Brown the pork on all sides in the heated butter and oil in a Dutch oven. Remove to a flameproof platter. Heat the brandy in a large metal ladle or saucepan. Ignite the brandy and pour over the pork; allow the flames to subside.

Add the onions to the drippings in the Dutch oven. Sauté for 4 or 5 minutes or until tender but not brown. Add the apples. Cook over medium-high heat until the apples and onions are golden brown. Stir in the flour and cook for several minutes.

Add the chicken stock, rosemary, salt and pepper. Bring to a boil and cook until slightly thickened, stirring constantly. Return the pork to the saucepan. Bake at 350 degrees for 1 1/2 to 2 hours or until the pork is tender. Remove the pork to a heated platter; cover and keep warm.

Strain the sauce. Purée the sauce in a food processor. Return to the Dutch oven and bring to a boil. Cook until reduced to a sauce that will coat the spoon. Add the cream and cook just until heated through. Adjust the seasonings.

Carve the pork diagonally into 1/4-inch slices. Spoon the sauce over the slices.

Yield: 8 servings

PORK ROAST AND DUMPLINGS

Dumplings
- 2   eggs
- 2   cups flour
- 1   cup cold milk
- 2   tablespoons butter, melted
- 1/4 teaspoon salt
- 4   slices white bread, cubed

Sauerkraut
- 1   small onion, chopped
- 1   teaspoon butter
- 1   (16-ounce) jar sauerkraut, drained
- 1   small apple, chopped
- 1/2 teaspoon sugar
- 1/4 teaspoon caraway seeds

Pork and Gravy
- 1   garlic clove
- 1   teaspoon salt
- 1   (1 1/2- to 2-pound) pork tenderloin
- 1/2 teaspoon caraway seeds
- 2   tablespoons flour
- 2   cups chicken broth
- Salt and pepper to taste

For the dumplings, beat the eggs in a bowl. Add the flour, milk, butter and salt gradually. Beat for 5 minutes with a wooden spoon. Let stand for 30 minutes.

Bring a large saucepan of water to a boil. Stir the bread cubes into the dough and mix well. Shape into 2 ovals on a floured surface. Drop into the boiling water and cook, covered, for 15 minutes. Turn the dumplings and cook for 15 minutes longer; the dumplings will rise to the surface of the water.

For the sauerkraut, sauté the onion in the butter in a saucepan until translucent. Add the sauerkraut, apple, sugar and caraway seeds. Simmer, covered, for 20 minutes.

For the pork and gravy, mash the garlic with 1 teaspoon salt in a small bowl. Spread over the pork. Place fat side up on a rack in a lightly oiled shallow roasting pan; sprinkle with the caraway seeds. Roast at 375 degrees for 1 1/4 hours or to 170 degrees on a meat thermometer. Remove the pork from the roasting pan and drain the pan, reserving 2 tablespoons of the drippings and browned bits. Add the flour to the drippings, stirring to deglaze the pan. Cook on the stove top over medium heat until light brown. Stir in the chicken broth. Simmer for 5 minutes or until thickened, stirring constantly. Season with salt and pepper to taste. Carve the pork and slice the dumplings. Serve with the sauerkraut and gravy.

Yield: 6 servings

GRAVY OR SAUCE *should be used sparingly and only on the intended dish. If you desire to soak up remaining gravy, use small pieces of bread with a fork.*

153

ROAST PORK WITH FRUIT STUFFING

COOK PORK *using a meat thermometer to determine when it is done to taste.*

Medium . . . . 150°
Well done . . . . 160° to 165°

1 cup dried apricots
  Strained juice and grated zest of 1 orange
  Strained juice and grated zest of 1 lemon
1/4 cup (1/2 stick) butter, melted
4 cups soft bread crumbs
1/2 cup chopped walnuts
1 1/2 teaspoons salt
1/2 teaspoon pepper
1 (5-pound) boneless pork loin roast, butterflied

Soak the apricots in enough water to cover in a bowl for 10 minutes. Drain and chop the apricots. Combine with the orange juice, orange zest, lemon juice and lemon zest in a bowl.

Pour the butter over the bread crumbs in a bowl and toss to mix well. Add the walnuts, salt and pepper and mix well. Add to the apricot mixture, adding additional fruit juices if needed for the desired consistency.

Spread the stuffing mixture on the cut sides of the roast and roll to enclose the stuffing; secure with string or skewers. Place in a roasting pan. Roast at 400 degrees until brown on all sides, turning to brown evenly. Reduce the oven temperature to 325 degrees and roast for 25 minutes per pound or until done to taste.

Yield: 10 servings

MARINATED PORK BARBECUE

1 cup soy sauce
1/2 cup pineapple juice
1/4 cup sherry
1 tablespoon brown sugar
1/2 teaspoon garlic powder
1/4 teaspoon ginger
1 (4- to 4 1/2-pound) rolled boneless pork loin roast
  Salt and pepper to taste

Combine the soy sauce, pineapple juice, wine, brown sugar, garlic powder and ginger in a shallow dish and mix well. Add the pork roast, turning to coat well. Marinate at room temperature for 2 hours or in the refrigerator for 8 to 12 hours, turning occasionally.

Remove the roast from the marinade, reserving the marinade. Season with salt and pepper. Place on a spit over hot coals and grill for 40 to 45 minutes per pound, rotating to cook evenly and brushing frequently with the reserved marinade.

Yield: 8 servings

PORK ROAST WITH PEARS

Pork

    1   (2¼-pound) boneless pork roast
    4   garlic cloves, very thinly sliced
    1   tablespoon very thinly sliced candied gingerroot
    1   tablespoon dried rosemary
        Salt and pepper to taste

Glazed Pears

    1   tablespoon butter
    3   cups peeled thin pear wedges
  ¼   cup red wine
    2   tablespoons red wine vinegar
    2   tablespoons soy sauce
    3   tablespoons red currant jelly
  ½   teaspoon cayenne pepper

For the pork, cut slits in the roast and insert the garlic and ginger slices into the slits. Rub the roast with rosemary, salt and pepper. Place in a roasting pan and insert a meat thermometer into the thickest portion. Roast at 350 degrees for 1 hour or to 170 degrees on the meat thermometer.

For the pears, melt the butter in a skillet. Add the pears and sauté until tender. Remove the pears with a slotted spoon to a bowl. Add the wine to the skillet and stir to deglaze. Stir in the vinegar, soy sauce, jelly and cayenne pepper. Cook over medium-high heat for 10 minutes or until reduced to the desired consistency. Add the pears and mix gently. Cook until heated through. Serve with the sliced pork.

Yield: 6 servings

GRILLED PORK CHOPS

    1   cup soy sauce
  ½   cup water
    1   bunch green onions, sliced
    1   teaspoon garlic powder
    4   pork chops

Combine the soy sauce, water, green onions and garlic powder in a shallow dish and mix well. Add the pork chops, turning to coat well. Marinate in the refrigerator for 3 hours or longer.

Remove the pork chops from the marinade and place on a rack over medium-low coals. Grill until done to taste.

Yield: 4 servings

PROPER ETIQUETTE *recommends eating a pork, veal, or lamb chop by cutting into the center of the chop with a fork and a sharp knife. One may cut the meat while grasping the chop with the fingers if the chop bone is in a paper sleeve. It is considered poor form to pick up the bone and chew on it in a formal setting. Informally, one may nibble at the bone.*

PESTO PORK CHOPS

PESTO *may be made in large amounts and frozen in ice cube trays. After freezing, place pesto cubes in a freezer bag. Freeze for up to six months.*

Spicy Rub

- 1/2 teaspoon celery seeds
- 1/2 teaspoon fennel seeds
- 1/4 teaspoon dried thyme
- 2 teaspoons minced garlic
- 1/4 teaspoon ground cumin
- 1 teaspoon freshly ground black pepper
- 1/2 teaspoon ground red pepper

Pork Chops

- 1/4 cup crumbled feta cheese
- 2 tablespoons prepared pesto
- 2 tablespoons pine nuts, toasted
- 4 (1 1/4-inch) pork loin chops or boneless pork loin chops

Jalapeño Pesto Glaze

- 2 tablespoons jalapeño pepper jelly
- 2 to 3 tablespoons prepared pesto
- 1 tablespoon balsamic vinegar

For the rub, crush the celery seeds, fennel seeds and thyme in a small bowl. Add the garlic, cumin, black pepper and red pepper and mix well.

For the pork chops, combine the cheese, pesto and pine nuts in a small bowl and mix well. Trim the fat from the pork. Cut pockets in the pork chops, slicing horizontally from the outer edge almost to the bone. Spoon the cheese mixture into the pockets and secure the cut sides with wooden picks. Coat evenly with the rub.

For the glaze, melt the jelly in a small saucepan over low heat. Stir in the pesto and vinegar and cook until heated through.

To grill, heat coals to medium and arrange around a drip pan. Place the pork chops on a rack over the drip pan. Grill, covered, for 35 to 40 minutes or until the juices run clear, basting occasionally with the glaze during the last 10 minutes of grilling time. Garnish with basil leaves.

Photograph for this recipe is on page 136 and opposite.

Yield: 4 servings

MEXICAN PORK CHOPS

3/4 cup uncooked rice
1 1/2 cups water
1 (8-ounce) can tomato sauce
1/2 envelope (2 tablespoons) taco seasoning mix
6 (1/2-inch) pork loin chops
2 tablespoons vegetable oil
Seasoned salt and pepper to taste
1 medium green bell pepper, chopped
1/2 cup shredded Cheddar cheese

Combine the rice, water, tomato sauce and taco seasoning mix in a greased 9×13-inch baking dish and mix well. Brown the pork chops on both sides in the oil in a large skillet. Sprinkle with seasoned salt and pepper. Arrange over the rice mixture and top with the bell pepper.

Bake, covered, at 350 degrees for 1 1/2 hours. Sprinkle with the cheese and bake, uncovered, just until the cheese melts.

Yield: 6 servings

REMOVE FOOD *from your mouth using the same utensil it went in with. Place the piece of food on the edge of your plate. If possible, cover it with some other food from your plate. Never spit a piece of unwanted food or tough gristle into your napkin.*

PORK CHOPS WITH SAUSAGES

  4 pork chops
  1 tablespoon flour
  2 tablespoons butter
  1 fresh sage sprig
  1 large tomato, peeled, seeded, chopped
     Salt to taste
  4 small fresh sausages

Coat the pork chops lightly with the flour. Add to the heated butter and sage in a skillet and cook over medium-high heat until brown on both sides. Sprinkle with the tomato and salt.

Reduce the heat and cook, covered, for 30 minutes. Pierce the sausages with a fork and add to the skillet. Cook for 15 minutes longer. Remove the pork chops and sausages to serving plates. Degrease the pan drippings and serve with the pork chops.

Yield: 4 servings

BAKED HAM WITH PINEAPPLE GLAZE

    1 (4-pound) ham butt or shank portion
    1 (16-ounce) can juice-pack pineapple slices
  1/4 cup packed brown sugar
    1 teaspoon soy sauce
    1 tablespoon cornstarch
  1/2 teaspoon ground ginger
     Whole cloves (optional)

Place the ham fat side up on a rack in a shallow baking pan. Insert a meat thermometer into the thickest portion, taking care not to touch the bone. Bake at 325 degrees for 1 3/4 hours.

Drain the pineapple, reserving the juice. Blend the reserved juice with the brown sugar, soy sauce, cornstarch and ginger in a small saucepan. Cook until thickened, stirring constantly.

Remove the ham from the oven and pour off the drippings. Remove and discard the skin. Score the top into diamonds and place a clove in the center of each diamond. Cut the pineapple slices in one place and twist; arrange on the ham. Brush with the brown sugar mixture.

Bake the ham for 30 minutes longer or to 160 degrees on the meat thermometer, brushing with the remaining brown sugar mixture after 15 minutes.

Yield: 12 servings

CHICKEN PICCATA

 8 boneless skinless chicken breast halves
 1/2 cup flour
 1/2 teaspoon paprika
 1 1/2 teaspoons salt
 1/2 teaspoon white pepper
 1/4 cup (1/2 stick) unsalted butter
 1 tablespoon olive oil
 1/3 cup white sherry
    Juice of 1 lemon, about 3 tablespoons
 8 ounces button mushrooms, cut into halves
 3 tablespoons drained capers

Pound the chicken 1/2 inch thick between sheets of waxed paper with a meat mallet. Mix the flour, paprika, salt and white pepper together. Coat the chicken on both sides with the seasoned flour. Heat the butter and olive oil in a 12-inch skillet over medium-high heat until the foam subsides. Add the chicken several pieces at a time and sauté for 2 to 3 minutes on each side. Remove to a warm platter and blot with paper towels.

Drain the skillet, reserving 2 tablespoons of the drippings in the skillet. Add the wine and cook over medium-high heat for several minutes, stirring to deglaze the skillet. Add the lemon juice and mushrooms. Simmer for 3 to 5 minutes. Return the chicken to the skillet and add the capers. Cook just until the chicken is glazed. Garnish with lemon slices and parsley. Serve with hot pasta tossed with butter and garlic.

Note: *You may microwave the lemon to more easily yield the juice. Pierce the lemon and microwave on High for 1 minute.*

Yield: 8 servings

DEGLAZING *is done after meat or others foods have been sautéed and the excess grease or oil removed. Liquid (broth or wine) is then added to the pan and extra browned bits of food are loosened with a turner. This becomes the base for gravy or sauces.*

GRILLED CHICKEN GRAND MARNIER

Grand Marnier is a dark amber, brandy-based French liqueur flavored with orange peel.

$3/4$ cup Grand Marnier
$1 1/4$ cups apricot jam
$3/4$ cup white vinegar
$4 1/2$ tablespoons Worcestershire sauce
3 tablespoons honey
3 tablespoons Dijon mustard
1 tablespoon dried red pepper flakes
3 whole boneless chicken breasts, split into halves
Olive oil

Combine the Grand Marnier, apricot jam, vinegar, Worcestershire sauce, honey, Dijon mustard and red pepper flakes in a saucepan and mix well. Simmer until the jam melts, stirring to mix well. Cool to room temperature.

Combine the Grand Marnier mixture with the chicken in a shallow dish. Marinate, covered, in the refrigerator for 4 hours or longer; drain.

Place the chicken skin side down on a rack over medium-hot coals. Grill for $3 1/2$ minutes. Brush the chicken with olive oil and turn. Grill for 3 or 4 minutes longer or until cooked through.

Yield: 6 servings

SAUTERNE CHICKEN

6 boneless skinless chicken breast halves
3 slices boiled ham
3 slices Swiss cheese
3 tablespoons butter
4 ounces fresh mushrooms
$1/2$ cup sauterne
$1/2$ cup water
2 cups chicken broth
$1/3$ cup sauterne

Pound the chicken with a meat mallet to flatten. Cut the ham and cheese into halves. Layer 1 piece of ham and 1 piece of cheese on each chicken breast. Roll the chicken to enclose the filling and secure with a wooden pick or string. Brown the rolls on all sides in the butter in a skillet. Remove to a baking dish.

Add the mushrooms to the skillet and sauté until tender. Stir in $1/2$ cup wine, water and chicken broth. Bring to a simmer. Pour over the chicken rolls. Pour $1/3$ cup wine over the top. Bake at 350 degrees for 1 hour.

Yield: 6 servings

RED PEPPER FLAKES *are the result of grinding or flaking hot, red chile peppers.*

SAUTERNES *are sweet wines from western France. Ideal dessert wines, they have been created by using only the ripest, sweetest grapes of the Sauvignon Blanc or Semillon grapes.*

PHYLLO-WRAPPED GREEK CHICKEN

Wine Marinade

- 1 cup white wine
- ½ cup olive oil
- 3 garlic cloves, chopped
- 1 bay leaf
- ½ teaspoon oregano
- ½ teaspoon salt
- ¼ teaspoon pepper

Chicken

- 4 whole chicken breasts, split into halves
- 12 ounces feta cheese, crumbled
- 2 tablespoons grated Parmesan cheese
- 1 egg
- ¼ cup white wine
- ¼ teaspoon salt
- ¼ teaspoon pepper
- 16 sheets frozen phyllo dough, thawed
- 1 cup (2 sticks) butter, melted

For the marinade, combine the wine, olive oil, garlic, bay leaf, oregano, salt and pepper in a shallow dish and mix well.

For the chicken, remove and discard the chicken skin and bones. Pound the chicken flat with a meat mallet. Add to the marinade, turning to coat well. Marinate in the refrigerator for 8 to 12 hours. Remove the chicken, discarding the marinade.

Mix the feta cheese, Parmesan cheese, egg, wine, salt and pepper in a bowl. Spoon onto the chicken and roll the chicken to enclose the filling.

Layer 2 sheets of phyllo dough on a work surface, brushing each sheet with butter and covering the remaining phyllo dough with a damp towel to prevent drying out. Fold the bottom edge up 2 inches. Place 1 chicken breast on the folded portion and fold in the sides; roll to enclose the chicken in the phyllo dough. Repeat with the remaining phyllo dough and chicken. If the phyllo should fall apart a bit, simply piece it back together.

Arrange the rolls seam side down in a 9×13-inch baking dish. Brush the tops with butter. Bake, uncovered, at 325 degrees for 1 hour. Bake at 350 degrees if using a metal baking pan.

Yield: 8 servings

PHYLLO *is very delicate Greek pastry and needs to be kept moist during handling. To seal edges, use a small amount of milk or beaten egg as with piecrust. Wrap the contents as you would a gift.*

LIME TEQUILA CHICKEN FAJITAS

Lime Tequila Marinade

- 1/2 cup fresh lime juice
- 1/4 cup tequila
- 2/3 cup olive oil
- 2 tablespoons Triple Sec
- 1 jalapeño pepper, seeded, minced
- 1/4 cup chopped fresh cilantro

Fajitas

- 6 boneless skinless chicken breast halves
- 2 red bell peppers, sliced
- 2 yellow bell peppers, sliced
- 2 cups thinly sliced red onions
- 3 tablespoons vegetable oil
- 12 flour tortillas, warmed

For the marinade, combine the lime juice, tequila, olive oil, Triple Sec, jalapeño pepper and cilantro in a shallow nonreactive dish and mix well. Do not use an aluminum pan.

For the fajitas, add the chicken to the marinade, turning to coat evenly. Marinate, covered, in the refrigerator for 4 hours, turning the chicken several times. Let stand at room temperature for 30 minutes.

Drain the chicken and place on the grill. Grill for 4 minutes on each side or until cooked through. Remove from the grill and slice into strips.

Sauté the bell peppers and onions in the heated oil in a heavy skillet over high heat until tender and caramelized. Add the chicken strips and cook until heated through. Spoon onto the warm tortillas. Serve with guacamole, chopped tomatoes, shredded cheese and salsa.

Yield: 6 servings

PHEASANT IN PLUM SAUCE

Asian plum sauce is a thick sweet-and-sour sauce made from plums, apricots, sugar, and seasonings. It is also known as duck sauce.

Pheasant

 2 cups dry red wine
  Breasts and thighs of 2 pheasant, boned
 1 green bell pepper, sliced
 1/2 white onion, sliced
 1 cup chopped prunes

Plum Sauce

 1 cup plum jam
 1/2 cup sliced green onions
 2 tablespoons cornstarch
 1/4 cup dry red wine
 1/4 cup soy sauce
 2 tablespoons vinegar

For the pheasant, pour the red wine over the pheasant in a shallow dish and turn to coat well. Marinate, covered, in the refrigerator for 8 to 9 hours, turning occasionally; drain. Arrange in a single layer in a roasting pan. Top with the bell pepper, onion and prunes.

For the sauce, combine the plum jam, green onions and cornstarch in a small saucepan and mix well. Add the wine, soy sauce and vinegar. Cook over medium heat until thickened, stirring constantly. Pour over the pheasant.

Roast at 375 degrees for 1 hour, basting occasionally. Serve with wild rice. You may substitute chicken or turkey for the pheasant.

Yield: 4 servings

ASIAN FLAVORINGS can now be found in most large markets. Some common Asian flavorings are:

Cinnamon Stick
Coriander
Cornstarch
Dried Hot Chile Peppers
Dried Tangerine Peel
Duck Sauce
Fermented Black Beans
 (Salted Black Beans)
Five-Spice Powder
Ginger
Hoisin Sauce
Hot Bean Sauce
Hot Chili Oil
Hot Chili Sauce
Hot Mustard Powder
Madras Curry Powder
Master Sauce
Monosodium Glutamate
 (MSG)
Oil—Corn, Safflower,
 Soy, or Peanut
Rice Wine
Rock Sugar
Scallions
Sesame Oil
Sesame Paste
Szechuan Peppercorns
Soy Sauce
Star Anise
White Pepper

CORNISH GAME HENS

CARVE BIRDS *properly by cutting off the wings and legs of a Cornish game hen, quail, pigeon, or squab, then eating the body with a knife and fork. Never pick up the body, although you can lift the wings and legs to your mouth using your fingers.*

Game Hens

 4 (1¼- to 1½-pound) Cornish game hens, giblets removed
    Salt and pepper to taste
 4 fresh sage leaves
 1 lemon, cut into 4 wedges
 3 tablespoons chopped fresh sage

Tomato Sauce

 ¾ ounce dried porcini mushrooms
 ¾ cup hot water
 1 tablespoon chopped fresh sage
 2 garlic cloves, minced
 2 tablespoons olive oil
 1 (14-ounce) can whole tomatoes
 ½ cup chicken broth
    Salt and pepper to taste

For the game hens, sprinkle the cavities of the hens with salt and pepper. Place 1 sage leaf and 1 lemon wedge in each cavity. Truss the legs and tuck the wing tips under the hens. Place on a rack in a roasting pan and sprinkle with the chopped sage, salt and pepper. Roast at 450 degrees for 50 minutes or until the juices run clear.

For the sauce, soak the mushrooms in the hot water in a bowl for 30 minutes. Drain and coarsely chop the mushrooms, reserving the soaking liquid. Sauté the sage and garlic in the heated olive oil in a medium skillet over medium heat for 1 minute.

Purée the undrained tomatoes in a food processor. Combine with the mushrooms, reserved soaking liquid, chicken broth, sage and garlic in a saucepan. Simmer over medium-low heat for 25 minutes or until of the desired consistency.

To finish, remove the game hens to a platter and tent with foil to keep warm. Pour the pan drippings into a cup, scraping the pan. Degrease the drippings and add to the tomato sauce. Simmer for 2 minutes longer. Season with salt and pepper. Spoon the sauce onto a serving platter and arrange the hens in the sauce.

You may substitute one 15-ounce can of puréed tomatoes for the whole tomatoes. You may also strain out the tomato seeds from the whole tomatoes to reduce bitterness if preferred.

Photograph for this recipe is on page 137 and opposite.

Yield: 4 servings

SWISS CRAB BAKE

　1/2　cup chopped celery
　1/2　cup chopped onion
　1/4　cup chopped green bell pepper (optional)
　　3　tablespoons butter
　　3　tablespoons flour
　　3　chicken bouillon cubes
2 1/2　cups boiling water
　　1　cup uncooked quick-cooking rice
　　2　(7-ounce) cans crab meat, drained, flaked
　　2　cups shredded Swiss cheese
　　1　(4-ounce) can sliced mushrooms, drained
　1/4　cup sliced almonds
　　1　cup buttered bread crumbs
　1/2　cup shredded Swiss cheese

Sauté the celery, onion and bell pepper lightly in the butter in a skillet. Remove from the heat and stir in the flour. Dissolve the bouillon cubes in the boiling water. Add to the skillet and bring to a boil, stirring constantly. Cook over medium heat for 2 minutes or until slightly thickened, stirring constantly.

Combine the rice, crab meat, 2 cups cheese, mushrooms and almonds in a slow cooker and toss to mix well. Stir in the sauce gently. Cook on Low for 4 to 6 hours.

Spoon into a shallow ovenproof serving dish. Sprinkle with the bread crumbs and 1/2 cup cheese. Broil until the cheese melts and the bread crumbs are crisp and golden brown.

Yield: 6 servings

BOUILLON *is the broth produced by cooking vegetables, poultry, meat, or fish in water. Bouillon is often used as a base for gravy, sauces, or soups.*

SEAFOOD GUMBO

GUMBO *is a Creole specialty from New Orleans. It is a thick, stewlike dish with numerous ingredients, including vegetables such as okra, tomatoes, and onions, and one or several meats or shellfish such as chicken, sausage, ham, shrimp, crab, or oysters. All gumbos start with a dark roux, which adds a rich flavor. Okra serves to thicken the mixture, as does filé powder, which must be stirred in just before serving, after removing from the heat.*

1 pound okra, sliced
2 to 4 tablespoons vegetable oil
1 to 2 tablespoons vinegar
6 to 8 slices bacon, chopped
1 cup finely chopped ham
2 tablespoons butter
1 medium to large onion, chopped
6 green onions, sliced
2 garlic cloves, crushed
2 to 3 tablespoons flour
1 (28-ounce) can tomatoes
4 dashes of Tabasco sauce
1/4 cup chopped parsley
1/2 teaspoon sugar
1 teaspoon thyme
1 teaspoon salt
1/2 teaspoon pepper
4 to 5 cups water
1 1/2 pounds (50- to 60-count) shrimp
2 (7-ounce) cans crab meat
2 tablespoons chopped parsley
3 cups hot cooked rice

Cook the okra in the oil and vinegar in a large saucepan over medium heat for 20 to 30 minutes or until tender, stirring frequently.

Cook the bacon and ham in a medium saucepan until the bacon is crisp. Add the butter, onion, green onions and garlic and sauté until tender. Stir in the flour. Cook until the flour is light brown, stirring constantly. Add the tomatoes, crushing to break up. Add the Tabasco sauce, 1/4 cup parsley, sugar, thyme, salt and pepper and mix well. Add a small amount of water if needed for the desired consistency. Simmer for 20 to 25 minutes, stirring occasionally.

Add to the okra and stir in 4 to 5 cups water. Bring to a boil and add the shrimp and 1 can of the crab meat. Simmer for 30 minutes.

Add the remaining crab meat and 2 tablespoons parsley at serving time. Spoon into serving bowls. Spoon the rice into the center of the gumbo and garnish the rice with additional parsley.

Yield: 6 servings

SHRIMP CREOLE

 1 cup flour
1¼ cups vegetable oil
3½ cups chopped scallions with 2 to 3 inches of the green portions
 ⅔ cup chopped celery
 2 cups chopped onions
 1 cup chopped green bell pepper
 8 teaspoons chopped garlic
 6 tablespoons minced fresh parsley
 2 (16-ounce) cans tomatoes, drained
 1 (15-ounce) can tomato sauce
 ½ cup dry red wine
 8 teaspoons fresh lemon juice
 2 tablespoons minced chives
 8 bay leaves, crumbled
12 whole allspice
 4 whole cloves
 ½ teaspoon ground mace
 ½ teaspoon dried basil
 1 teaspoon dried thyme
 ½ teaspoon chili powder
 1 tablespoon salt
 1 teaspoon cayenne pepper
1½ teaspoons freshly ground black pepper
 4 cups water
 4 pounds fresh shrimp, peeled

Stir the flour into the heated oil in a 10- to 12-quart stockpot. Cook over medium-low heat until the flour is the color of peanut butter, stirring constantly. Remove from the heat and stir in the scallions, celery, onions, bell pepper, garlic and parsley. Cook for 10 minutes or until the vegetables are tender, stirring constantly.

Stir in the tomatoes and tomato sauce. Add the wine, lemon juice, chives, bay leaves, allspice, cloves, mace, basil, thyme, chili powder, salt, cayenne pepper and black pepper. Increase the heat and bring to a low boil. Add the water and return to a boil. Reduce the heat and simmer for 45 minutes.

Add the shrimp and bring to a simmer. Reduce the heat slightly and simmer, covered, for 20 minutes. Remove from the heat and let stand, covered, for 10 minutes before serving; discard the whole allspice and cloves. Serve over rice.

You may substitute precooked shrimp for the fresh shrimp, adding them 5 minutes before removing from the heat to stand. You may also substitute chopped partially cooked chicken breast for the fresh shrimp or reduce the recipe by half. You may tie the whole allspice and cloves in a cheesecloth bag for easy removal.

Yield: 12 servings

CREOLE COOKERY *encompasses the best of French, Spanish, and African cooking. It has an emphasis on butter and cream and is more refined than Cajun cooking (which relies heavily on pork fat). An additional distinction between the two cuisines is that Creole cooking uses more tomatoes and Cajun cooking uses more spices. Both cuisines rely on the "holy trinity" of chopped green peppers, onions, and celery, and make generous use of filé powder.*

*I*OWA has the pleasure of offering four seasons that give pause in their natural beauty. The romance of the first snow falling like crystal glimmering on a brisk evening is a memory etched into the hearts and minds of many. Sitting by the fire with hot chocolate or warm cider watching the glitter accumulate lends as much anticipation for adults as it did as a child waiting to make snow angels or snow sculptures. The snowfall covers the ground like flawless frosting until the first deer, rabbit, or squirrel marks its path. It is difficult to equate this scene to any other experience, as winter is a quiet time, one of solace.

Winter in Iowa—crisp, cold, and undeniably pristine. It offers not only a change in climate but the opportunity to take advantage of winter activities. Hockey, ice-skating, sledding, ice-fishing, or cross-country skiing are all eagerly anticipated winter alternatives.

First impressions . . . the aroma of home- baked bread with a hearty soup and a bottle of wine shared with good friends on a winter night—the trees covered in ice. Simple elegance . . . the snow outside imitates the fluffy white frosting on the dessert. Simple pleasures . . . the glow of the fire. This is Iowa.

Photograph by:
David Cavagnaro

CREOLE SHRIMP AND CHICKEN

DINNER NAPKINS *should be placed on the lap folded in half with the fold close to the body. If it is a luncheon-size napkin, open it completely. When you leave the table during a meal, always place it, casually folded, on either the right or left of your plate. Do not place your napkin on the chair.*

1 pound medium shrimp, peeled, deveined
   Salt to taste
4 chicken breast halves
3 tablespoons vegetable oil
1/2 cup chopped green bell pepper
1 small onion, chopped
1 (8-ounce) can chunky tomato sauce
1/2 cup dry sherry
1 tablespoon Worcestershire sauce
1 to 2 tablespoons chopped parsley
1/4 teaspoon thyme
1 1/2 teaspoons salt
1/4 teaspoon pepper
1 cup half-and-half

Cook the shrimp in salted boiling water in a saucepan for 2 to 3 minutes or until cooked through; drain and chill.

Sauté the chicken in the oil in a skillet until brown on both sides. Drain on paper towels and cut into bite-size pieces. Add the bell pepper and onion to the drippings in the skillet and sauté until tender.

Return the chicken to the skillet and add the tomato sauce, sherry, Worcestershire sauce, parsley, thyme, salt and pepper and mix well. Spoon into a 4-quart baking dish.

Bake at 350 degrees for 45 minutes. Stir in the shrimp and half-and-half. Bake until heated through. Serve over rice.

Yield: 6 servings

Scampi

1 pound uncooked large shrimp
1 cup (2 sticks) butter
1/4 cup olive oil
1 garlic clove, minced
1 tablespoon parsley flakes
3/4 teaspoon basil
1/2 teaspoon oregano
1 tablespoon fresh lemon juice
   Salt to taste

Peel and devein the shrimp, leaving the tails intact. Butterfly the shrimp if desired. Arrange with the tails up in a shallow baking dish.

Melt the butter with the olive oil in a saucepan. Add the garlic, parsley flakes, basil, oregano, lemon juice and salt and mix well. Cook just until heated through, stirring to mix well. Pour over the shrimp.

Bake at 450 degrees for 5 minutes. Broil for 5 minutes longer or until golden brown. Serve with rice pilaf.

Yield: 4 servings

Baked Salmon with Mustard Chive Butter

3/4 cup (1 1/2 sticks) unsalted butter, softened
3 1/2 tablespoons lemon juice
3 tablespoons chopped chives
1 1/2 tablespoons country-style Dijon mustard
1 1/2 teaspoons grated lemon zest
3/4 teaspoon salt
1/4 teaspoon pepper
6 (6-ounce) salmon fillets
2 tablespoons lemon juice

Combine the butter, 3 1/2 tablespoons lemon juice, chives, Dijon mustard, lemon zest, salt and pepper in a food processor or mixing bowl. Process or beat until smooth.

Line a baking sheet with foil. Spread 1 tablespoon of the butter mixture over the foil. Place the salmon fillets skin down on the prepared foil. Drizzle each fillet with 1 teaspoon of the 2 tablespoons lemon juice. Spread with the remaining butter mixture. Bake at 450 degrees for 10 to 20 minutes or until the fish flakes easily. Garnish with additional chopped chives.

Yield: 6 servings

SERVE SALT in a shaker, grinder, or saltcellar. A saltcellar (small bowl) should include a spoon for serving, although one may use the tip of the knife to serve. If one has food to be dipped in salt, place it on the butter plate or on the edge of the dinner plate. If the table setting includes individual saltcellars, one may season by taking a pinch with the fingers.

HAZELNUT-ENCRUSTED SALMON

1 cup uncooked rice
1 1/2 cups water
1/2 cup hazelnuts
2 tablespoons flour
4 (6-ounce) salmon fillets
1/2 teaspoon salt
2 tablespoons vegetable oil
1/2 tablespoon butter
1 shallot, chopped
8 ounces snow peas, trimmed, strings removed
Juice of 2 oranges
2 teaspoons chopped fresh tarragon
1/2 tablespoon butter

Combine the rice with the water in a medium saucepan and bring to a simmer. Simmer, covered, over low heat for 30 minutes or until the rice is tender.

Combine the hazelnuts and flour in a food processor container and pulse until fine crumbs form. Sprinkle the salmon with salt. Place the salmon skin side down on a work surface and press the hazelnut mixture over the side that is up.

Heat the oil in a large sauté pan over high heat and place the salmon hazelnut side down in the pan. Reduce the heat slightly and cook for 3 minutes or until the salmon is golden brown. Remove to a platter and keep warm.

Wipe the sauté pan and add 1/2 tablespoon butter. Cook over medium-high heat until the butter melts. Add the shallot and snow peas. Sauté for 1 minute. Remove the snow peas.

Pack the rice into moistened individual molds. Invert onto warm serving plates. Spoon the snow pea mixture onto the plates. Arrange the salmon fillets on the snow peas.

Add the orange juice, tarragon and 1/2 tablespoon butter to the sauté pan and cook until heated through. Spoon the sauce around the salmon.

Yield: 4 servings

LEMON PEPPER BAKED SALMON

4 salmon fillets
   Lemon juice to taste
   Lemon pepper to taste
1/4 cup mayonnaise

Arrange the salmon skin side down in a baking pan sprayed with nonstick cooking spray. Sprinkle with lemon juice and lemon pepper. Spread with mayonnaise and sprinkle again with lemon pepper.

Bake at 350 degrees for 15 minutes or until the salmon flakes easily. Broil until the top is brown if desired.

Yield: 4 servings

SALMON WITH CARAMELIZED GLAZE

1/2 cup packed brown sugar
2 tablespoons margarine
3 tablespoons lemon juice
1 (1-pound) salmon fillet

Melt the brown sugar and margarine with the lemon juice in a 9×13-inch baking dish and stir to mix well. Arrange the salmon in the prepared dish and spoon the brown sugar mixture over it.

Bake at 350 degrees for 30 minutes or until the salmon flakes easily, basting with the brown sugar mixture every 10 minutes to glaze. Serve with the remaining glaze spooned over the fillet.

Note: *Remember that every time you open the oven door, the oven temperature drops 25 to 50 degrees.*

Yield: 2 servings

GRILLED SALMON

Select thinner 4-ounce fillets cut from the tail portions of the salmon. Sprinkle with a small amount of seasoned salt and grill over medium-hot coals for about 5 minutes or until the fillets flake easily. Serve on split focaccia lightly spread with mayonnaise. Top with tomato slices and leaf lettuce.

173

GRILL PANS *are used to grill indoors. They resemble heavy cast-iron skillets with ridges that simulate the effect of an outdoor grill. To prevent food from sticking to the pan, apply a light coating of oil or butter to the food and the pan.*

GRILL BASKETS *are shallow metal baskets with a woven lid and handle used to grill small or unstable items such as shrimp, fish, chicken wings, or vegetables. The handle and lid allow foods to be turned with ease.*

GRILL TRAYS *are metal trays with small openings positioned close in proximity to allow small food items to cook securely on a conventional grill.*

GRILLED SEA BASS

Sea Bass
- 4 (6- to 8-ounce) sea bass fillets
- 2 tablespoons vegetable oil
- Salt and pepper to taste

Leeks
- 2 tablespoons olive oil
- White and pale green portions of 6 small leeks, sliced 1/4 inch thick
- 2 tablespoons water
- Salt and pepper to taste

Assembly
- Tomato Pepper Relish (page 175)
- Wine Sauce (page 175)

For the sea bass, brush the sea bass fillets with oil and season with salt and pepper. Place on a heated grill pan and cook over high heat for 1 minute on each side, turning once. Remove to a large baking dish. Bake at 400 degrees for 5 to 10 minutes or until the fillets flake easily. Remove from the oven and tent with foil to keep warm.

For the leeks, heat the olive oil in a skillet over medium heat. Add the leeks and water. Cook for 5 to 8 minutes or until tender, stirring frequently. Season with salt and pepper.

To serve, spoon the leeks onto 4 serving plates. Arrange the fish over the leeks. Top with the Tomato Pepper Relish and spoon the Wine Sauce around the fish.

Yield: 4 servings

TOMATO PEPPER RELISH

  1 large red bell pepper
  4 plum tomatoes
  2 tablespoons olive oil
     Salt and pepper to taste
  1 large shallot, chopped
  2 tablespoons olive oil
12 niçoise olives, chopped
  2 anchovies, chopped

Place the bell pepper on a baking sheet and broil until charred on all sides, turning 3 or 4 times. Place in a paper bag and let stand until cool. Peel, seed and chop the bell pepper.

Cut the tomatoes into halves and discard the seeds. Place on a baking sheet; drizzle with 2 tablespoons olive oil and season with salt and pepper. Broil until the tomatoes are tender. Chop coarsely.

Sauté the shallot in 2 tablespoons heated olive oil in a skillet for 2 minutes or until tender. Add the olives, anchovies and chopped bell pepper. Sauté for 30 seconds. Stir in the tomatoes and sauté for 30 seconds longer. Remove from the heat and season with salt and pepper; keep warm.

Yield: 4 servings

WINE SAUCE

1/4 cup lemon juice
1/2 cup dry white wine
  1 medium shallot, chopped
1/2 cup (1 stick) unsalted butter, sliced into tablespoons
    Saffron, salt and pepper to taste

Combine the lemon juice, wine and chopped shallot in a medium saucepan. Bring to a boil and cook for 5 minutes or until reduced by 3/4. Reduce the heat and whisk in the butter 1 tablespoon at a time. Season with saffron, salt and pepper.

Yield: 4 servings

SAFFRON *is the most expensive spice in the world. It takes 14,000 hand-picked stigmas from the purple crocus to yield one ounce. The intense spice is used to tint and flavor foods. Only a small amount is necessary due to its intense flavor. It is packaged in powder form or whole stigmas. Storage requires an airtight container kept in a cool dark place.*

CRUSTY PARMESAN SNAPPER FILLETS

THE HOSTESS *should always be the last to finish eating, and should always take a second small portion to encourage others to do so.*

- 1/3 cup oil-pack sun-dried tomatoes
- 1/2 cup finely chopped walnuts
- 2 tablespoons chopped fresh chives
- 2 to 4 tablespoons stone-ground mustard, or to taste
- 1/4 teaspoon pepper
- 1/4 to 1/3 cup water
- 4 (6-ounce) snapper fillets, 1 inch thick
- 3 tablespoons freshly grated Parmesan cheese
- 3 tablespoons dried unseasoned bread crumbs
- 1 garlic clove, minced
- 1 tablespoon olive oil

Drain the sun-dried tomatoes and rinse under warm water. Combine with the walnuts, chives, mustard and pepper in a food processor container and process to form a paste. Add enough of the water to make of spreading consistency, processing constantly.

Pat the fillets dry and arrange in a 9×13-inch baking pan sprayed with nonstick cooking spray. Spread with the tomato mixture. Mix the cheese, bread crumbs and garlic in a bowl. Sprinkle over the fish and drizzle with the olive oil.

Bake at 400 degrees for 15 to 18 minutes or until the fish flakes easily. Serve with lemon wedges.

Yield: 4 servings

TUNA STEAKS WITH ROSEMARY BUTTER

Rosemary Butter
- 2 teaspoons chopped fresh rosemary
- 1 tablespoon chopped black olives
- 1/4 teaspoon Dijon mustard
- 1/4 cup (1/2 stick) butter

Tuna
- 1/2 cup olive oil
- 1/4 cup soy sauce
- 2 tablespoons minced gingerroot
- 1/4 teaspoon pepper
- 6 tuna steaks

For the butter, mix the rosemary, olives, Dijon mustard and butter in a bowl.

For the fish, combine the olive oil, soy sauce, gingerroot and pepper in a shallow dish and mix well. Add the tuna and marinate for 30 minutes; drain. Grill for 4 minutes on each side.

Serve the tuna with the butter. Garnish with sprigs of fresh rosemary.

Yield: 6 servings

MARINATED AHI TUNA WITH PINEAPPLE SALSA

Pineapple Salsa

1 large pineapple, peeled, cored, chopped
1 papaya, peeled, seeded, chopped
1 red bell pepper, seeded, chopped
1/2 green bell pepper, seeded, chopped
3 green onions, finely chopped
1 cup finely chopped red onion
1 habanero chile, finely chopped
3 tablespoons minced fresh cilantro
2 tablespoons fresh lime juice
1 1/2 teaspoons rice vinegar
1/8 teaspoon cayenne pepper
   Salt and black pepper to taste

Tuna

1/2 cup rice vinegar
4 green onions, finely chopped
2 teaspoons Dijon mustard
1/2 teaspoon red pepper flakes
3 tablespoons olive oil
6 ahi (yellowfin) tuna steaks

For the salsa, combine the pineapple, papaya, bell peppers, green onions, red onion, chile, cilantro, lime juice and vinegar in a nonreactive bowl and mix well. Do not use an aluminum pan. Season with the cayenne pepper, salt and black pepper. Store in the refrigerator.

For the tuna, combine the vinegar, green onions, Dijon mustard and red pepper flakes in a nonreactive bowl. Whisk in the olive oil gradually. Add the tuna steaks and coat well. Marinate in the refrigerator for 1 to 4 hours, turning occasionally. Let stand at room temperature for 30 minutes before cooking.

Drain the tuna and place on a rack in a broiler pan or on a grill. Broil or grill for 4 to 5 minutes on each side for rare to medium-rare. Serve immediately with the salsa.

The salsa is best if prepared on the day to be served, but it can be stored in the refrigerator for up to 1 week.

Yield: 6 servings

PAPAYA *is a tropical fruit that has a sweet golden skin and varies in weight from one to two pounds. Its juicy pulp is tangy and smooth. The center cavity is full of glossy dark seeds that make an excellent salad dressing. Unripened fruit will ripen at room temperature, while ripe fruit should be refrigerated.*

Lasting Impressions...

DESSERTS

This photograph is sponsored by:
Mary Liebscher
Amy Lockard
Doris Miller

Lasting Impressions...

Special events are made even more so by giving small gifts or mementos to mark notable experiences. The favor may be a photo used as a place card, a jar of your best jam, or a bottle of wine. Whatever the gift, it should not be so substantial that it requires special recognition or reciprocation, nor should it cause embarrassment. Some ideas for gifts or favors may come from your menu or theme and might include:

Candy	Nuts
Gourmet coffee	Fruit-infused vinegars
Flowers	Dried fruit
Seeds in a small clay pot	Potpourri
Herb-infused cooking oils	Homemade breadsticks
Miniature topiaries	Holiday ornament
Specialty teas	Sachets
Biscotti	Disposable cameras
Special cookies	Small frames used as place cards
Candles	

Perhaps the most important thought to hold on to is that despite how much time and effort is put into an event, the most important factor is hospitality. Everyone wants to feel special. The gracious nature of the host and hostess coupled with the extraordinary level of comfort and ease will create an environment that people are drawn to time and again. Take time to enjoy entertaining and sharing your culinary and creative self. Also, take time to relax. The best gift you give your guests is your undivided and cordial attention.

Take a few moments after the event is completed to write a note to those attending to share how splendid it was to spend time together. This form of affirmation is well appreciated.

Finally, use the knowledge that you gain every time you entertain to build a collection of entertaining resources. Record your guest list, theme, decorating ideas, favors, beverages, flowers, tableware, tablecloths, and any other details that may prove useful for future events. A journal or note card may serve as a great future entertaining asset.

Johnny Appleseed Cake with Caramel Sauce

Cake

    2¼ cups flour
    ¾   cup sugar
    ¾   cup packed brown sugar
    2   teaspoons baking powder
    ½   teaspoon baking soda
    1   tablespoon cinnamon
    1   teaspoon nutmeg
    1   teaspoon salt
    ¾   cup vegetable oil
    3   eggs, lightly beaten
    2   teaspoons vanilla extract
    2   large tart cooking apples, cut into ½-inch pieces, about 2½ cups
    ¾   cup finely chopped walnuts

Caramel Sauce

    1   cup packed brown sugar
    ½   cup heavy cream
    3   tablespoons butter
    1   teaspoon vanilla extract

For the cake, mix the flour, sugar, brown sugar, baking powder, baking soda, cinnamon, nutmeg and salt in a large mixing bowl. Beat at low speed for 1 to 2 minutes to mix well. Add the oil, eggs and vanilla and beat at medium speed for 1 to 2 minutes or until smooth. Stir in the apples and walnuts by hand.

Spoon into a greased and floured 9×13-inch cake pan. Bake at 350 degrees for 40 to 45 minutes or until the top springs back when lightly touched in the center. Cool on a wire rack.

For the sauce, combine the brown sugar, cream and butter in a 1-quart saucepan. Cook over medium heat for 3 to 4 minutes or until the brown sugar dissolves, stirring constantly. Stir in the vanilla. Drizzle over cake slices to serve. Garnish with Vanilla Whipped Cream (at right) or whipped topping.

Yield: 15 servings

Vanilla Whipped Cream

Combine 1 cup chilled whipping cream, 1 tablespoon confectioners' sugar and ½ teaspoon vanilla extract in a large mixing bowl and beat until soft peaks form. Chill, covered, for up to 4 hours.

BUTTERMILK SPICE CAKE

Cake

- 1¾ cups flour
- ½ cup sugar
- ¾ cup packed brown sugar
- 1 teaspoon baking powder
- ¾ teaspoon baking soda
- 1½ teaspoons cinnamon
- ½ teaspoon ground cloves
- 1 teaspoon salt
- 1¼ cups buttermilk
- ¾ cup (1½ sticks) unsalted butter, softened
- 3 eggs

Brown Sugar Frosting

- ½ cup (1 stick) butter
- 1 cup packed brown sugar
- ¼ cup milk
- 3¼ cups sifted confectioners' sugar

For the cake, mix the flour, sugar, brown sugar, baking powder, baking soda, cinnamon, cloves and salt in a large mixing bowl. Add the buttermilk and butter and beat at medium speed for 2 minutes. Add the eggs and beat for 2 minutes longer.

Spoon into 2 greased and floured cake pans. Bake at 350 degrees for 20 minutes. Cool in the pans for 5 minutes; remove to a wire rack to cool completely.

For the frosting, melt the butter in a heavy saucepan. Add the brown sugar and cook until bubbly. Cook for 1 minute, stirring constantly. Cool slightly and add the milk. Beat until smooth. Add enough confectioners' sugar to make of the desired consistency and mix well. Spread between the layers and over the top and side of the cake.

Reduce the frosting recipe by ½ for a cake baked in a 9×13-inch cake pan or baking dish. Reduce the oven temperature to 325 degrees for a baking dish.

Yield: 16 servings

Carrot Pecan Cake with Cream Cheese Frosting

Cake

1¹/₂ cups vegetable oil
2 cups sugar
3 eggs
2 teaspoons vanilla extract
2 cups flour
2 teaspoons baking soda
2 teaspoons cinnamon
1 teaspoon salt
2 cups shredded carrots
1 cup chopped pecans
¹/₂ cup crushed pineapple
1 cup raisins

Cream Cheese Frosting

1 cup (2 sticks) butter, softened
16 ounces cream cheese, softened
2 teaspoons vanilla extract
2 (1-pound) packages confectioners' sugar

For the cake, combine the oil, sugar, eggs and vanilla in a mixing bowl and beat until smooth. Add the flour, baking soda, cinnamon and salt and mix well. Stir in the carrots, pecans, pineapple and raisins.

Spoon into 2 greased and floured 9-inch cake pans. Bake at 350 degrees for 50 to 55 minutes or until the layers test done. Cool in the pans for 5 minutes. Remove to a wire rack to cool completely.

For the frosting, beat the butter and cream cheese in a mixing bowl until light. Beat in the vanilla. Add the confectioners' sugar gradually, beating constantly until smooth. Spread between the layers and over the top and side of the cake.

You may add a small amount of milk to the frosting if needed for the desired consistency.

Yield: 16 servings

CONFECTIONERS' SUGAR, *a product from sugar cane or sugar beets, is granulated sugar that has been finely crushed to a powder form. Cornstarch is added to prevent clumping. Powdered sugar labeled XXXX is finer than that labeled XXX. Confectioners' sugar may require sifting prior to use.*

FLOURLESS CHOCOLATE CAKE

CHOCOLATE *should be kept in a cool, dry place. Storage temperature should be between 60 and 75 degrees and at less than 50 percent humidity. Chocolate can be refrigerated, but it requires a tight wrapping to avoid absorbing odors from the refrigerator and to prevent condensation when it is removed from the refrigerator. Chocolate becomes very brittle when cold.*

Chocolate can develop "bloom," which is a gray film from cocoa butter that has softened and risen to the surface, when stored in a warm place. These chocolates will be rather unattractive but are safe to eat. The flavor is not affected. The chocolate will regain its attractive color when melted.

Chocolate Tart Dough
- 1/2 cup (1 stick) butter, softened
- 1/2 cup sugar
- 1 egg
- 1 cup flour
- 1/3 cup baking cocoa
- 1/2 teaspoon salt

Cake
- 1 cup heavy cream
- 2 tablespoons instant espresso granules
- 1 teaspoon vanilla extract
- 12 1/2 (1-ounce) squares bittersweet chocolate
- 1/3 cup sugar
- 5 eggs
- 1/4 cup sugar

Chocolate Ganache
- 1 cup (2 sticks) butter
- 8 ounces good-quality semisweet chocolate, chopped

For the dough, cream the butter and sugar in a mixing bowl until light and fluffy. Beat in the egg. Sift the flour, baking cocoa and salt together. Add to the creamed mixture, stirring just until smooth. Wrap with plastic wrap and chill for 1 hour or longer.

Roll the dough on a lightly floured surface. Fit into a deep 9-inch round cake pan. Bake at 325 degrees for 20 minutes.

For the cake, combine the cream, espresso granules and vanilla in a saucepan and bring to a boil. Remove from the heat and add the chocolate and 1/3 cup sugar; stir until smooth.

Beat the eggs with 1/4 cup sugar in a mixing bowl until tripled in volume and pale yellow. Fold into the chocolate mixture. Pour into the tart shell.

Place the cake pan in a large pan and add enough hot water to reach halfway up the side of the cake pan. Bake at 325 degrees for 30 to 40 minutes or until the top appears dull and feels set when lightly touched. Remove to a wire rack to cool for several minutes. Remove the cake from the pan to the wire rack and cool completely.

For the ganache, combine the butter and chocolate in a double boiler. Cook over hot water over very low heat until the butter and chocolate melt, stirring to mix well. Place a piece of foil under the cake on the rack. Spoon the ganache over the cake.

Yield: 12 servings

SINFULLY RICH CHOCOLATE CAKE

      10 ounces bittersweet or semisweet chocolate
       1 cup (2 sticks) unsalted butter, softened
       5 large eggs, beaten
    1¼ cups sugar
       5 tablespoons flour
    1½ teaspoons baking powder

Combine the chocolate and butter in a microwave-safe dish. Microwave on High for 2 minutes or until melted; stir until smooth. Combine the eggs and sugar and beat until mixture begins to thicken. Sift the flour and baking powder over the egg mixture and fold in gently. Fold in the chocolate mixture gradually.

Spoon into a buttered and floured 10-inch springform pan with a side 2¾ inches deep. Bake at 325 degrees for 20 minutes. Cover with foil and bake for 30 minutes longer or until a tester inserted in the center comes out with moist crumbs still attached.

Remove the foil and cool in the pan on a wire rack; the cake will fall as it cools. Loosen the pan side with a knife and remove. Garnish with a sifting of confectioners' sugar. Serve with sweetened or mocha-flavor whipped cream.

Yield: 10 servings

COCOA POWDER *can be used to dust cake pans when making chocolate cakes. The cakes will not be highlighted with white flour on the outside.*

AMARETTI TORTE

Amaretti are light, crisp macaroon cookies made with either bitter-almond paste or apricot-kernel paste.

      10 amaretti
       1 cup (2 sticks) unsalted butter, softened
       1 cup sugar
       5 egg yolks
    ½ cup flour
       4 (1-ounce) squares semisweet chocolate, finely grated
       5 egg whites, stiffly beaten
    ½ cup amaretto

Process the amaretti in a blender until finely crushed; measure ½ cup. Cream the butter and sugar in a mixing bowl until light and fluffy. Add the egg yolks one at a time, beating for 10 minutes. Add the flour and the crushed amaretti gradually, mixing well after each addition. Fold in the chocolate and egg whites.

Spoon into a greased and lightly floured round 10-inch baking pan. Bake at 350 degrees for 35 to 45 minutes or until the top springs back when lightly touched. Cool in the pan on a wire rack for 10 minutes. Remove to the wire rack to cool completely. Serve slices drizzled with 1 tablespoon amaretto and topped with fresh fruit or top with Cherry Almond Glaze (at right).

Yield: 8 servings

CHERRY ALMOND GLAZE

Mix ½ cup sugar and 2 tablespoons cornstarch in a small saucepan. Blend in 1 cup water and ¾ cup juice from canned cherries gradually. Bring to a boil and cook for 1 minute or until thickened, stirring constantly. Stir in ¼ teaspoon almond extract and enough red food coloring to color as desired. You may also add cherries when the mixture boils.

COFFEE-BUTTERED THIN-LAYER CAKE

Cake

   1 cup (2 sticks) butter, softened
   1 cup sugar
   4 eggs
   1 teaspoon vanilla extract
$1^1/_2$ cups sifted flour

Coffee Butter Filling

   1 cup (2 sticks) butter, softened
   4 cups sifted confectioners' sugar
$1^1/_2$ teaspoons instant coffee granules
  $^1/_4$ teaspoon fresh lemon juice
   2 teaspoons vanilla extract
   4 egg yolks or equivalent egg substitute

For the cake, cream the butter and sugar in a mixing bowl until light and fluffy. Beat in the eggs one at a time until light and fluffy. Beat in the vanilla. Add the flour gradually, beating just until smooth after each addition.

Invert a round 9-inch cake pan. Use the bottom of the pan as a cooking platform. Butter and lightly flour. Spread a $^1/_8$-inch-thick layer of the batter to within $^1/_4$ inch of the edge of the pan. Bake at 350 degrees for 7 to 9 minutes or just until the edge is light brown. Loosen the layer carefully with a flexible spatula and remove to a wire rack to cool. Repeat the process with the remaining batter to make 10 to 12 thin layers.

For the filling, cream the butter and confectioners' sugar in a mixing bowl until light and fluffy. Beat in the coffee granules, lemon juice and vanilla until creamy. Beat in the egg yolks one at a time until the mixture is fluffy.

To assemble, place one layer on a serving platter, spread with some of the filling. Top with another layer and continue building layers of cake and filling, ending with a cake layer. Chill, covered, for 3 to 12 hours. Let stand at room temperature for 15 minutes before serving. Garnish with confectioners' sugar.

Yield: 18 servings

DECADENT CAPPUCCINO CAKE

Nut Crust

5	graham crackers
1/2	cup each almonds and pecans
1/4	cup sugar
6	tablespoons unsalted butter
1/8	teaspoon salt

Chocolate Ganache

2	cups heavy cream
16	ounces semisweet chocolate
2	tablespoons light corn syrup
1/2	cup (1 stick) butter

Cappuccino Buttercream

1	cup sugar
1/3	cup water
8	egg yolks, or equivalent egg substitute
1	tablespoon each instant coffee granules and hot water
3	ounces semisweet chocolate, melted, cooled
1	teaspoon vanilla extract
1 1/2	cups (3 sticks) unsalted butter

CAPPUCCINO WHIPPED CREAM

Dissolve 2 teaspoons coffee granules in 1 tablespoon whipping cream and 1/2 teaspoon vanilla extract in a small bowl. Beat 1 cup plus 3 tablespoons whipping cream in a mixing bowl until the mixture begins to thicken. Add the coffee mixture and 5 tablespoons confectioners' sugar and beat until soft peaks form.

For the crust, process the graham crackers, almonds and pecans in a food processor until crumbly. Add the sugar, butter and salt and process until well mixed. Press over the bottom of a buttered 10-inch springform pan with a 3-inch side. Bake at 350 degrees for 15 minutes. Cool on a wire rack.

For the ganache, bring the cream just to a boil in a saucepan and reduce the heat to low. Add the chocolate. Cook until the chocolate melts, stirring to blend well. Stir in the corn syrup. Add the butter gradually, stirring to blend well after each addition. Cool to room temperature. Pour into the prepared crust. Chill, covered, for 2 hours or longer.

For the buttercream, mix the sugar with the water in a small saucepan. Cover and bring to a boil. Reduce the heat to medium and boil for 1 to 2 minutes or to 240 degrees on a candy thermometer.

Beat the egg yolks in a large mixing bowl. Add the sugar syrup gradually, beating constantly at medium speed. Place in the freezer until cool.

Dissolve the coffee granules in the hot water. Stir into the egg yolk mixture. Add the chocolate and vanilla and stir to mix well. Beat in the butter 1 tablespoon at a time until smooth and creamy. Spread over the ganache.

Chill, covered, until firm. Place on a serving plate and remove the side of the pan. Spread Cappuccino Whipped Cream (at right) over the top and garnish with chocolate leaves or curls and chocolate-covered espresso beans.

Photograph for this recipe is on page 178 and opposite.

Yield: 12 servings

GLAZED LEMON SOUR CREAM POUND CAKE

DUST CAKES *with baking cocoa, ground cinnamon, or very finely ground toasted almonds or hazelnuts in place of confectioners' sugar.*

    3 tablespoons fine bread crumbs
3½ cups flour
    1 teaspoon baking powder
½ teaspoon baking soda
½ teaspoon salt
    2 cups (4 sticks) butter, softened
    2 tablespoons finely grated lemon zest
    3 cups sugar
    2 tablespoons lemon juice
    1 teaspoon vanilla extract
    6 egg yolks, at room temperature
1⅓ cups sour cream, at room temperature
    6 egg whites, at room temperature
⅓ cup sugar
⅓ cup fresh lemon juice

Grease a fluted 10-inch tube pan and sprinkle with the bread crumbs, shaking out the excess. Mix the flour, baking powder, baking soda and salt together.

Cream the butter and lemon zest at medium-high speed in a large mixer bowl for 30 seconds. Add 3 cups sugar gradually, beating constantly for 10 minutes and scraping the bowl frequently. Beat in 2 tablespoons lemon juice and vanilla.

Beat in the egg yolks one at a time. Add the flour mixture alternately with the sour cream, beating at medium-low speed just until well mixed. Beat the egg whites at medium speed in a large mixing bowl until soft peaks form. Fold into the batter ⅓ at a time.

Spoon into the prepared tube pan. Bake at 325 degrees for 1 hour and 5 minutes to 1 hour and 10 minutes or until the cake tests done. Cool in the pan on a wire rack for 10 minutes. Remove to a serving plate.

Combine ⅓ cup sugar and ⅓ cup lemon juice in a small saucepan. Heat until the sugar dissolves, stirring to blend well. Brush warm glaze over the cake. Store, covered, for 24 hours before serving. Serve sliced cake with whipped cream and fresh raspberries.

Yield: 16 servings

Lemon Buttercream Cake

Lemon Filling

- 1 cup water
- ¼ cup cornstarch
- 1 cup sugar
- 4 large egg yolks, beaten
- ⅓ cup lemon juice
- 2 tablespoons unsalted butter

Cake

- 1 cup (2 sticks) unsalted butter, softened
- 2 cups sugar
- Finely grated zest of 1 lemon
- 4 large egg yolks
- 3 cups flour
- 1 tablespoon baking powder
- 1 cup milk
- 1 teaspoon lemon extract
- 4 large egg whites
- ⅛ teaspoon salt
- Fluffy Butter Frosting or Buttercream Frosting (at right)

For the filling, bring the water to a boil in a medium saucepan. Stir in a mixture of the cornstarch and sugar. Cook over medium heat until thickened and smooth, stirring constantly until the sugar is dissolved. Whisk a small amount of the hot mixture into the egg yolks; whisk the egg yolks into the hot mixture. Whisk in the lemon juice.

Cook until thickened, stirring constantly. Remove from the heat and stir in the butter until melted. Cool to room temperature, stirring occasionally.

For the cake, beat the butter at medium speed in a mixing bowl until fluffy. Add a mixture of the sugar and lemon zest gradually, beating until light. Beat in the egg yolks one at a time.

Mix the flour and baking powder together. Add to the beaten mixture alternately with the milk, beating at low speed until well mixed after each addition. Fold in the lemon extract.

Beat the egg whites with the salt in a large mixing bowl until stiff peaks form. Fold into the batter.

Spoon into 3 greased and floured round cake pans. Bake at 350 degrees for 18 to 22 minutes or until a wooden pick inserted into the center comes out clean. Cool in the pans on wire racks for 10 minutes. Remove to the wire racks to cool completely.

To assemble, spread the filling between the cake layers, stacking on a serving plate. Spread frosting over the top and side of the cake.

Photograph for this recipe is on page 178.

Yield: 16 servings

Fluffy Butter Frosting

Beat ⅔ cup softened butter in a mixing bowl until fluffy. Add 4 cups sifted confectioners' sugar gradually, beating until smooth. Beat in ½ cup milk and 1 tablespoon vanilla extract gradually. Add 5 cups sifted confectioners' sugar gradually and beat until smooth, adding a small amount of additional milk if needed for spreading consistency.

Buttercream Frosting

Combine 2 cups sugar and ⅔ cup water in a saucepan and mix well. Cover and bring to a boil. Reduce heat to medium and boil for 1 to 2 minutes until a candy thermometer reads 240 degrees. Using an electric mixer, beat 16 egg yolks and 2 teaspoons vanilla. Add hot syrup mixture to the yolks very slowly while mixing on medium speed. Cool. Add 6 sticks of butter, 1 tablespoon at a time until creamy.

HICKORY NUT CAKE

SEVEN-MINUTE FROSTING

Combine 1³/4 cups sugar, 1/2 teaspoon cream of tartar, 2 egg whites and 6 tablespoons cold water in a double boiler. Place over boiling water and cook for 7 minutes or until the mixture triples in volume and forms soft peaks, beating constantly. Remove from the heat and stir in 2 teaspoons vanilla extract.

Cake
- 3¹/2 cups cake flour
- 4 teaspoons baking powder
- ¹/2 teaspoon salt
- ²/3 cup butter, softened
- 2 cups sugar
- 2 teaspoons vanilla extract
- 2 tablespoons boiling water
- 1¹/2 cups cold water
- ³/4 cup chopped hickory nuts
- 4 egg whites, stiffly beaten

Fresh Fruit Filling
- 3 cartons whipping cream
- 3 tablespoons confectioners' sugar
- 1¹/2 teaspoons vanilla extract
- 1 (8- or 9-ounce) jar strawberry or currant jelly
- 1 pint fresh strawberries, raspberries or other fruit in season

Frosting
Seven-Minute Frosting (at left) (optional)

For the cake, grease and flour three 9-inch cake pans and line with baking parchment.

Sift the cake flour, baking powder and salt together 3 times. Cream the butter and sugar in a mixing bowl until light and fluffy. Beat in the vanilla and boiling water. Add the sifted dry ingredients alternately with the cold water, mixing well after each addition. Add the hickory nuts. Fold in the stiffly beaten egg whites.

Spoon into the prepared cake pans. Bake at 350 degrees for 20 to 25 minutes or until the layers test done. Cool in the pans on wire racks for 10 minutes. Remove to the wire racks to cool completely.

For the filling, combine the whipping cream with the confectioners' sugar and vanilla in a mixing bowl and beat until stiff peaks form. Heat the jelly in a small saucepan until of spreading consistency. Slice the strawberries.

To assemble, spread a thin layer of the jelly on the top of one cake layer and place on a serving plate. Spread with some of the whipped cream and some of the strawberries. Spread both sides of the middle cake layer with the jelly. Top with additional whipped cream. Top with the remaining cake layer. Top with remaining strawberries and frost top and sides with remaining whipped cream.

If you do not wish to use the fresh fruit filling and whipped cream, frost the top and side of the cake with Seven-Minute Frosting. Garnish with additional fresh fruit. Store in the refrigerator.

Yield: 16 servings

OATMEAL CAKE

Cake
- 1½ cups boiling water
- 1 cup rolled oats
- ½ cup (1 stick) margarine or butter, softened
- 1 cup sugar
- 1 cup packed brown sugar
- 2 eggs
- 1 teaspoon vanilla extract
- 1½ cups flour
- 1 teaspoon baking soda
- 1 teaspoon cinnamon
- ½ teaspoon salt
- 1 cup raisins
- ½ cup chopped pecans or walnuts

Cream Cheese Frosting
- ½ cup (1 stick) margarine or butter, softened
- 8 ounces cream cheese, softened
- 1 (1-pound) package confectioners' sugar
- 1 teaspoon vanilla extract
- ½ cup chopped pecans or walnuts

For the cake, pour the boiling water over the oats in a bowl and let stand until cool.

Cream the margarine, sugar and brown sugar in a mixing bowl until light and fluffy. Beat in the eggs and vanilla. Add the flour, baking soda, cinnamon and salt and mix well. Mix in the oats, raisins and pecans.

Spoon into a greased and floured 9×13-inch cake pan. Bake at 350 degrees for 30 to 35 minutes or until the cake tests done. Cool in the pan on a wire rack.

For the frosting, beat the margarine and cream cheese in a mixing bowl until smooth. Add the confectioners' sugar and beat until light. Beat in the vanilla and pecans. Spread over the cooled cake.

Yield: 15 servings

OAT GROATS are refined oats that still contain most of the original nutrients. They can be cooked and served as cereal, or prepared for use in other dishes. After groats have been steamed and flattened with huge rollers, they become regular rolled oats or old-fashioned oats, taking about 15 minutes to cook. Quick-cooking rolled oats are groats that have been cut into several pieces before being steamed and rolled into thinner flakes.

They cook in about 5 minutes, yet the flavor and texture are never quite the same as with regular rolled oats. Old-fashioned oats and quick-cooking oats can usually be interchanged in recipes. Instant oats are not interchangeable as they're processed with cut groats that have been precooked and dried before being rolled. This precooking process softens the oat pieces.

PINEAPPLE MERINGUE CAKE

MERINGUE is a mixture of egg whites and granulated sugar that has been beaten until stiff peaks form. Sugar should be added very gradually to promote a smooth consistency. Meringues may be used as a topping for pies or a baked confection.

By turning off the oven when the meringue begins to turn brown and leaving the door slightly ajar, pies will cool slowly and prevent the meringue from splitting.

Cake
$1/2$	cup (1 stick) butter, softened
$1/2$	cup sugar
4	egg yolks, beaten
$1/2$	cup cake flour, sifted
$1/4$	cup milk
$1/4$	teaspoon salt
$1\ 1/2$	teaspoons baking powder
2	tablespoons sifted cake flour

Meringue Topping
3	egg whites
$3/4$	cup sugar
1	teaspoon vanilla extract
1	cup (or more) English walnuts, crushed

Pineapple Filling
1	cup whipping cream
2	teaspoons confectioners' sugar
1	cup drained crushed pineapple
$1/4$	teaspoon vanilla extract

For the cake, cream the butter and sugar in a mixing bowl until light and fluffy. Beat in the egg yolks. Add $1/2$ cup flour, milk and salt and mix well. Mix the baking powder with 2 tablespoons flour and add to the batter; mix well. Spoon into 2 parchment-lined 8-inch cake pans.

For the topping, beat the egg whites in a mixing bowl until frothy. Add the sugar gradually, beating constantly until soft peaks form. Beat in the vanilla. Spread over the unbaked cake layers. Sprinkle with the walnuts.

Bake the cake layers at 325 degrees for 30 minutes or until the layers test done. Cool in the cake pans on wire racks for 10 minutes. Remove to the wire racks to cool completely.

For the filling, beat the whipping cream in a mixing bowl until it begins to thicken. Add the confectioners' sugar gradually, beating constantly until soft peaks form. Fold in the pineapple and vanilla.

To assemble, place 1 cake layer meringue side down on a cake plate. Spread the filling over the top and place the remaining cake layer meringue side up on the filling. Store in the refrigerator.

Yield: 16 servings

BÛCHE DE NOËL (YULE LOG)

Cake

     5 egg whites
     1/2 cup confectioners' sugar
     5 egg yolks
     3 tablespoons baking cocoa
     1/2 cup confectioners' sugar

Mocha Filling

     1 cup whipping cream
     1/4 cup each confectioners' sugar and baking cocoa
     1 tablespoon instant coffee granules (optional)

Chocolate Buttercream Frosting

     1/4 cup (1/2 stick) butter, softened
     2 cups confectioners' sugar
     2 tablespoons milk
     1 egg yolk or equivalent egg substitute
     1 (1-ounce) square unsweetened chocolate, melted, cooled
     1 teaspoon vanilla extract

For the cake, grease a 10×15-inch cake pan and line the bottom with waxed paper. Grease and flour the waxed paper.

Beat the egg whites at high speed in a large mixing bowl until soft peaks form. Add 1/2 cup confectioners' sugar gradually, beating until stiff peaks form.

Beat the egg yolks at high speed in a small mixing bowl until thickened. Add the baking cocoa and 1/2 cup confectioners' sugar and beat at low speed until well mixed. Fold into the egg white mixture.

Spread in the prepared cake pan. Bake at 400 degrees for 15 minutes or until the top springs back when lightly touched. Invert onto a towel sprinkled with baking cocoa and remove the waxed paper. Roll the cake in the towel from the narrow side. Place seam side down on a wire rack to cool.

For the filling, beat the whipping cream in a mixing bowl until it begins to thicken. Add the confectioners' sugar, baking cocoa and coffee granules gradually, beating constantly until stiff peaks form.

For the frosting, cream the butter and confectioners' sugar in a mixing bowl until light and fluffy. Add the milk, egg yolk, chocolate and vanilla and beat until smooth.

To assemble, unroll the cake and spread with the filling. Roll without the towel from the narrow side to enclose the filling. Place seam side down on a serving platter. Spoon the frosting into a decorating bag fitted with a large star tip. Pipe the frosting in rows down the length of the cake roll. Store in the refrigerator.

     Yield: 14 servings

SAVE TIME *by channeling rosettes or dollops of whipped cream onto foil-covered baking sheets and freezing. Store them in a freezer bag in the freezer. Use them to accent desserts, placing one on each portion; they'll thaw in approximately ten minutes.*

PUMPKIN ROLL

Cake

Cake
- 3 eggs
- 1 cup sugar
- 3/4 cup flour
- 1 teaspoon baking soda
- 1 teaspoon lemon juice
- 2/3 cup canned pumpkin
- 2 teaspoons pumpkin pie spice
- 1/2 cup finely chopped pecans

Cream Cheese Filling
- 8 ounces cream cheese, softened
- 1/4 cup (1/2 stick) butter, softened
- 1/2 cup confectioners' sugar
- 1 teaspoon vanilla extract

BAKING SODA *is a leavening agent used in baked goods causing ingredients to rise. It requires an acid agent such as buttermilk or yogurt to activate the chemical process. Because the reaction is immediate it should be mixed with other dry ingredients prior to adding the acidic liquid. The completed mixture should be placed immediately in the oven.*

For the cake, beat the eggs in a mixing bowl until frothy. Add the sugar gradually, beating until light yellow. Fold in the flour, baking soda, lemon juice, pumpkin and pumpkin pie spice. Spoon into a greased and floured 10×15-inch cake pan.

Bake at 350 degrees for 15 minutes. Loosen the sides of the cake from the pan immediately with a spatula and invert onto a towel sprinkled with confectioners' sugar and pecans. Roll up in the towel from the long side. Cool on a wire rack for 20 minutes.

For the filling, beat the cream cheese, butter and confectioners' sugar in a mixing bowl until smooth. Beat in the vanilla.

To assemble, unroll the cake and spread with the filling. Roll the cake without the towel to enclose the filling. Freeze, wrapped in foil, until serving time.

Cut the frozen cake into slices. Place on serving plates and let stand until room temperature to serve.

You may substitute 1 teaspoon cinnamon, 1/2 teaspoon ground cloves and 1/4 teaspoon nutmeg for the pumpkin pie spice if preferred.

Yield: 12 servings

DOUBLE-DECADENT BROWNIE TORTE

Torte

- ¹⁄₂ cup (1 stick) butter
- ¹⁄₂ cup light corn syrup
- 6 ounces (1 cup) semisweet chocolate chips
- ¹⁄₂ cup sugar
- 3 eggs, beaten
- 1 cup flour
- 1 cup chopped walnuts or pecans
- 1 teaspoon vanilla extract

Chocolate Glaze

- 3 ounces (¹⁄₂ cup) semisweet chocolate chips
- 2 tablespoons butter
- 1 tablespoon light corn syrup
- 1 teaspoon vanilla extract

For the torte, melt the butter with the corn syrup in a saucepan, stirring to blend well. Stir in the chocolate chips and cook until the chips melt, stirring constantly. Remove from the heat and add the sugar and eggs; mix well. Stir in the flour, walnuts and vanilla.

Spoon into a buttered and floured 9-inch round baking pan or springform pan. Bake at 350 degrees for 30 minutes or until the center springs back when lightly touched. Cool in the pan on a wire rack for 10 minutes. Remove to the wire rack to cool completely.

For the glaze, melt the chocolate chips and butter with the corn syrup in a saucepan over low heat, stirring to mix well. Remove from the heat and stir in the vanilla. Spread over the top and side of the torte. Chill, covered, until set. Garnish with whipped cream, edible flowers, strawberry fans or chocolate leaves.

Note: *You can make Chocolate Leaves by brushing tempered chocolate on the underside of leaves of such nontoxic plants as rose, mint or strawberry. Chill until set. Peel the leaf carefully away from the chocolate.*

Yield: 8 servings

STRAWBERRY FANS *add lovely color to any dish. Hold a firm, ripe strawberry with the stem down on a cutting board. Using a sharp knife, make cuts* ¹⁄₈ *inch through the strawberry to about* ¹⁄₈ *inch from the stem. Gently spread apart the slices to form the fan. Leave the stem on the strawberry or remove it and replace it with a fresh mint leaf.*

Lemon Meringue Torte

Meringue Shell

    3 egg whites
    1/2 teaspoon vinegar
    1/8 teaspoon salt
    1 cup sugar

Lemon Filling

    4 egg yolks
    2/3 cup sugar
    1/3 cup fresh lemon juice
    2 teaspoons grated lemon zest
    2 tablespoons sugar
    1 cup whipped cream

For the meringue shell, place a sheet of baking parchment on a baking sheet and draw a 9-inch circle; butter the circle.

Combine the egg whites, vinegar and salt in a mixing bowl and beat until soft peaks form. Add the sugar gradually, beating constantly after each addition and continuing to beat until stiff peaks form.

Spread over the circle on the baking parchment, mounding the edges and swirling in ridges with the back of the spoon. Bake at 300 degrees for 45 minutes or until the surface appears dry. Remove to a serving plate.

For the filling, beat the egg yolks in a double boiler until thickened. Add 2/3 cup sugar gradually, beating constantly. Beat in the lemon juice and lemon zest. Place over hot water and cook for 5 minutes or until thickened, stirring constantly; do not boil. Cool to room temperature. Mix 2 tablespoons sugar with the whipped cream.

To assemble, spread half the whipped cream over the meringue shell. Spread the lemon mixture over the whipped cream in the meringue shell and spread the remaining whipped cream over the top.

Yield: 8 servings

SCHAUM TORTES

Caramel Sauce

 2 tablespoons butter
 1/2 cup packed brown sugar
 1/4 cup light cream or half-and-half
 2 tablespoons toasted chopped walnuts
 1/2 teaspoon vanilla extract

Meringues

 6 egg whites
 1/4 teaspoon cream of tartar
 2 cups sugar
 1 tablespoon vinegar
 1 teaspoon vanilla extract
 12 scoops vanilla ice cream

For the sauce, melt the butter in a small saucepan. Stir in the brown sugar and cook just until dissolved. Remove from the heat and stir in the cream gradually. Return to the heat and cook for 1 minute, stirring constantly. Combine with the walnuts and vanilla in a small bowl and mix well.

For the meringues, beat the egg whites with the cream of tartar in a mixing bowl until frothy. Add the sugar gradually, beating constantly until stiff peaks form. Beat in the vinegar and vanilla.

Spoon into a pastry bag fitted with a #31 tip. Pipe into individual 2½-inch meringue shells on a greased aluminum baking sheet, leaving 2 inches between shells. Bake at 275 degrees for 10 minutes or until firm but not brown. Remove to a wire rack to cool.

To serve, place 1 scoop of ice cream in each meringue. Spoon the sauce over the top.

The sauce may be served cold or reheated to serve. You may also serve the meringues filled with fresh fruit and whipped cream. Unfilled meringues may be stored in an airtight container at room temperature or in the freezer.

Yield: 12 servings

CREAM OF TARTAR *is a white powder produced from a crystalline acid found in wine barrels. It makes frostings and candy creamy and provides volume and stability to meringue.*

CASHEW BUTTER CRUNCH

Combine 1 cup sugar, 1 cup butter and 1 tablespoon light corn syrup in a heavy 2-quart saucepan. Cook over medium heat for 25 to 30 minutes or to 290 degrees on a candy thermometer, brittle stage, stirring constantly. Remove from the heat and stir in 1¹/₂ cups salted cashews. Spread ¹/₄ inch thick on a 10×15-inch baking sheet lined with waxed paper. Let stand until completely cooled. Break into pieces and store in an airtight container.

Another test for the brittle stage is to drop a small amount of the hot mixture into cold water. It will form breakable threads at the brittle stage.

FIVE-POUND FUDGE

  1 (12-ounce) can evaporated milk
4¹/₂ cups sugar
1¹/₂ cups (3 sticks) butter
  1 (10³/₄-ounce) chocolate bar without nuts, broken
 24 ounces (4 cups) semisweet chocolate chips
  2 cups (or more) marshmallow creme
  1 teaspoon vanilla extract
  1 cup chopped English walnuts

Combine the evaporated milk, sugar and butter in a heavy saucepan and bring to a boil. Cook for 5 minutes, stirring constantly. Remove from the heat and stir in the broken chocolate and chocolate chips until melted.

Add the marshmallow creme and beat until smooth. Stir in the vanilla and walnuts. Pour into 2 greased 9×13-inch dishes. Let stand until cool and cut into squares. Store in the refrigerator or freezer.

Yield: 10 dozen

PECAN CLUSTERS

¹/₂ cup evaporated milk
¹/₂ cup sugar
  1 tablespoon light corn syrup
  6 ounces (1 cup) semisweet chocolate chips
  1 cup pecan halves

Combine the evaporated milk, sugar and corn syrup in a heavy saucepan. Bring to a rolling boil over medium heat, stirring constantly. Cook for 2 minutes longer, stirring constantly. Remove from the heat and stir in the chocolate chips until melted. Stir in the pecans.

Drop by 2 teaspoonfuls onto a parchment-lined baking sheet. Chill until firm.

Yield: 2 dozen

ALMOND MACAROONS

    2¾ cups blanched almonds, ground
    2½ cups sugar
         Grated zest of 1 lemon
    4   egg whites

Line cookie sheets with oiled baking parchment. Mix the almonds, sugar and lemon zest in a large bowl. Beat the egg whites until stiff peaks form. Add to the almond mixture and mix well.

Drop by 2 teaspoonfuls onto the prepared cookie sheets, spreading into 1-inch circles and flattening slightly with the back of the spoon. Bake at 300 degrees for 25 minutes or at 325 degrees for 12 minutes or until light brown but still moist and chewy. Remove to a wire rack to cool.

Yield: 3 dozen

ALMOND ESPRESSO BISCOTTI

    2   cups (or more) flour
    1   cup sugar
    ½   teaspoon each baking powder and baking soda
    ½   teaspoon each cinnamon, ground cloves and salt
    2   tablespoons instant espresso granules
    ⅓   cup water
    1   egg yolk
    1   tablespoon milk
    1   teaspoon vanilla extract
    ¾   cup coarsely chopped toasted almonds
    3   ounces (½ cup) chocolate chips

Mix 2 cups flour, sugar, baking powder, baking soda, cinnamon, cloves and salt in a large mixing bowl. Dissolve the espresso granules in the water in a medium mixing bowl. Add the egg yolk, milk and vanilla and whisk until smooth. Add to the flour mixture and beat to form a dough. Mix in the almonds and chocolate chips.

Knead on a floured surface, kneading in additional flour if needed to prevent sticking. Divide into 2 portions and shape each portion into a roll 12 inches long and 2 inches in diameter.

Place the rolls 3 inches apart on a greased and floured cookie sheet. Bake at 350 degrees for 35 minutes. Cool on the cookie sheet for 10 minutes.

Reduce the oven temperature to 300 degrees. Cut the rolls into ¾-inch slices. Arrange on the cookie sheet. Bake for 8 to 10 minutes on each side or until crisp. Remove to a wire rack to cool. Store in an airtight container.

Yield: 2½ dozen

GRIND FOOD *to reduce it to small particles. Coffee beans can be ground in a coffee grinder, while meats such as beef must be run through a meat grinder. A food processor fitted with a metal blade can also grind some foods. Food can be ground to various degrees—fine, medium, and coarse.*

PECAN AND CRANBERRY BISCOTTI

CRAISINS *are dried cranberries. They can be substituted for raisins in recipes to add a more tart flavor.*

2¹/2 cups flour
1¹/4 cups sugar
1 teaspoon baking powder
¹/8 teaspoon salt
3 large eggs plus 2 large egg yolks
1 teaspoon vanilla extract
1¹/2 cups toasted pecan halves, coarsely chopped
1 cup dried cranberries or other dried fruit
Grated zest of 1 lemon or orange

Mix the flour, sugar, baking powder and salt in a small bowl. Combine the eggs, egg yolks and vanilla in a mixing bowl and beat until smooth. Add the flour mixture and mix well. Mix in the pecans, cranberries and lemon zest.

Knead for 2 or 3 minutes on a floured surface. Shape into 2 rolls 9 inches long and 3¹/2 inches in diameter. Place on a cookie sheet. Bake at 350 degrees for 25 to 30 minutes or until golden brown. Cool on the cookie sheet for 10 minutes. Reduce the oven temperature to 275 degrees.

Cut the rolls into ¹/2-inch slices. Arrange on the cookie sheet. Bake for 18 to 20 minutes on each side or until crisp. Remove to a wire rack to cool.

Yield: 3 dozen

CHOCOLATE MARSHMALLOW COOKIES

CHOCOLATE FROSTING

Combine ¹/4 cup milk, ¹/4 cup margarine and 1 cup sugar in a saucepan. Bring to a boil. Stir in ¹/2 cup chocolate chips until melted. Stir until of spreading consistency.

2¹/2 cups flour
¹/2 cup baking cocoa
1 teaspoon each baking powder and baking soda
¹/4 teaspoon salt
1 cup (2 sticks) margarine, softened
1¹/2 cups sugar
2 eggs
Vanilla extract to taste
18 marshmallows, cut into halves
Chocolate Frosting (at left)

Sift the flour, baking cocoa, baking powder, baking soda and salt together. Cream the margarine and sugar in a mixing bowl until light and fluffy. Beat in the eggs and vanilla. Add the dry ingredients and mix well.

Drop by teaspoonfuls onto a greased cookie sheet. Bake at 350 degrees for 8 minutes. Remove from the oven and press 1 marshmallow half cut side down into the top of each cookie. Bake for 2 minutes longer. Remove from the oven. Press down lightly on the marshmallows. Cool on the cookie sheet for several minutes. Remove to a wire rack to cool completely. Spread with Chocolate Frosting.

Yield: 3 dozen

CAPPUCCINO BROWNIES

Brownies

- 1 tablespoon instant espresso granules
- 1/2 tablespoon boiling water
- 4 (1-ounce) squares bittersweet chocolate, chopped
- 6 tablespoons (3/4 stick) unsalted butter
- 3/4 cup sugar
- 1 teaspoon vanilla extract
- 2 large eggs
- 1/2 cup flour
- 1/4 teaspoon salt
- 1/2 cup chopped walnuts

Cinnamon Cream Cheese Frosting

- 4 ounces cream cheese, softened
- 3 tablespoons unsalted butter, softened
- 3/4 cup confectioners' sugar, sifted
- 1/2 teaspoon cinnamon
- 1/2 teaspoon vanilla extract
- Mocha Glaze (at right)

For the brownies, dissolve the espresso granules in the boiling water in a small bowl. Combine with the chocolate and butter in a 1 1/2-quart saucepan. Cook over low heat until the chocolate and butter melt, stirring to blend well; remove from the heat and cool to lukewarm.

Whisk in the sugar and vanilla. Whisk in the eggs one at a time. Whisk until the mixture is glossy and smooth. Add the flour and salt and mix just until moistened. Stir in the walnuts.

Spread in a buttered and floured 8x8-inch baking pan. Place on a rack in the middle of an oven heated to 350 degrees and bake for 22 to 25 minutes or until a wooden pick inserted in the center comes out with moist crumbs. Cool in the pan on a wire rack.

For the frosting, beat the cream cheese and butter in a mixing bowl until light. Add the confectioners' sugar, cinnamon and vanilla gradually, beating until fluffy.

Spread the frosting over the brownie layer. Chill for 1 hour or until firm. Spread the Mocha Glaze over the top. Cut into 24 brownies and remove from the pan.

Yield: 2 dozen

MOCHA GLAZE

Dissolve 2 1/4 teaspoons instant espresso granules in 1/2 tablespoon boiling water in a small bowl. Melt 1 tablespoon unsalted butter and 3 ounces bittersweet chocolate in a double boiler over hot water. Add 1/4 cup heavy cream and the espresso mixture. Cook until heated through, stirring constantly. Cool to room temperature.

RASPBERRY FUDGE BROWNIES

A QUICK DESSERT can be created by spooning chunks of fresh fruit or whole berries into long-stemmed wine glasses and covering the fruit with a sparkling mineral water or Champagne.

Brownies

- ½ cup (1 stick) butter
- 3 (1-ounce) squares unsweetened chocolate
- 1 cup packed brown sugar
- ½ cup flour
- 2 eggs, beaten
- 1 teaspoon vanilla extract
- ½ cup raspberry jam
- Confectioners' sugar to taste

Raspberry Sauce

- 1 (16-ounce) package frozen raspberries, thawed
- ⅔ cup sugar
- 1 tablespoon Grand Marnier

For the brownies, melt the butter and chocolate in a saucepan over low heat, stirring constantly; remove from the heat. Mix in the brown sugar, flour, eggs and vanilla. Spread in a greased 8×8-inch baking pan. Spread the jam over the top and swirl lightly to mix. Bake at 350 degrees for 25 minutes. Cool in pan on a wire rack. Sprinkle with confectioners' sugar and cut into squares.

For the sauce, purée the raspberries, sugar and Grand Marnier in a blender or food processor; strain. Drizzle over the brownies.

Yield: 16 servings

BLACK WALNUT ICEBOX COOKIES

- 1 cup (2 sticks) butter, softened
- 2 cups packed brown sugar
- 2 eggs
- 2½ teaspoons vanilla extract
- 4 cups flour
- ¼ cup black walnuts, ground
- 1 teaspoon baking soda
- ⅛ teaspoon salt
- 1 cup black walnuts, chopped

Cream the butter and brown sugar in a mixing bowl until light and fluffy. Beat in the eggs and vanilla. Sift in the flour, ground black walnuts, baking soda and salt and mix well. Mix in the chopped black walnuts. Shape the dough into rolls. Chill, wrapped in waxed paper, in the refrigerator or store in the freezer.

Slice the rolls ¼ inch thick and place the slices on lightly greased cookie sheets. Bake at 350 degrees for 8 to 8½ minutes or until golden brown. Cool on the cookie sheets for 5 minutes. Remove to a wire rack to cool completely.

Yield: 5 dozen

CARAMEL PEANUT BARS

1½ cups each quick-cooking oats and flour
1¼ cups packed brown sugar
¾ teaspoon baking soda
¼ teaspoon salt
¾ cup (1½ sticks) butter or margarine, melted
1 (14-ounce) package caramels
½ cup heavy cream
9 ounces (1½ cups) semisweet chocolate chips
¾ cup chopped peanuts

Combine the oats, flour, brown sugar, baking soda and salt in a mixing bowl. Add the butter and mix well. Reserve 1 cup of the mixture for the topping. Press the remaining mixture into a greased 9×13-inch baking pan. Bake at 350 degrees for 10 minutes or until light brown.

Combine the caramels with the cream in a heavy saucepan or microwave-safe bowl. Cook over low heat or microwave until melted, stirring frequently.

Sprinkle the chocolate chips and peanuts over the baked layer. Spread the caramel mixture over the top and sprinkle with the reserved oats mixture. Bake for 15 to 20 minutes or until golden brown. Cool completely and cut into bars.

Yield: 3 dozen

CHOCOLATE MINT SNAPPERS

6 ounces (1 cup) mint-flavor chocolate chips
2½ cups flour
2 teaspoons baking soda
1 teaspoon cinnamon
½ cup (1 stick) butter, softened
½ cup sugar
1 egg
¼ cup light corn syrup
½ cup (or more) sugar

Melt the chocolate chips in a double boiler over hot water; remove from the heat and cool. Sift the flour, baking soda and cinnamon together.

Cream the butter and ½ cup sugar in a mixing bowl until light and fluffy. Beat in the egg. Blend in the corn syrup and melted chocolate. Add the sifted dry ingredients gradually, mixing well after each addition.

Shape into 1-inch balls and roll in ½ cup sugar, coating well. Arrange 3 inches apart on an ungreased cookie sheet. Bake at 350 degrees for 15 minutes. Cool on the cookie sheet for 5 minutes. Remove to a wire rack to cool completely.

Yield: 4 dozen

CORN SYRUP *is available in light or dark varieties. Light corn syrup has had all color and cloudiness removed through a clarification process; dark corn syrup has a deeper color and stronger flavor similar to caramel. Because it prevents crystallization, it's perfect for desserts or preserves.*

COLA FROSTING

Combine 1 ounce unsweetened chocolate, 3 tablespoons cola and 1/4 cup margarine in a saucepan and bring to a boil. Boil for 1 minute; remove from the heat. Add 2 cups confectioners' sugar and beat until smooth. Mix in 1 teaspoon vanilla extract.

Cola is a sweet carbonated beverage containing cola-nut extract and additional flavorings.

CITRUS EXTRACTS may be used if you don't have fresh citrus zest. If your recipe calls for 1 teaspoon of grated orange or lemon zest, substitute 1/2 teaspoon of the corresponding extract. Add the extract to liquid ingredients in the recipe.

FROSTED CHOCOLATE COLA BARS

1 1/2 (1-ounce) squares unsweetened chocolate
1 cup cola
1/2 cup (1 stick) margarine
2 cups each sifted flour and sugar
2 eggs
1/2 cup sour cream
1 teaspoon each baking soda and salt
Cola Frosting (at left)

Combine the chocolate, cola and margarine in a saucepan and bring to a boil, stirring to blend well; remove from the heat. Stir in a mixture of the flour and sugar. Add the eggs, sour cream, baking soda and salt and mix well.

Spoon into a greased and floured 10×15-inch baking pan. Bake at 350 degrees for 25 to 30 minutes or until set. Spread Cola Frosting over the warm baked layer. Cut into bars. Do not use diet cola in this recipe.

Yield: 5 dozen

CRANBERRY CHEESE BARS

2 cups flour
1 1/2 cups quick-cooking oats
3/4 cup packed brown sugar
1 cup (2 sticks) butter, softened
8 ounces cream cheese, softened
1 (14-ounce) can sweetened condensed milk
1/4 cup lemon juice
2 tablespoons cornstarch
1 tablespoon brown sugar
1 (16-ounce) can whole cranberry sauce

Mix the flour, oats, 3/4 cup brown sugar and butter in a bowl until crumbly. Remove and reserve 1 1/2 cups of the mixture. Press the remaining crumbs over the bottom of a greased 9×13-inch baking pan. Bake at 350 degrees for 15 minutes.

Beat the cream cheese in a small mixing bowl until light. Add the condensed milk gradually, beating constantly until smooth. Mix in the lemon juice. Spread evenly over the crust.

Mix the cornstarch and 1 tablespoon brown sugar in a small bowl. Add the cranberry sauce and mix well. Spread over the cream cheese layer.

Sprinkle the reserved crumbs over the layers. Bake at 350 degrees for 40 minutes or until golden brown. Cool on a wire rack. Chill, covered, for 1 hour. Cut into bars to serve. Store, covered, in the refrigerator.

Yield: 2 dozen

Orange Drop Cookies

Cookies

- 2¾ cups flour
- 1 teaspoon baking powder
- ½ teaspoon baking soda
- ½ teaspoon salt
- ½ cup (1 stick) butter, softened
- ½ cup shortening
- ½ cup sugar
- ½ cup packed brown sugar
- 1 egg
- 2 tablespoons orange juice
- 2 tablespoons grated orange zest
- ½ cup chopped walnuts

Orange Frosting

- 2½ tablespoons butter, softened
- 1½ cups confectioners' sugar
- 1½ tablespoons orange juice
- 2 tablespoons grated orange zest

For the cookies, sift the flour, baking powder, baking soda and salt together. Cream the butter, shortening, sugar and brown sugar in a mixing bowl until light and fluffy. Beat in the egg. Mix in the orange juice and orange zest. Add the dry ingredients and mix well. Mix in the walnuts.

Drop by teaspoonfuls onto ungreased cookie sheets. Bake at 350 to 375 degrees for 10 to 12 minutes or until golden brown. Remove to wire racks to cool.

For the frosting, cream the butter and confectioners' sugar in a mixing bowl until light and fluffy. Add the orange juice and orange zest and mix well. Spread over the cooled cookies.

Yield: 3 dozen

Lemon Pistachio Cookies

Mix 4½ cups flour, 1 teaspoon baking soda, 1 teaspoon cream of tartar and 1 teaspoon salt together. Cream 1 cup butter, 1 cup sugar and 1 cup confectioners' sugar in a bowl until light. Beat in 2 eggs one at a time. Add 1 cup oil, 1 teaspoon grated lemon zest and 1 teaspoon lemon extract; beat until smooth. Add dry ingredients gradually. Wrap in plastic wrap and chill. Divide dough into 3 equal portions. Work with 1 portion at a time; chill remaining portions. Shape by teaspoonfuls into balls and place on greased cookie sheets. Press with a glass dipped in sugar to flatten. Bake at 325 degrees for 11 minutes. Beat 3½ cups confectioners' sugar, 7 tablespoons butter and 3 tablespoons lemon juice in a bowl. Spread over the cooled cookies. Sprinkle with ½ cup finely chopped pistachios.

Mocha Filling

Combine ²/₃ cup confectioners' sugar, 2 tablespoons butter, 2 teaspoons instant coffee granules and 1 teaspoon boiling water in a bowl and mix well.

Mocha-Filled Spritz Cookies

    1 cup (2 sticks) butter, softened
 ¹/₂ cup sifted confectioners' sugar
 ¹/₂ teaspoon vanilla extract
    2 cups flour
 ¹/₄ teaspoon baking powder
       Mocha Filling (at left)

Cream the butter and confectioners' sugar in a mixing bowl until light. Beat in the vanilla. Add the flour and baking powder and mix well. Spoon into a cookie press and press into 2- to 3-inch strips on a cookie sheet. Bake at 375 degrees for 7 minutes. Remove to a wire rack to cool. Spread the Mocha Filling over the smooth side of half the cookies and top with the remaining cookies. Garnish with a sprinkling of additional confectioners' sugar.

Yield: 1¹/₂ dozen

Jam-Filled Sandwich Cookies

 2¹/₂ cups flour
     1 teaspoon each baking soda and cream of tartar
     1 cup (2 sticks) butter, softened
 1¹/₂ cups sifted confectioners' sugar
     1 egg
     1 teaspoon vanilla extract
  ¹/₂ teaspoon almond extract
  ²/₃ cup seedless raspberry jam

Sift the flour, baking soda and cream of tartar together. Beat the butter in a mixing bowl until light. Add the confectioners' sugar and beat until fluffy. Beat in the egg and flavorings. Add the sifted dry ingredients to the butter mixture and fold in thoroughly. Wrap in plastic wrap and chill for 2 hours to 4 days.

Divide the dough into 4 portions. Roll 1 portion at a time to an 8×8-inch square about ³/₁₆ inch thick on a lightly floured surface, keeping the remaining portions chilled. Cut with a 1- to 1¹/₂-inch cutter, reserving and chilling the scraps and rerolling. Place the cookies 1 inch apart on lightly floured or parchment-lined cookie sheets. Cut three ³/₈-inch circles from the centers of half the cookies with a plain pastry tip or thimble. Bake at 375 degrees for 7 to 8 minutes or until golden brown. Heat the jam in a saucepan over low heat for 1 to 2 minutes or until thickened slightly. Spread ¹/₄ to ¹/₂ teaspoon jam on each solid cookie and top with a cut-out cookie. Sift confectioners' sugar over the top. Store cookies between layers of waxed paper or parchment in an airtight container for up to 2 weeks.

Photograph for this recipe is on page 178 and opposite.

Yield: 1¹/₂ dozen

WHITE WALNUT BARS

- ²/₃ cup shortening
- ³/₄ cup sugar
- ³/₄ cup packed brown sugar
- 2 eggs
- 1 teaspoon vanilla extract
- 1¼ teaspoons baking soda
- ½ teaspoon salt
- 2½ cups (scant) flour
- 1 cup chopped black walnuts or English walnuts
- 1 cup golden raisins
- 1 egg, beaten

Cream the shortening, sugar and brown sugar in a mixing bowl until light and fluffy. Beat in 2 eggs one at a time. Mix in the vanilla. Add the baking soda and salt and as little flour as possible to form a dough; mix well. Mix in the walnuts and raisins.

Shape into 4 rolls the length of the cookie sheet. Place on the cookie sheet and flatten to a thickness of ¼ inch. Brush the tops with the beaten egg. Bake at 375 degrees for just 13 minutes; do not overbake. Cool on a wire rack. Cut into bars.

Yield: 3 dozen

WALNUTS *come in different varieties; two of the more popular varieties are English and Black. English walnuts are the most readily available; they come in many types, depending on the texture and thickness of the shell. They come in three main sizes: large, medium, and babies, and are available year-round. Choose walnuts free of cracks or holes. Those already shelled should be plump, meaty, and crisp. Walnuts in the shell can be stored in a cool, dry place for up to three months. Shelled nutmeats should be refrigerated, tightly covered, for up to six months. They can be frozen for up to a year.*

DUTCH APPLE PUMPKIN PIE

Pie

- 1 unbaked pie shell (see page 209)
- 1/4 cup sugar
- 2 teaspoons flour
- 1 teaspoon lemon juice
- 1/4 teaspoon cinnamon
  Nutmeg to taste
- 2 medium apples, peeled, sliced
- 1 1/2 cups canned pumpkin
- 1/2 cup sugar
- 2 tablespoons butter, melted
- 3/4 teaspoon cinnamon
- 1/4 teaspoon nutmeg
- 1/4 teaspoon salt
- 2 eggs
- 1 cup evaporated milk

Pecan Crumb Topping
- 1/2 cup flour
- 1/3 cup packed brown sugar
- 1/3 cup chopped pecans
- 3 tablespoons butter

For the pie, bake the pie shell at 375 degrees for 10 minutes or just until it begins to brown; cool to room temperature.

Combine 1/4 cup sugar, 2 teaspoons flour, lemon juice, 1/4 teaspoon cinnamon and nutmeg to taste in a bowl. Add the apples and toss to coat well. Spoon into the pie shell.

Combine the pumpkin, 1/2 cup sugar, melted butter, 3/4 teaspoon cinnamon, 1/4 teaspoon nutmeg and salt in a bowl. Add the eggs and beat lightly. Add the evaporated milk and mix well. Spread evenly over the apples. Bake for 30 minutes.

For the topping, combine the flour, brown sugar, pecans and butter in a bowl and mix with a pastry blender. Sprinkle over the pie.

Bake for 25 to 30 minutes longer, covering the crust with foil if necessary to prevent overbrowning. Cool to room temperature. Store in the refrigerator.

Yield: 8 servings

APPLES *for cooking and baking should remain flavorful and firm. Baldwin, Cortland, Northern Spy, Rome Beauty, Winesap, and York Imperial are good baking apples. Store apples in a cool, dark place. They store well when placed in a plastic bag in the refrigerator. Other varieties include: Braeburn, Cashew Apple, Crabapple, Criterion, Empire, Fuji, Gala, Golden Delicious, Granny Smith, Gravenstein, Jonathan, Lady, Macoun, May, McIntosh, Newton Pippin, Red Delicious, Rhode Island Greening, Spygold, and Stayman.*

CHOCOLATE SILK PIE

  1 cup (2 sticks) butter, softened
1 1/2 cups superfine sugar
  3 (1-ounce) squares semisweet chocolate, melted
  2 teaspoons vanilla extract
  4 eggs or equivalent egg substitute
  1 baked pie shell (at right)

Cream the butter and sugar in a mixing bowl until light and fluffy. Add the chocolate and vanilla and mix well. Add the eggs one at a time, beating for 5 minutes after each addition. Spoon into the pie shell. Chill, covered, in the refrigerator.

Serve on plates drizzled with chocolate sauce and garnish with chocolate curls.

Yield: 10 servings

PECAN PIE

  3 eggs, beaten
  1 cup white corn syrup
  5 tablespoons butter, melted
  1 cup packed brown sugar
1/8 teaspoon vanilla extract
    Salt to taste
  1 cup pecans
  1 unbaked (9-inch) pie shell (at right)

Combine the eggs, corn syrup, butter, brown sugar, vanilla and salt in a mixing bowl and beat until smooth. Add the pecans and mix well. Spoon into the pie shell. Bake at 375 degrees for 40 to 50 minutes or until set. Cool to room temperature. Store in the refrigerator.

Yield: 8 servings

PIECRUST

Combine 1 1/2 cups flour and 1 teaspoon salt in a bowl and mix well. Cut in 1/2 cup plus 1 tablespoon shortening until crumbly. Add 3 to 4 tablespoons chilled water 1 tablespoon at a time, mixing with a fork until the mixture forms a ball. Chill, wrapped in plastic wrap, for 30 minutes or longer. Roll into a 12-inch circle on a lightly floured surface. Fit into a pie plate. Prick with a fork.

To use as an unbaked pie shell, proceed as recipe directs. To use as a baked pie shell, freeze for 20 minutes before baking. Bake at 400 degrees for 10 to 12 minutes or until golden brown.

SWEET POTATO PIE

MASH *foods such as cooked sweet potatoes into a smooth, evenly textured mixture to use in recipes.*

Pie

    2 tablespoons flour
    1 cup sugar
    1 teaspoon cinnamon
    1 (48-ounce) can sweet potatoes, drained and mashed
    3 eggs
  $\frac{1}{2}$ cup (1 stick) butter, melted
  $\frac{1}{2}$ cup half-and-half
    2 teaspoons (or more) vanilla extract

Brown Sugar Pecan Topping

    1 cup packed brown sugar
  $\frac{1}{4}$ cup flour
  $\frac{1}{2}$ cup (1 stick) butter
    1 cup (or more) chopped pecans

For the pie, mix the flour, sugar and cinnamon in a bowl. Add the sweet potatoes and mix well. Combine the eggs, butter, half-and-half and vanilla in a bowl and mix well. Fold into the sweet potato mixture.

Spoon into a 10-inch pie plate sprayed with nonstick cooking spray. Bake at 350 degrees for 40 minutes or until the center appears set when the pie plate is gently shaken.

For the topping, combine the brown sugar, flour, butter and pecans in a bowl and mix until crumbly. Sprinkle over the pie. Bake for 20 to 30 minutes longer or until the topping is golden brown.

Yield: 8 servings

CARAMEL CASHEW CHEESECAKE

Cashew Crust
- 2 cups finely crushed vanilla wafers
- 1/4 cup sugar
- 6 tablespoons (3/4 stick) butter, melted
- 1/2 cup finely chopped cashews

Filling
- 24 ounces cream cheese, softened
- 1 (14-ounce) can sweetened condensed milk
- 3 eggs
- 1 1/2 tablespoons rum
- 1 tablespoon vanilla extract
- 1/2 tablespoon butter flavoring

Caramel Cashew Topping
- 2 1/4 teaspoons sugar
- 6 tablespoons brown sugar
- 3 tablespoons heavy cream
- 1 1/2 tablespoons butter
- 3/4 teaspoon vanilla extract
- 1/3 cup finely chopped cashews

CASHEWS *are kidney-shape nuts that have a sweet, buttery flavor and contain about 48 percent fat. They should be stored tightly wrapped in the refrigerator due to their high fat content to retard rancidity. Like all nuts, roasting brings out their nutty flavor.*

For the crust, combine the vanilla wafer crumbs, sugar, butter and cashews in a bowl and mix well. Press over the bottom and up the side of a 9-inch springform pan.

For the filling, beat the cream cheese in a mixing bowl until light and fluffy. Beat in the condensed milk gradually. Add the eggs, rum and flavorings and mix well.

Spoon the filling into the prepared crust. Bake at 325 degrees for 55 to 60 minutes or until the center is set. Cool on a wire rack.

For the topping, combine the sugar, brown sugar, cream and butter in a small saucepan. Bring to a boil, stirring to dissolve the sugar and brown sugar. Cook over low to medium heat until the mixture reaches 225 degrees on a candy thermometer. Remove from the heat and add the vanilla. Stir until creamy.

Sprinkle the cashews over the top of the cheesecake. Drizzle the cooked mixture over the cashews. Chill for 8 hours or longer. Place the cheesecake on a serving plate and remove the side of the pan.

Yield: 12 servings

$\mathcal{I}$OWA is a land of gentle balance: black fertile soil and pristine white snow; warm humid summer days and fresh crisp winter nights; lush green springs and brittle vivid autumns; the commitment and dedication to work and the joyful passion for the arts. Iowa has a profound background and energetic pursuit of the arts in many forms.

The Iowa Arts Council estimates that there are over 11,000 Iowa artists. Many are well known nationally, and those that are perhaps not as well known are deeply respected by their peers and are acknowledged on a more local basis. Iowans are fortunate to have a wide selection from which to choose: writers, designers, musicians, composers, actors, directors, painters, sculptors, craft artists, photographers, dancers, and performers. We are fortunate to have opportunities to thrive through the various arts and embrace a multitude of options.

Our urban areas offer various dimensional arts: crafts, design arts, folk arts, interdisciplinary and multi-disciplinary art. All forms of music are appreciated, and they include opera, music theatre, symphonic, chamber, and contemporary, to name just a few. Visual arts include photography, multiple genres of theatre, and two-dimensional forms. Our venues vary from performing arts centers to universities, and from private colleges to public schools, as well as local festivals and private homes.

Artistic balance is an integral part of Iowa and its people.

Photograph by:
David Cavagnaro

CHOCOLATE ALMOND CHEESECAKE

MINT SPRIGS dusted lightly with confectioners' sugar before garnishing a dessert plate or platter add a festive touch.

Chocolate Crust
1½ cups crushed chocolate graham crackers
¼ cup sugar
¼ cup (½ stick) butter, melted

Filling
16 ounces cream cheese, softened
1 cup (8 ounces) sour cream
1¼ cups sugar
3 eggs
½ cup baking cocoa
1 teaspoon almond extract

Almond Topping
1 cup whipping cream
¼ cup confectioners' sugar
¼ teaspoon almond extract
¼ cup sliced almonds

For the crust, mix the graham cracker crumbs, sugar and butter in a bowl. Press over the bottom of a 9-inch springform pan.

For the filling, combine the cream cheese, sour cream and sugar in a mixing bowl and beat until light. Beat in the eggs one at a time. Add the baking cocoa and almond extract and mix well.

Spoon the filling into the prepared crust. Bake at 350 degrees for 45 to 50 minutes or until set. Cool to room temperature. Chill, covered, in the refrigerator for 8 hours or longer. Place on a serving plate and remove the side of the pan.

For the topping, beat the whipping cream in a mixing bowl until soft peaks form. Fold in the confectioners' sugar and almond extract. Spread over the cheesecake just before serving. Sprinkle with the almonds.

Yield: 16 servings

CHOCOLATE CHIP CHEESECAKE

Walnut Crust
- 3/4 cup graham cracker crumbs
- 1/4 cup (1/2 stick) butter
- 2 tablespoons sugar
- 3/4 cup ground walnuts

Filling
- 1/2 cup (1 stick) butter, softened
- 24 ounces cream cheese, softened
- 1/2 cup sugar
- 3 eggs
- 2 teaspoons grated orange zest
- 3/4 teaspoon almond extract
- 3 ounces (1/2 cup) chocolate chips or miniature chocolate chips

Chocolate Cream Cheese Topping
- 3 ounces (1/2 cup) chocolate chips
- 1 1/2 tablespoons butter
- 2 tablespoons water
- 6 ounces cream cheese, softened

For the crust, mix the graham cracker crumbs, butter, sugar and walnuts in a bowl. Press over the bottom of a 10-inch springform pan.

For the filling, cream the butter and cream cheese in a mixing bowl until light. Add the sugar, eggs, orange zest and almond extract and beat until smooth. Fold in the chocolate chips. Spoon the filling into the prepared crust. Bake at 325 degrees for 1 hour. Turn off the oven and let the cheesecake stand in the closed oven for 15 minutes longer. Cool on a wire rack.

For the topping, melt the chocolate chips and butter with the water in a small saucepan; remove from the heat. Beat the cream cheese in a small mixing bowl until light. Add to the chocolate mixture and beat until smooth. Spread over the cheesecake.

Chill, covered, in the refrigerator for 4 hours. Place on a serving plate and remove the side of the pan.

Yield: 12 servings

GRATE CHOCOLATE with a hand grater or a hand-cranked grater that would be used to grate nuts or cheese. Chocolate should be cool and firm. Clean the surface of the grater often to prevent clogging. To grate in an electric blender, first cut chocolate into small pieces.

IRISH CREAM CHOCOLATE CHIP CHEESECAKE

Chocolate garnishes add eye appeal to desserts. Chocolate can be grated, shredded, curled, or chopped to make garnishes. For best results, handle chocolate as little as possible. Make sure implements are totally dry. When not using chocolate garnish immediately refrigerate to prevent lumping. To shred, use a vegetable or potato peeler. Chocolate should be in large pieces that are cool and firm. Shave surface with peeler blade. To chop, use a sharp, heavy knife or cleaver. Put chocolate on a wooden cutting board and chop to desired size.

Graham Cracker Crust
- 1/2 cup graham cracker crumbs
- 1/4 cup sugar
- 2 tablespoons unsalted butter

Filling
- 24 ounces cream cheese, softened
- 1 cup plus 2 tablespoons sugar
- 3 large eggs, at room temperature
- 2/3 cup Irish Cream liqueur
- 1/2 teaspoon vanilla extract
- 4 ounces (2/3 cup) chocolate chips

Mocha Whipped Cream
- 1 cup whipping cream, chilled
- 2 tablespoons sugar
- 1 teaspoon instant coffee granules

For the crust, combine the graham cracker crumbs and sugar in a bowl. Add the butter and mix well. Press over the bottom and 1 inch up the side of a 9-inch springform pan sprayed with nonstick cooking spray. Bake at 350 degrees for 7 minutes or until light brown.

For the filling, beat the cream cheese in a mixing bowl until smooth. Add the sugar gradually, beating until light. Beat in the eggs one at a time. Blend in the Irish Cream and vanilla.

Sprinkle half the chocolate chips over the crust. Spoon the filling over the chocolate chips and top with the remaining chocolate chips.

Bake at 350 degrees for 15 minutes. Reduce the oven temperature to 300 degrees and bake for 1 1/2 hours longer or until the filling is puffed in the center and golden brown. Cool on a wire rack. Chill, covered, in the refrigerator. Place on a serving plate and remove the side of the pan.

For the whipped cream, beat the whipping cream with the sugar and coffee granules in a mixing bowl until soft peaks form. Spread over the cheesecake at serving time. Garnish with chocolate curls.

Yield: 12 servings

Chocolate Coconut Cheesecake

Coconut Crust
- 3/4 cup finely crushed vanilla wafers
- 1/2 cup coconut, lightly toasted
- 1/4 cup sugar
- 1/4 cup (1/2 stick) butter, melted

Filling
- 24 ounces cream cheese, softened
- 1 (14-ounce) can sweetened condensed milk
- 2 eggs
- 1/4 cup Chococo liqueur

Chocolate Coconut Glaze
- 1 (1-ounce) square semisweet chocolate
- 1 tablespoon butter
- Salt to taste
- 3/4 cup sifted confectioners' sugar
- 1 tablespoon boiling water
- 2 teaspoons Chococo liqueur

For the crust, combine the vanilla wafer crumbs, coconut, sugar and butter in a bowl and mix well. Press over the bottom of a 9-inch springform pan.

For the filling, beat the cream cheese in a mixing bowl until light. Add the condensed milk gradually, beating constantly until smooth. Beat in the eggs and liqueur.

Spoon the filling into the prepared crust. Bake at 300 degrees for 1 hour or until the center is set. Cool on a wire rack.

For the glaze, melt the chocolate with the butter and salt in a heavy small saucepan over low heat, stirring constantly to blend well; remove from the heat. Stir in the confectioners' sugar, boiling water and liqueur. Mix until smooth. Spread over the cheesecake immediately.

Chill, covered, in the refrigerator. Place on a serving plate and remove the side of the pan.

Yield: 12 servings

CHOCOCO *is a chocolate and coconut liqueur that is only available in the US Virgin Islands. Be sure to purchase this liqueur when you are visiting an island where this is available. And bring back plenty for your friends!*

CREAMY COCONUT CHEESECAKE

CREAM OF COCONUT
*is an ingredient produced by
taking four parts shredded
coconut and one part water
and simmering until foamy.
After the foam surfaces, the
mixture is strained through
cheesecloth. To make a richer
product recombine used
coconut with strained fluid and
repeat the process. Milk may
be substituted for water for a
creamier result. Asian markets
may offer canned or frozen
cream of coconut.*

32 ounces cream cheese, softened
1 1/2 cups sugar
1 (15-ounce) can cream of coconut
1/8 teaspoon grated lemon zest
1/4 teaspoon salt
1/2 vanilla bean
5 large eggs
1 cup shredded coconut

Beat the cream cheese in a mixing bowl until smooth. Add the sugar and beat until light and fluffy. Add the cream of coconut, lemon zest and salt and mix well. Split the vanilla bean lengthwise and scrape the seeds into the batter. Add the eggs one at a time, beating just until combined after each addition. Fold in the coconut.

Spoon into a 9-inch springform pan. Place a shallow 10×15-inch pan of water on the lower rack of an oven heated to 450 degrees. Place the cheesecake on the center rack. Bake for 10 minutes. Reduce the oven temperature to 350 degrees and bake for 40 to 50 minutes or until the center appears nearly set; do not overbake. Cool on a wire rack.

Chill, covered, in the refrigerator for 8 hours or longer. Loosen from the side of the pan with a sharp knife. Place on a serving plate and remove the side of the pan. Serve topped with whipped cream and toasted coconut.

You may also bake this in a traditional Graham Cracker Crust (page 216) or a Coconut Crust (page 217) if preferred.

Yield: 12 servings

WHITE CHOCOLATE RASPBERRY CHEESECAKE

Raspberry Glaze

    1 cup fresh raspberries
    1 tablespoon cornstarch
    2 tablespoons Chambord
    $\frac{1}{2}$ cup sugar
    $\frac{1}{2}$ cup red currant jelly

Vanilla Wafer Crust

    $1\frac{1}{4}$ cups vanilla wafer crumbs
    $\frac{1}{4}$ cup sugar
    $\frac{1}{4}$ cup ($\frac{1}{2}$ stick) butter, melted

Filling

    24 ounces cream cheese, softened
    1 cup plus 2 tablespoons sugar
    3 eggs
    $\frac{1}{2}$ cup heavy cream
    $\frac{1}{2}$ cup flour
    $\frac{1}{4}$ cup Godet, or other white chocolate liqueur
    1 tablespoon Raspberry Glaze

For the glaze, purée the raspberries in a food processor or blender. Mix the cornstarch, liqueur, sugar and jelly in a small saucepan. Add the raspberries and bring to a boil. Cook over low heat until thickened, stirring constantly. Strain into a bowl and discard the seeds. Cool to room temperature. Reserve 1 tablespoon for the filling and chill the remainder in the refrigerator for 8 hours or longer.

For the crust, mix the vanilla wafer crumbs, sugar and butter in a bowl. Press over the bottom of a 9-inch springform pan.

For the filling, beat the cream cheese in a mixing bowl until smooth. Add the sugar and beat until light and fluffy. Add the eggs, cream, flour and liqueur and mix well.

Spoon half the filling into the prepared crust. Spread the reserved tablespoon of Raspberry Glaze over the center of the filling and spread the remaining filling over the top. Bake at 350 degrees for 1 hour or until the center is set. Cool on a wire rack. Chill, covered, in the refrigerator for 8 hours or longer. Place on a serving plate and remove the side of the pan. Serve with the Raspberry Glaze. Garnish with fresh raspberries.

You may omit spooning the Raspberry Glaze into the center of the cheesecake before baking if preferred. For a thinner sauce, purée 20 ounces of thawed and drained frozen raspberries in a food processor and strain into a saucepan. Add 6 tablespoons sugar and cook until heated through. Remove from the heat and stir in $\frac{1}{4}$ cup Chambord.

Photograph for this recipe is on page 179 and opposite.

Yield: 12 servings

SPRINGFORM PANS *have a round base with high sides ($2\frac{1}{2}$ to 3 inches) that expand by releasing a spring or clamp. This provides a clean removal for cheesecakes, cakes, or tortes.*

CHOCOLATE SWIRL CHEESECAKE

Graham Cracker Crust

- 1¼ cups graham cracker crumbs
- 2 tablespoons sugar
- ¼ cup (½ stick) butter, melted

Filling

- 6 ounces (1 cup) semisweet chocolate chips
- ½ cup sugar
- 16 ounces cream cheese, softened
- ¾ cup sugar
- ½ cup (4 ounces) sour cream
- 1 teaspoon vanilla extract
- 4 eggs

For the crust, combine the graham cracker crumbs, sugar and butter in a bowl and mix well. Press over the bottom and 1 inch up the side of a 9-inch springform pan.

For the filling, melt the chocolate chips with ½ cup sugar in a double boiler over hot water, stirring to blend well; remove from the heat. Beat the cream cheese in a mixing bowl until light. Add ¾ cup sugar and beat until smooth. Add the sour cream and vanilla and mix well. Beat in the eggs one at a time.

Divide the filling into 2 portions. Stir the melted chocolate mixture into 1 portion. Spread half the chocolate filling in the prepared crust. Spread the plain filling over the chocolate filling. Dollop the remaining chocolate filling over the top and swirl with a knife to marbleize.

Bake at 325 degrees for 50 minutes or until all but a 2- to 3-inch area in the center is set. Cool on a wire rack. Chill, covered, in the refrigerator. Place on a serving plate and remove the side of the pan.

Yield: 12 servings

VANILLA *comes from a long, thin pod which must be hand-picked. The pods are green and are absent of the familiar vanilla flavor and fragrance. They require curing, a three- to six-month process that begins with a twenty-second bath in boiling water and is followed by sun heating. Once the beans are hot, they're wrapped and allowed to sweat. During months of drying in the sun by day and sweating at night, the beans ferment, shrinking by 400 percent and turning dark brown. The three most common types of vanilla beans are Bourbon-Madagascar, Mexican, and Tahitian.*

For best flavor in your recipes, be sure to use pure vanilla extract instead of imitation vanilla extract.

Pumpkin Cheesecake

Ginger Pecan Crust

    6 ounces pecans
1 1/2 cups gingersnap crumbs
  1/4 cup packed brown sugar
  1/4 cup (1/2 stick) unsalted butter, melted

Filling and Topping

  32 ounces cream cheese, softened
1 2/3 cups sugar
1 1/2 cups canned pumpkin
  1/4 cup heavy cream
    1 teaspoon ground cinnamon
    1 teaspoon ground ginger
    4 large eggs
    5 tablespoons heavy cream
    1 tablespoon caramel sauce
    1 cup (8 ounces) sour cream

For the crust, spread the pecans on a baking sheet. Toast at 300 degrees for 10 to 15 minutes or until golden brown, stirring occasionally. Combine with the gingersnap crumbs and brown sugar in a food processor container and process until ground. Add the butter and process to mix well. Press over the bottom and up the side of a 10-inch springform pan. Bake at 350 degrees for 8 minutes. Cool on a wire rack.

For the filling, beat the cream cheese and sugar at low speed in a mixing bowl until light. Remove 3/4 cup of the mixture for the topping and reserve in the refrigerator. Add the pumpkin, 1/4 cup cream, cinnamon and ginger to the remaining cream cheese mixture and mix well. Beat in the eggs one at a time.

Spoon the filling into the prepared crust. Bake at 350 degrees for 1 1/4 hours or until the filling is puffed and golden brown; center will not be set completely. Cool on a wire rack for 10 minutes. Loosen the side from the pan with a knife. Let stand until completely cool. Chill, covered, in the refrigerator for 8 hours or longer. Press down the edge of the filling to even the top.

For the topping, bring the reserved 3/4 cup cream cheese to room temperature. Combine with 5 tablespoons cream in a bowl and mix well. Spread over the cheesecake. Drizzle the caramel sauce in lines over the top and swirl the sauce with the tip of a knife.

Place the cheesecake on a serving plate and remove the side of the pan. Spoon the sour cream into a pastry bag fitted with a star tip and pipe into a decorative border around the edge.

Yield: 10 to 12 servings

Cinnamon is a warm, sweet, pungent spice that is actually tree bark. It is sold as rolled dried sticks or ground.

PUMPKIN PIE SPICE
can be made by mixing
1 teaspoon ground cinnamon,
1/2 teaspoon ground nutmeg,
1/4 teaspoon ground ginger,
and 1/4 teaspoon ground cloves.

BROWN SUGAR *that has*
hardened can be softened by
placing it in a plastic bag with
an apple wedge and sealing it
for 1 to 2 days.

PUMPKIN CHEESECAKE WITH CRANBERRY GLAZE

Graham Cracker Crust
- 3/4 cup graham cracker crumbs
- 3 tablespoons butter, melted
- 2 tablespoons brown sugar
- 1 teaspoon cinnamon

Filling
- 32 ounces cream cheese, softened
- 1 1/2 cups sugar
- 5 eggs
- 1/4 cup flour
- 2 teaspoons pumpkin pie spice
- 1 (16-ounce) can pumpkin
- 2 tablespoons rum

Cranberry Glaze
- 2 cups fresh cranberries
- 1 cup sugar
- 1/2 cup water
- 1 tablespoon cornstarch
- 1/4 cup sugar

For the crust, mix the graham cracker crumbs, butter, brown sugar and cinnamon in a bowl. Press over the bottom of a 9-inch springform pan.

For the filling, beat the cream cheese in a mixing bowl until smooth. Add the sugar gradually, beating until light and fluffy. Beat in the eggs one at a time. Add a mixture of the flour and pumpkin pie spice gradually and mix well. Add the pumpkin gradually, mixing well. Stir in the rum.

Spoon the filling into the prepared crust. Bake at 325 degrees for 1 1/4 hours or just until the center is slightly firm to the touch, checking after 45 minutes; do not overbake. Cool on a wire rack.

For the glaze, combine the cranberries, 1 cup sugar and water in a saucepan. Bring to a boil and cook for 2 minutes. Mix the cornstarch with 1/4 cup sugar and stir into the cranberries. Bring to a boil and cook until thickened, stirring constantly. Cool to room temperature.

Spread the glaze over the cheesecake. Chill, covered, in the refrigerator for 8 hours or longer. Place on a serving plate and remove the side of the pan.

Yield: 16 servings

Pumpkin Flan

3/4 cup sugar
 6 eggs
1/2 cup sugar
1/2 teaspoon cinnamon
1/4 teaspoon ground ginger
1/8 teaspoon ground cloves
1/2 teaspoon salt
 2 teaspoons vanilla extract
1/3 cup brandy or rum
 1 cup canned pumpkin
 1 cup milk
 1 cup light cream

Sprinkle 3/4 cup sugar into a heavy large skillet. Cook over medium heat until the sugar melts and forms a light brown syrup, stirring constantly. Pour immediately into a heated round 8-inch baking dish, rotating to coat the bottom evenly.

Beat the eggs lightly in a large mixing bowl. Add 1/2 cup sugar, cinnamon, ginger, cloves, salt, vanilla and brandy and mix well. Combine the pumpkin, milk and cream in a medium saucepan. Cook over low heat until bubbles appear around the edge. Add to the egg mixture gradually, stirring constantly to mix well.

Pour into the prepared dish. Set in a larger pan and fill with 1/2 inch boiling water. Bake at 325 degrees for 50 to 60 minutes or until a silver knife inserted in the center comes out clean. Cool on a wire rack.

Chill, covered, in the refrigerator for 8 hours or longer. Loosen the side from the dish with a knife and invert onto a serving plate. Serve with sweetened whipped cream.

You may also prepare the flan in 12 individual ramekins and bake for a shorter time.

Yield: 12 servings

SUGAR comes in various forms. Granulated or white sugar is produced by refining sugar cane or sugar beets. Superfine sugar is perfect for making meringues and sweetening cold liquids, as it dissolves almost instantly. Confectioners' or powdered sugar is granulated sugar that has been crushed into a fine powder. To prevent clumping, a small amount of cornstarch has been added. One and 3/4 cups confectioners' sugar equals 1 cup granulated sugar. Decorating or coarse sugar has granules about four times larger than granulated sugar. Brown sugar is white sugar combined with molasses. It offers a soft texture. The two most common types of brown sugar are light and dark. Generally, the lighter the brown sugar the more subtle the flavor. Dark has a more powerful molasses flavor. A tightly packed cup of brown sugar may be substituted for 1 cup granulated sugar.

CRÈME BRÛLÉE

CARAMELIZED SURFACES *may be achieved under the broiler of the oven or by using a professional propane hand-held torch (available in kitchen shops). Caution should be used to prevent scorching.*

5 egg yolks
1/2 cup sugar
2 cups heavy cream
1 tablespoon vanilla extract
2 ounces (1/3 cup) semisweet chocolate chips
2 tablespoons sugar

Whisk the egg yolks and 1/2 cup sugar together in a large bowl. Bring the cream to a simmer over low heat. Add to the egg yolk mixture very gradually, whisking constantly. Whisk in the vanilla.

Divide the chocolate chips evenly between 4 custard cups. Spoon the cream mixture into the cups. Place in a baking pan and add enough hot water to reach halfway up the sides of the cups.

Bake at 300 degrees for 55 minutes or just until the custards are set in the center. Remove to a wire rack and let stand until cool. Chill, covered, for 8 hours or longer.

Sprinkle 1/2 tablespoon sugar over the top of each custard. Broil for 2 minutes or until the sugar melts and browns slightly. Let stand for 5 minutes before serving.

You may substitute fresh strawberries or raspberries for the chocolate chips.

Yield: 4 servings

STRAWBERRY GRAND MARNIER SORBET

6 cups fresh strawberries, stemmed
2 cups sugar
3/4 cup fresh lemon juice
1 1/2 cups fresh orange juice
1/3 cup Grand Marnier

Combine the strawberries, sugar, lemon juice and orange juice in a bowl and mix gently. Let stand for 2 1/2 hours. Purée the mixture in a blender or food processor. Add the liqueur and mix well.

Pour into 2 large freezer trays. Freeze until the mixture is frozen for 1 inch on all sides. Spoon into a mixing bowl and beat until smooth. Return to the freezer trays and freeze until firm.

You may also freeze this in an ice cream freezer using the manufacturer's instructions.

Photograph for this recipe is on the cover.

Yield: 8 servings

FRENCH VANILLA ICE CREAM

  2 cups heavy cream
 3/4 cup sugar
 2/3 cup half-and-half
  1 teaspoon vanilla extract

Combine the cream, sugar, half-and-half and vanilla in a bowl and mix well. Pour into the container of a small ice cream freezer and freeze for 20 minutes using the manufacturer's instructions. Place in the freezer for 2 to 3 hours before serving.

    Yield: 4 servings

    For *Cinnamon Ice Cream*, add 2 teaspoons cinnamon.

    For *Chocolate Ice Cream*, add 1/2 cup melted milk chocolate.

    For *Strawberry Ice Cream*, add 1 cup chopped fresh strawberries and omit the vanilla.

    For *Raspberry Ice Cream*, add 2 cups fresh raspberries and omit the vanilla.

RICH HOMEMADE VANILLA ICE CREAM

 3/4 cup sugar
  2 tablespoons flour
 1/4 teaspoon salt
  2 cups milk
  2 eggs, lightly beaten
  2 cups heavy cream
1 1/2 tablespoons vanilla extract

Mix the sugar, flour and salt in a saucepan. Stir in the milk gradually, blending until smooth. Cook over low heat until the mixture is thickened and bubbly, stirring constantly. Stir a small amount of the hot mixture into the eggs and mix well; stir the eggs into the hot mixture. Cook for 1 minute longer, stirring constantly. Chill in the refrigerator.

    Stir the cream and vanilla into the chilled mixture. Pour into an ice cream freezer container and freeze using the manufacturer's instructions.

    Yield: 4 servings

CRANBERRY MAPLE WALNUT SAUCE

Warm 1 cup of real maple syrup in a small saucepan. Add 1/2 cup dried cranberries and 1/2 cup chopped walnuts and mix well. Serve over vanilla or coffee ice cream in Champagne or parfait glasses.

RASPBERRY TOPPING

Combine 2 cups fresh red raspberries or one 10-ounce package frozen raspberries with 2/3 cup brown sugar and 1/2 cup corn syrup in a saucepan and mix well. Bring to a boil and cook for 2 minutes, stirring constantly. Press through a strainer into a bowl. Chill until serving time. Serve over ice cream.

Best-Ever Cream Puffs

SEPARATE EGGS *by cracking the egg shell into halves and gently pouring the yolk from one half of the shell to the other over a small bowl until only the yolk remains.*

Puffs

- 1/2 cup (1 stick) butter or margarine
- 1 cup water
- 1 cup flour
- 4 eggs

Cream Filling

- 5 tablespoons cornstarch
- 1/2 cup sugar
- 1/8 teaspoon salt
- 3 cups half-and-half
- 2 egg yolks, lightly beaten
- 1 teaspoon vanilla extract
- 2 egg whites

For the puffs, combine the butter and water in a saucepan and bring to a rolling boil. Stir in the flour all at once. Cook over low heat for 1 minute or until the mixture leaves the side of the saucepan and forms a ball, stirring constantly. Remove from the heat and stir in the eggs one at a time. Beat until smooth.

Drop by spoonfuls onto an ungreased baking sheet. Bake at 400 degrees for about 30 minutes or until dry. Remove to a wire rack to cool.

For the filling, mix the cornstarch, sugar and salt in a saucepan. Stir in the half-and-half gradually. Bring to a boil and cook until thickened, stirring constantly. Stir a small amount of the hot mixture into the egg yolks; stir the egg yolks into the hot mixture. Bring to a boil. Cook for 1 minute longer, stirring constantly.

Cool to lukewarm and fold in the vanilla. Beat the egg whites until stiff but not dry; fold into the cooled mixture.

To fill the cream puffs, cut off and reserve the tops of the puffs. Spoon the filling into the puffs and replace the tops. Garnish with a sifting of confectioners' sugar.

Yield: 16 servings

Profiteroles au Chocolat

  2 tablespoons sugar
 1/2 cup (1 stick) butter, sliced
  1 cup water
 1/2 teaspoon salt
  1 cup flour
  4 eggs, at room temperature
  1 egg
  3 cups vanilla ice cream
     Chocolate Sauce (below)
     Roasted almonds to taste

Combine the sugar, butter, water and salt in a saucepan and bring to a rolling boil. Remove from the heat and stir in the flour all at once; beat until the mixture leaves the side of the saucepan and forms a ball. Add 4 eggs one at a time, beating well after each addition.

Spoon into a pastry tube and pipe into 1-inch mounds on a buttered baking sheet. Brush with a mixture of 1 egg and a small amount of water. Bake at 425 degrees for 20 minutes or until doubled in size and the surface is firm, crusty and golden brown. Pierce each puff on the side to release steam. Turn off the oven and let the puffs stand in the oven for 10 minutes to dry. Remove to a wire rack to cool.

To serve, cut the tops from the puffs and reserve. Fill the puffs with ice cream and replace the tops. Place on serving plates and drizzle the lukewarm Chocolate Sauce over the tops. Sprinkle with roasted almonds.

Yield: 24 servings

Chocolate Sauce

 1 1/2 cups half-and-half
  2 cups sugar
  4 (1-ounce) squares chocolate
  1 tablespoon instant coffee granules
  3 tablespoons butter
  1 teaspoon vanilla extract
  2 tablespoons rum
 1/2 teaspoon salt

Bring the half-and-half and sugar to a boil in a saucepan and boil for several minutes. Add the chocolate and coffee granules. Cook until the chocolate melts and the coffee granules dissolve, whisking constantly. Remove from the heat and stir in the butter, vanilla, rum and salt. Cool to lukewarm.

Yield: 24 servings

ROLLING BOIL *refers to heating liquid over high heat until many large bubbles erupt from the bottom of the pan.*

PEACH AND BERRY SHORTCAKES

      1   cup flour
  1 1/2   teaspoons baking powder
    1/4   cup sugar
    1/8   teaspoon grated nutmeg
    1/4   teaspoon salt
    1/4   cup (1/2 stick) unsalted butter, softened
      1   small egg
    1/4   cup milk
      3   large peaches, peeled, sliced
      2   pints mixed berries
          Cream Sauce (below)

Mix the flour, baking powder, sugar, nutmeg and salt in a large bowl. Cut in the butter with a pastry blender until the mixture resembles fine cornmeal; make a well in the center. Beat the egg with the milk in the measuring cup. Add to the well and mix with a fork just until moistened.

Drop by large forkfuls into 6 mounds on a greased baking sheet. Bake at 400 degrees for 15 to 20 minutes or until golden brown.

Split the shortcakes and place the bottoms on serving plates. Spoon the peaches onto the bottoms and replace the tops. Spoon the berries over each top. Spoon the warm Cream Sauce over the tops.

Yield: 6 servings

CREAM SAUCE

    1/4   cup (1/2 stick) unsalted butter
    1/4   cup sugar
      2   cups heavy cream

Combine the butter, sugar and cream in a heavy saucepan and bring to a boil over low heat. Stir down and return to a boil. Reduce the heat and simmer for 15 to 20 minutes for a thin sauce. Simmer longer for a thicker sauce.

You may thin the sauce with a small amount of additional cream if necessary for the desired consistency.

Yield: 6 servings

SHORTCAKE *can be made by substituting scones, shortbread, or cinnamon rolls from the bakery for homemade shortcakes.*

Many think of shortcake as being "strawberry shortcake" exclusively. Try substituting one of the following: akala, blackberry, blueberry, boysenberry, cape gooseberry, cranberry, dewberry, elderberry, gooseberry, huckleberry, lingonberry, loganberry, mulberry, olallieberry, raspberry, thimbleberry, and youngberry.

You can also omit the sugar from a dessert shortcake and substitute an herb for the spices to use it as a base for creamed chicken or beef.

Glazed Cardamom Pears with Honey Cream Sauce

Honey Cream Sauce

- 1/2 cup whipping cream
- 1 cup sour cream
- 1/3 cup honey
- 1 tablespoon grated orange zest

Pears

- 1/3 cup packed light brown sugar
- 1/3 cup honey
- 1 teaspoon ground cardamom
- 8 pears, peeled
- 2/3 cup water
- 3 tablespoons butter

For the sauce, beat the whipping cream in a mixing bowl until soft peaks form. Add the sour cream, honey and orange zest and mix well. Chill, covered, for 1 hour or longer.

For the pears, mix the brown sugar, honey and cardamom in a bowl. Cut the pears into halves, discarding the cores. Arrange cut side up in a 9×13-inch baking pan filled with the water. Spoon the honey mixture over the pears and dot with butter.

Bake at 450 degrees for 30 minutes or until the pears are glazed and fork tender, basting with the pan juices occasionally and adding additional water to the pan if needed. Remove the pears to serving plates and spoon the sauce over the top.

You may prepare the pears in advance and store in the refrigerator for up to 24 hours. Reheat to serve if desired.

Yield: 8 servings

CARDAMOM is a strong and pungent member of the ginger family. Cardamom pods contain seventeen to twenty small seeds. This spice may be purchased whole or ground and adds an intense warm, spicy, and sweet taste. Whole pods retain freshness that ground cardamom loses after grinding. Whole pods may be freshly ground for a more intense flavor.

POACHED PEARS should be eaten with a spoon and a fork. The fork holds the pear down against the plate while the spoon is used to cut the fruit into pieces. The fork may be used to rotate the pear around to access the entire pear. If only a spoon is available, rotate the dish by hand. Leave the core in the dish. Use a spoon to drink the wine or syrup.

Wine Guide

THE PAIRING *of good food with fine wine is one of the great pleasures of life. The rule that you drink white wine only with fish and fowl and red wine with meat no longer applies— just let your own taste and personal preference be the guide. Remember to serve light wines with lighter foods and full-bodied wines with rich foods so the food and wine will complement rather than overpower each other.*

SEMIDRY WHITE WINES

These wines have a fresh fruity taste and are best served young. Serve with dove, quail, or shellfish in cream sauce; roast turkey, duck, or goose; seafood, pasta, or salad; fish in an herbed butter sauce.

- Johannisberg Riesling – (Yo-hann-is-burg Rees-ling)
- Frascati – (Fras-kah-tee) • Gewürztraminer – (Guh-vurts-trah-mee-ner)
- Bernkasteler – (Barn-kahst-ler)
- Sylvaner Riesling – (Sihl-van-uhr Rees-ling) • Fendant – (Fahn-dawn)
- Dienheimer – (Deen-heim-er) • Kreuznach – (Kroytz-nock)

DRY WHITE WINES

These wines have a crisp, refreshing taste and are best served young. Serve with chicken, turkey, and cold meat; roast young gamebirds and waterfowl; shellfish; fried or grilled fish; ham and veal.

- Vouvray – (Voo-vray) • Chablis – (Sha-blee)
- Chardonnay – (Shar-doh-nay) • Pinot Blanc – (Pee-noh Blahn)
- Chenin Blanc – (Shen-ihn Blahn) • Pouilly-Fuissé – (Poo-yee Fwee-say)
- Orvieto Secco – (Ohr-vyay-toh Say-koh)
- Piesporter Trocken – (Peez-porter Trawk-uhn) • Meursault – (Mehr-soh)
- Hermitage Blanc – (Ehr-mee-tahzh Blahn)
- Pinot Grigio – (Pee-noh Gree-jo) • Verdicchio – (Vehr-deek-kyoh)
- Sancerre – (Sahn-sehr) • Sauvignon Blanc – (Soh-vihn-yohn Blahn)
- Soave – (So-ah-veh)

Light Red Wines

These wines have a light taste and are best served young.
Serve with grilled chicken; fowl with highly seasoned stuffings; soups
and stews; Creole foods; veal or lamb.

- Beaujolais – (Boh-zhuh-lay) • Bardolino – (Bar-doh-lee-noh)
- Valpolicella – (Vahl-paw-lee-chehl-lah)
- Moulin-à-Vent Beaujolais – (Moo-lan-nah-vahn Boh-zhuh-lay)
- Barbera – (Bar-beh-rah) • Lambrusco – (Lam-broos-koh)
- Lirac – (Lee-rak) • Nuits-Saint-Georges "Villages" – (Nwee San Zhawrzh)
- Gamay Beaujolais – (Ga-may Boh-zhuh-lay)
- Santa Maddalena – (Sahn-tah Mahd-dah-leh-nah)
- Merlot del Ticino – (Mehr-loh dehl Tee-chee-noh)

Hearty Red Wines

These wines have a heavier taste, improve with age, and are best opened
thirty minutes before serving. Serve with game including duck, goose,
venison, and hare; pot roast; red meats including beef, lamb, and veal;
hearty foods; cheese and egg dishes, pastas, and highly seasoned foods.

- Barbaresco – (Bar-bah-ress-koh) • Barolo – (Bah-roh-loh)
- Burgundy – (Ber-gun-dee) • Zinfandel – (Zihn-fuhn-dehl)
- Chianti Riserva – (Kee-ahn-tee Ree-zehr-vah) • Bordeaux – (Bohr-doh)
- Côte-Rotie – (Koht Roh-tee) • Hermitage – (Ehr-mee-tahzh)
- Taurasi – (Tow-rah-zee) • Merlot – (Mehr-loh)
- Syrah – (See-rah) • Châteauneuf-du-Pape – (Shah-toh-nuhf-doo-Pahp)
- Petite Sirah – (Peh-teet Sih-rah) • Côte de Beaune – (Koht duh Bohn)
- Cabernet Sauvignon – (Ka-behr-nay Soh-vihn-yohn)

THE BEST WINE *with which to cook is the one you will be serving at the table. The real secret is to cook with a good wine, as the alcohol evaporates during the cooking process leaving only the actual flavor of the wine. A fine wine with rich body and aroma will insure a distinct and delicate flavor. When used in cooking, the wine should accent and enhance the natural flavor of the food while adding its own inviting fragrance and flavor.*

Edible Flowers

ALLIUM
A perennial herb that blooms during May and June with pretty lilac-pink flowers that can be used, in addition to the hollow leaves, as a garnish or substitute for scallions.

BEE BALM
Bees and hummingbirds are attracted to this citrus-tasting herb whose leaves and colorful scarlet flowers can be used with fruits, duck, and pork, or in salads, teas, and jellies.

BORAGE
The bright blue star-shape flowers have a cucumber-like flavor and are often used in salads. The flowers may also be floated in drinks or candied for a dessert garnish.

CALENDULA
The ray petal is the edible portion of the blossom and provides an attractive garnish. It is often used to color butter and cheese and is commonly known as the pot marigold. It can be used as a substitute for saffron and has a tangy, peppery taste.

CLOVE PINKS
This wild ancestor of the modern carnation has a spicy, mild clove flavor. The semi-double fragrant flowers of this perennial can be used fresh to flavor syrups, fruit cups, or beverages, but be sure to remove the bitter white base first.

DAISY
A perennial flower that has a mild flavor, the daisy can be eaten fresh in salads or used as a garnish.

DANDELION
This familiar yellow flower can be minced and added to butters, spreads, and vinegar.

DAY LILY
The yellow, tawny orange flowers of all day lilies are edible, but sample first to determine taste before chopping into salads or soups. Pick the flower buds after they have elongated but before they open, as the smaller buds tend to taste better.

FENNEL
Fennel's mild licorice-flavor leaves and large yellow ublema flowers should be used fresh, not dried, in soups and salads.

SCENTED GERANIUMS
A perennial grown as an annual or houseplant, these come in a wide variety of colors and scents, which are released by being rubbed or by the hot sun. Use for baked goods, ice creams, jellies, candied garnishes, and scented sugar.

HOLLYHOCKS
The flowers are best used as an attractive container for a dish or as a garnish, but they can also be made into fritters or be used as flavoring for tea.

HONEYSUCKLE
Known for its delightful fragrance and sweet taste, the honeysuckle can be used in puddings, ice creams, or syrups.

JOHNNY-JUMP-UPS
These flowers make a pretty candied garnish on a dessert or can brighten up a spring salad or punch bowl. Their mild taste is reminiscent of sweet baby lettuce.

LAVENDER

A perennial shrub with graceful purple flowers and a scent that is associated more with potpourri than cooking. However, its leaves and flowers can be used in vinegar or jellies, or used sparingly in salads, ice creams, and custards.

LILAC

The pyramidal lavender clusters of its flowers are known for their scent, which carries over into their taste, and can be candied or used in herb butters, scented sugars, or as a garnish. The blossoms should be picked as soon as they open.

MARIGOLD

Although all are edible, the Tangerine Gem and Lemon Gem varieties have a more pleasant flavor; there is a Peruvian variety used in salsa. Most marigolds are a good accompaniment to salads, soups, and sauces.

NASTURTIUM

The slightly peppery taste of the young leaves, flowers, and buds, combined with their vibrant colors, brighten any green salad. The flowers also provide a unique container for cold salads, but the bitter-tasting base should be removed first.

PANSY

Similar in taste to Johnny-jump-ups, the flowers are often used as a garnish on desserts or floating in cold drinks or soups. They should be picked when they first open.

PINEAPPLE SAGE

Rough, dark green leaves and bright scarlet tubular flowers that bloom in late summer characterize this tender perennial. The flowery, pineapple taste, with a hint of sage muskiness, can season fruit salads, tea, desserts, and tea breads.

ROSES

Older varieties seem to have more scent and therefore more taste, but many varieties can be quite bitter, so sample first. The hips and petals can be used for making tea, jelly, jam, syrup, or wine. The petals can also be candied or used to make rosewater, scented sugar, or butter.

SQUASH BLOSSOMS

The golden-orange flowers should be picked when fully open, but don't pick them all or there'll be no squash. The blossoms can be chopped into soups, salads, or vegetable dishes. Be sure to remove stamens and pistils before cooking.

SWEET WOODRUFF

A staple of the May punch bowl, the tiny star-shape white flowers of this shade-loving perennial can also garnish tea cakes, desserts, salads, and fruits, especially berries.

THYME

The lilac-color flowers tend to be mild with a floral scent, perfect for garnishing salads, pastas, or desserts.

TULIP

Like the nasturtium, these brightly colored flowers are best used as a garnish or container for a cold dish, such as chicken or egg salad. Their light flavor is similar to peas. The best variety for culinary use is the Darwin hybrid.

VIOLET

Like the Johnny-jump-up and pansy, this hardy perennial has a sweeter, stronger scent. Its flowers and heart-shape leaves can be used as a garnish. The flowers can be made into violet water, which can flavor tea, breads, fruit compotes, and chilled soups.

Nutritional Profile Guidelines

The editors have attempted to present these recipes in a format that allows approximate nutritional values to be computed. Persons with dietary or health problems or whose diets require close monitoring should not rely solely on the nutritional information provided. They should consult their physician or a registered dietitian for specific information.

Abbreviations for Nutritional Profile

Cal — Calories	T Fat — Total Fat	Sod — Sodium
Prot — Protein	Chol — Cholesterol	g — grams
Carbo — Carbohydrates	Fiber — Dietary Fiber	mg — milligrams

Nutritional information for these recipes is computed from information derived from many sources, including materials supplied by the United States Department of Agriculture, computer databanks, and journals in which the information is assumed to be in the public domain. However, many specialty items, new products, and processed food may not be available from these sources or may vary from the average values used in these profiles. More information on new and/or specific products may be obtained by reading the nutrient labels. Unless otherwise specified, the nutritional profile of these recipes is based on all measurements being level.

- Artificial sweeteners vary in use and strength so should be used "to taste," using the recipe ingredients as a guideline. Sweeteners using aspartame (NutraSweet and Equal) should not be used as a sweetener in recipes involving prolonged heating, which reduces the sweet taste. For further information on the use of these sweeteners, refer to the package.
- Alcoholic ingredients have been analyzed for the basic information. Cooking causes the evaporation of alcohol, which decreases alcholic and caloric content.
- Buttermilk, sour cream, and yogurt are the types available commercially.
- Cake mixes which are prepared using package directions include 3 eggs and 1/2 cup oil.
- Chicken, cooked for boning and chopping, has been roasted, which yields the lowest caloric values.
- Cottage cheese is cream-style with 4.2 percent creaming mixture. Dry curd cottage cheese has no creaming mixture.
- Eggs are all large. To avoid raw eggs that may carry salmonella, as in eggnog or 6-week muffin batter, use an equivalent amount of commercial egg substitute.
- Flour is unsifted all-purpose flour.
- Garnishes, serving suggestions, ingredients and other optional information and variations are not included in the profile.
- Margarine and butter are regular, not whipped or presoftened.
- Milk is whole milk, 3.5 percent butterfat. Low-fat milk is 1 percent butterfat. Evaporated milk is whole milk with 60 percent of the water removed.
- Oil is any type of vegetable cooking oil. Shortening is hydrogenated vegetable shortening.
- Salt and other ingredients to taste as noted in the ingredients have not been included in the nutritional profile.
- If a choice of ingredients has been given, the profile reflects the first option. If a choice of amounts has been given, the profile reflects the greater amount.

234

Nutritional Profiles

Pg #	Recipe Title (Approx Per Serving)	Cal	Prot (g)	Carbo (g)	T Fat (g)	% Cal from Fat	Chol (mg)	Fiber (g)	Sod (mg)
17	Antipasto Appetizer	264	7	5	24	83	15	1	356
17	Crab Bruschetta	255	9	17	16	59	36	1	426
18	Greek-Style Bruschetta	114	4	14	5	38	9	1	619
18	Curried Chicken Canapés	221	8	12	17	66	22	2	293
19	Roquefort Grapes	64	1	3	6	78	6	1	24
19	Curried Deviled Eggs	84	4	<1	7	81	7	0	250
20	Sausage-Stuffed Mushrooms	169	11	10	10	50	22	1	556
20	Gruyère-Stuffed Mushrooms	75	1	3	6	72	17	<1	53
21	Hot Marinated Mushrooms	89	2	2	8	75	21	<1	285
21	Parmesan Knots	63	1	4	5	71	<1	<1	110
22	Country Pâté	179	8	2	15	77	42	<1	241
23	Creamy Garlic Snow Peas	14	<1	<1	1	82	4	<1	23
23	Herbed Cheese Spread	91	4	7	8	79	23	<1	110
24	Mediterranean Feta Stuffed Mushrooms	56	2	3	4	68	13	1	172
24	Mexican Chicken Pizza	226	17	23	8	15	42	1	556
25	Mediterranean Pizzas	Nutritional information for this recipe is not available.							
25	Basil Pesto	300	16	24	16	46	4	20	114
26	Pot Stickers with Asian Sauce	60	3	8	2	25	11	1	608
27	Miniature Focaccia Sandwiches	44	2	4	2	45	7	<1	102
27	Won Ton Sausage Stars[1]	56	2	4	4	58	8	<1	94
28	Curried Chicken Puffs	139	6	5	11	69	48	<1	128
29	Iowa Maytag Tart	183	4	10	14	69	53	1	146
30	Seafood Tartlets	179	4	13	11	59	26	0	248
30	Stuffed Phyllo Cups	82	3	4	6	65	26	<1	79
31	Grilled Shrimp Dijonnaise	131	7	1	11	72	24	<1	450
32	Chutney Cheese Spread	185	6	8	15	70	46	1	209
32	Crab Rangoon Spread with Won Ton Crackers	101	4	5	7	63	27	<1	168
33	Guacamole	170	2	9	15	75	0	5	593
33	Creamy Kahlúa Fruit Dip	164	2	16	8	44	24	0	60
34	Savory Hot Mushroom Dip	132	4	4	12	81	28	2	240
34	Reuben Dip[2]	180	8	2	16	80	52	0	316
35	Texas Caviar	193	5	23	10	45	0	5	601
35	Tortilla Stacks	446	12	34	29	59	63	2	860
36	Roasted Red Pepper Dip	276	1	4	28	92	33	<1	357
36	Hot Spinach Dip	136	6	4	11	72	34	1	426
37	Mexican Spinach Dip	157	6	4	14	76	34	1	201
37	Shrimp Dip	117	7	4	9	65	59	<1	208
38	Shrimp Mold	145	6	2	13	80	67	<1	150

NUTRITIONAL PROFILES

Pg #	Recipe Title (Approx Per Serving)	Cal	Prot (g)	Carbo (g)	T Fat (g)	% Cal from Fat	Chol (mg)	Fiber (g)	Sod (mg)
38	Grasshoppers by the Gallon	434	5	49	17	35	58	0	107
39	Raspberry Champagne Aperitif	159	<1	17	1	1	0	1	6
40	Sunrise Mimosa[3]	111	1	13	<1	1	0	<1	5
40	Margaritas Supreme	331	<1	41	<1	0	0	<1	3
40	Celebration Punch	94	<1	7	<1	1	0	<1	8
41	Holiday Punch	85	<1	16	<1	0	0	<1	13
41	Champagne Punch	148	<1	22	<1	0	0	<1	3
41	Poinsettia Punch	146	<1	14	<1	1	0	<1	6
45	Butterscotch Pecan Rolls[4]	452	7	69	17	33	22	1	179
46	Almond Coffee Cakes	297	5	37	15	44	50	2	147
47	Kolache Bread[5]	190	3	34	5	23	25	1	85
48	French Bread	73	2	15	<1	<1	0	<1	97
48	Streamlined White Bread	152	4	27	3	1	0	1	389
49	Apple Bread[6]	297	4	41	14	41	56	1	407
50	Banana Nut Bread	271	3	42	11	3	36	1	265
50	Cranberry Orange Bread	238	4	37	9	3	23	2	289
51	Fruit Bread	286	4	44	12	3	56	2	195
51	Blueberry Muffins	143	2	23	5	30	25	1	131
52	Honey-Glazed Bran Muffins	302	3	62	7	20	35	4	400
53	Bountiful Breakfast Muffins	431	5	51	24	50	53	3	341
53	Rhubarb Muffins	230	3	37	8	31	22	1	208
54	Glazed French Toast	580	14	78	24	37	227	2	810
54	Classic Buttermilk Pancakes	466	17	57	19	36	249	2	1129
55	Dutch Babies Baked Pancake	313	12	28	15	43	277	1	157
56	Crepes Iceland[7]	224	12	17	12	48	71	<1	481
57	Crepes Sylvia[7]	600	11	44	40	74	219	3	511
60	Layered Mushroom Crepes[7]	196	7	8	15	70	75	1	351
61	Quiche Ranchero	177	10	4	13	68	111	1	387
61	Spinach and Asiago Frittata	92	6	3	7	65	112	<1	107
62	Sausage and Egg Strata	405	22	18	27	60	306	1	764
62	Italian Zucchini Crescent Pie	428	13	21	33	68	100	2	849
63	Apple Lemon Crescent Braid	209	2	39	6	24	0	1	216
63	Fruit Compote[8]	399	1	97	<1	0	0	2	42
64	Raspberry Cream Cheese Coffee Cake	333	5	39	19	49	70	1	276
65	Apricot Orange Conserve	20	<1	5	1	10	0	<1	<1
65	Brunch Trifle	473	7	51	29	52	193	4	164
69	Blueberry Spinach Salad	245	5	8	23	81	11	3	260
69	Strawberry and Spinach Salad	293	3	20	24	71	0	2	104

236

NUTRITIONAL PROFILES

Pg #	Recipe Title (Approx Per Serving)	Cal	Prot (g)	Carbo (g)	T Fat (g)	% Cal from Fat	Chol (mg)	Fiber (g)	Sod (mg)
70	Arugula Salad with Pears and Beets	391	7	26	30	67	13	5	300
70	Spinach Salad with Garlic Vinaigrette	226	8	6	20	75	111	2	176
71	Southwest Caesar Salad with Red Chile Dressing	597	9	10	60	88	15	2	776
71	Red Cabbage Salad	405	5	29	32	68	14	3	253
72	Spinach and Orange Salad with Poppy Seed Dressing	369	2	28	29	68	0	2	322
72	Cranberry and Apple Salad	270	3	17	23	72	0	3	34
73	Apple Walnut Salad with Bacon Vinaigrette[9]	571	9	23	52	78	15	3	780
74	Black Bean and Bell Pepper Salad	205	7	29	8	33	0	8	381
75	Fresh Fruit Salad with Dates[10]	581	4	110	17	25	10	5	73
75	Broccoli and Almond Salad	393	6	27	31	73	25	3	279
76	Tomato and Cucumber Bread Salad	234	3	18	17	65	1	2	408
77	Creamy Potato Salad	390	9	37	23	54	207	4	708
77	Picnic Potato Salad	638	12	45	48	66	200	5	2185
78	Grilled Vegetable Salad with Pesto Vinaigrette	501	7	27	43	75	1	10	357
79	Orzo with Everything	459	16	39	27	53	29	2	523
79	Rotini and Vegetable Salad	745	14	94	36	43	58	7	971
80	Tropical Chicken Salad	324	15	38	14	37	45	3	218
80	Chicken and Fruit Salad	505	25	23	35	62	98	1	379
81	Grilled Chicken Caesar Salad	558	61	3	45	61	209	1	380
82	Shrimp and Fennel Spinach Salad with Vinaigrette[11]	375	16	11	30	71	126	3	291
83	Creamy Hot Bacon Dressing[12]	32	<1	4	2	52	2	<1	51
83	Bleu Cheese Dressing[12]	79	1	1	8	94	9	<1	104
84	Feta Cheese Salad Dressing[12]	59	1	<1	6	94	8	0	82
84	Honey Salad Dressing[12]	77	<1	6	6	69	0	<1	89
84	Maple Dijon Vinaigrette[12]	49	<1	4	4	63	0	<1	93
85	Peppercorn Parmesan Dressing[12]	45	1	<1	4	88	6	0	95
85	Peppercream Dressing[12]	81	<1	<1	9	99	8	0	83
85	Poppy Seed Dressing[12]	78	<1	4	7	79	0	<1	73
89	Iced Parsley Soup	451	7	25	37	72	130	3	1364
89	Strawberry Cantaloupe Soup	143	3	30	2	12	6	3	35
90	Cream of Brie Soup	437	16	21	33	67	106	2	480
90	Cream of Fennel Soup	363	9	18	28	67	85	4	857
91	Roasted Garlic Soup with Prosciutto and Gruyère	586	30	21	37	60	102	2	1294
92	Potato Soup	334	15	19	22	60	51	1	1030
92	Creamy Sweet Potato Soup	49	2	10	1	11	2	1	19
93	Tuscan Soup	257	8	20	17	57	48	2	1482
93	Provolone Spinach Soup	250	11	14	17	60	53	2	899
96	Wild Rice Soup	311	10	24	20	57	50	2	630

Nutritional Profiles

Pg #	Recipe Title (Approx Per Serving)	Cal	Prot (g)	Carbo (g)	T Fat (g)	% Cal from Fat	Chol (mg)	Fiber (g)	Sod (mg)
97	Acorn Squash Soup	212	8	29	8	31	20	4	971
98	Tortellini Soup	187	13	24	4	21	28	4	1365
99	Chili Blanco	808	64	55	37	41	140	19	1770
99	Turkey and Apple Pitas	390	57	35	3	6	141	4	376
100	Kraut Runza	230	11	26	9	36	22	2	805
100	Hot Italian Sandwiches	433	16	34	26	55	63	2	815
101	Pressed Picnic Sandwiches	210	11	18	11	46	23	1	471
102	Grilled Asparagus Pâté Sandwiches	316	12	32	16	44	41	3	753
102	Cranberry Chutney	46	<1	12	<1	0	0	1	43
103	Cornichons au Vinaigre	14	<1	1	<1	1	0	<1	90
107	Green Beans with Bacon	128	3	14	7	49	9	4	95
107	Scalloped Broccoli	224	10	14	15	60	31	2	562
108	Sweet-and-Sour Cabbage	112	2	27	1	4	1	2	1002
108	Carrots in Port Sauce	147	1	12	10	57	0	2	74
109	Honey-Glazed Carrots	122	1	13	8	55	21	2	105
109	Scalloped Carrots	392	13	38	21	48	58	4	1131
110	Scalloped Corn	205	6	26	9	40	56	2	484
110	Elegant Eggplant	190	5	17	12	56	33	3	209
111	Onion Casserole	274	7	17	20	66	47	2	356
111	Potatoes with Leeks and Gruyère Cheese	421	20	21	29	61	167	2	734
112	Murphy's Potatoes	412	13	32	26	56	78	3	566
112	Potato and Carrot Bake	284	8	41	11	33	32	4	526
113	Garlic Mashed Potatoes	255	3	22	18	61	54	2	138
113	Sweet Potato Puff	356	4	49	17	42	75	2	151
114	Baked Acorn Squash with Pears and Apples	362	3	79	7	19	16	11	44
114	Cider-Roasted Squash	91	1	16	4	32	0	2	150
115	Orange-Glazed Squash	359	2	67	12	28	31	3	232
115	Tomato Pie	399	9	16	33	74	42	1	254
116	Tomatoes Parmesan	155	5	10	11	60	27	1	504
116	Garlic Tomatoes	123	1	3	12	87	0	1	394
117	Couscous with Dried Fruits and Pecans	224	5	35	8	30	8	3	223
117	Quick-Cooking Couscous	Nutritional information for this recipe is not available.							
118	Risotto	307	5	40	13	38	34	1	395
118	Spinach and Wild Rice Casserole	245	9	22	15	51	44	3	733
119	Herbed Wild Rice and Cranberry Stuffing	230	5	36	7	26	12	3	777
123	Shrimp and Tortellini Casserole	674	59	47	27	36	428	1	1377
123	Chinese Vermicelli	471	14	55	22	42	62	5	908
124	Chicken and Pecan Fettuccini	642	28	34	46	62	156	4	818

NUTRITIONAL PROFILES

Pg #	Recipe Title (Approx Per Serving)	Cal	Prot (g)	Carbo (g)	T Fat (g)	% Cal from Fat	Chol (mg)	Fiber (g)	Sod (mg)
125	Ham and Asparagus Fettuccini	488	45	58	9	17	52	4	1954
125	Fettucini with Shrimp and Garlic	917	31	52	64	62	295	3	738
126	Spinach-Filled Lasagna Rolls	567	19	32	42	65	181	5	1115
127	Marinara Sauce	105	1	7	9	69	10	2	178
127	Balsamella Sauce	146	2	4	14	84	45	<1	270
128	Classic Lasagna	492	30	22	30	54	122	2	949
129	White Lasagna	568	44	16	35	55	158	1	480
130	Penne with Yellow Peppers and Tomatoes	364	11	64	6	15	0	3	242
130	Penne with Asiago Cream Sauce	372	9	26	25	60	82	1	356
131	Spaghetti with Shiitake and Tomato Cream Sauce	606	18	53	36	53	115	4	721
131	Pesto Spaghetti	700	28	103	19	25	20	17	199
132	Sensational Spaghetti	569	28	62	21	33	74	5	908
133	Angel Hair Pasta with Tomatoes and Ricotta Cheese	252	10	30	11	38	17	1	652
133	Shrimp and Farfalle Toss	685	44	83	19	25	275	7	1606
134	Vegetable Terrine on Linguini	508	19	60	23	39	197	7	695
135	Basic Pasta Dough	293	11	48	5	17	159	2	630
139	Beef Tenderloin with Bordelaise Sauce	428	48	4	23	49	157	<1	295
139	Pepper Steak	315	33	11	14	39	96	2	461
140	Fillet of Beef	319	43	<1	15	44	127	<1	95
140	Fillet of Beef Dijonnaise	456	49	1	27	55	153	<1	539
141	Oven-Barbecued Brisket	558	60	15	27	45	183	1	1445
142	Barbecued Beef Brisket	318	38	3	16	46	114	<1	1166
142	Beef Roast	387	48	3	19	46	141	1	109
143	Grilled Marinated Pot Roast[11]	1127	57	11	93	74	121	1	5387
143	London Broil[11]	525	49	9	31	55	117	<1	1465
144	Classic Beef Stroganoff	443	42	9	24	49	145	1	445
145	Leg of Lamb with Parsley and Crumb Crust	489	54	6	27	50	195	1	395
146	Rack of Lamb with Honey Mustard and Pecan Crust	728	22	13	65	78	174	1	476
147	Roast Lamb with Potato and Tomato Gratin	408	35	22	18	40	107	3	94
148	Rack of Lamb with Spicy Pepper Crust	709	38	2	60	77	173	<1	131
148	Fillet of Pork Amandine	664	49	20	42	57	130	7	219
149	Barbecued Pork Ribs	757	62	84	20	24	147	3	3348
152	Normandy-Style Pork Loin	452	50	12	19	39	140	2	231
153	Pork Roast and Dumplings	545	44	55	15	25	179	5	1543
154	Roast Pork with Fruit Stuffing	507	55	22	21	39	146	2	564
154	Marinated Pork Barbecue[11]	441	58	6	18	39	155	<1	2743
155	Pork Roast with Pears	364	40	23	12	29	105	2	520
155	Grilled Pork Chops	182	26	7	5	26	51	1	5308

Nutritional Profiles

Pg #	Recipe Title (Approx Per Serving)	Cal	Prot (g)	Carbo (g)	T Fat (g)	% Cal from Fat	Chol (mg)	Fiber (g)	Sod (mg)
156	Pesto Pork Chops[13]	286	26	4	18	58	65	1	281
157	Mexican Pork Chops	319	25	24	13	37	61	1	459
158	Pork Chops with Sausages	234	23	4	14	54	75	1	231
158	Baked Ham with Pineapple Glaze	225	27	11	7	28	84	<1	96
159	Chicken Piccata	393	55	8	14	32	162	<1	683
160	Grilled Chicken Grand Marnier[14]	657	54	79	7	9	146	1	493
160	Sauterne Chicken	432	61	2	17	37	178	<1	692
161	Phyllo-Wrapped Greek Chicken[11]	876	64	23	55	57	274	1	1277
162	Lime Tequila Chicken Fajitas[11]	1104	67	92	47	39	146	7	819
163	Pheasant in Plum Sauce[11]	1090	116	85	17	14	297	4	1535
164	Cornish Game Hens	929	96	11	53	53	298	3	1311
165	Swiss Crab Bake	465	27	35	24	47	99	2	1156
166	Seafood Gumbo	624	40	41	34	48	242	5	1475
167	Shrimp Creole	394	23	21	24	54	179	3	1129
170	Creole Shrimp and Chicken	384	47	7	16	39	202	1	822
171	Scampi	597	15	1	60	90	259	<1	625
171	Baked Salmon with Mustard Chive Butter	464	32	1	36	71	164	<1	461
172	Hazelnut-Encrusted Salmon	672	40	51	34	45	110	3	403
173	Lemon Pepper Baked Salmon	435	42	0	28	60	145	0	177
173	Salmon with Caramelized Glaze	651	43	56	29	39	136	<1	258
174	Grilled Sea Bass	763	40	23	56	65	145	4	353
176	Crusty Parmesan Snapper Fillets	329	30	12	17	48	46	3	446
176	Tuna Steaks with Rosemary Butter[11]	643	88	1	30	43	206	<1	1117
177	Marinated Ahi Tuna with Pineapple Salsa[11]	596	94	25	11	18	179	4	195
181	Johnny Appleseed Cake with Caramel Sauce	415	4	54	21	45	60	1	312
182	Buttermilk Spice Cake	395	3	62	16	35	80	<1	338
183	Carrot Pecan Cake with Cream Cheese Frosting	858	6	106	48	49	102	2	523
184	Flourless Chocolate Cake	681	9	54	51	64	197	4	373
185	Sinfully Rich Chocolate Cake	470	6	45	31	58	157	2	109
185	Amaretti Torte	606	9	62	36	51	201	1	136
186	Coffee-Buttered Thin-Layer Cake	375	3	41	23	54	150	<1	225
187	Decadent Cappuccino Cake	881	8	50	79	75	295	2	150
188	Glazed Lemon Sour Cream Pound Cake	541	6	65	29	48	150	1	422
189	Lemon Buttercream Cake	735	6	126	24	29	165	1	220
190	Hickory Nut Cake	487	5	65	24	36	51	2	304
191	Oatmeal Cake	543	5	81	24	39	45	2	364
192	Pineapple Meringue Cake	251	3	24	17	58	90	1	161
193	Bûche Noël (Yule Log)	247	4	31	13	47	124	1	64

Nutritional Profiles

Pg #	Recipe Title (Approx Per Serving)	Cal	Prot (g)	Carbo (g)	T Fat (g)	% Cal from Fat	Chol (mg)	Fiber (g)	Sod (mg)
194	Pumpkin Roll	299	5	31	18	54	84	1	217
195	Double-Decadent Brownie Torte	664	10	68	44	59	119	3	203
196	Lemon Meringue Torte	264	3	46	8	27	127	<1	67
197	Schaum Tortes	344	4	59	11	29	40	<1	106
198	Five-Pound Fudge	105	1	14	6	45	7	<1	30
198	Pecan Clusters	89	1	11	6	52	1	1	7
199	Almond Macaroons	121	3	16	6	41	0	1	7
199	Almond Espresso Biscotti	92	2	16	3	27	7	1	69
200	Pecan and Cranberry Biscotti	108	2	17	4	31	30	1	41
200	Chocolate Marshmallow Cookies	173	2	26	8	38	12	1	145
201	Cappuccino Brownies	169	2	17	11	56	40	1	46
202	Raspberry Fudge Brownies	241	2	40	9	33	42	2	77
202	Black Walnut Icebox Cookies	98	2	14	4	39	15	<1	62
203	Caramel Peanut Bars	198	3	27	10	42	16	1	133
203	Chocolate Mint Snappers	80	1	13	3	35	10	<1	76
204	Frosted Chocolate Cola Bars	90	1	15	4	34	10	<1	89
204	Cranberry Cheese Bars	269	4	36	13	42	37	1	164
205	Lemon Pistachio Cookies	141	1	17	8	50	16	<1	90
206	Mocha-Filled Spritz Cookies	178	2	17	12	58	31	<1	124
206	Jam-Filled Sandwich Cookies	219	2	29	11	43	39	1	183
207	White Walnut Bars	132	2	17	6	42	18	<1	84
208	Dutch Apple Pumpkin Pie	441	7	57	21	43	78	4	314
209	Chocolate Silk Pie	444	5	43	30	59	135	1	311
209	Pecan Pie	514	5	71	26	43	99	2	274
210	Sweet Potato Pie	744	8	99	37	44	147	4	403
211	Caramel Cashew Cheesecake	619	12	48	43	61	152	1	352
214	Chocolate Almond Cheesecake	372	6	32	25	60	106	2	214
215	Chocolate Chip Cheesecake	551	9	28	47	74	166	1	404
216	Irish Cream Chocolate Chip Cheesecake	511	7	40	36	61	150	1	236
217	Chocolate Coconut Cheesecake	474	9	39	31	58	125	<1	297
218	Creamy Coconut Cheesecake	499	9	34	37	66	172	1	337
219	White Chocolate Raspberry Cheesecake	535	7	58	30	50	144	1	263
220	Chocolate Swirl Cheesecake	421	7	43	26	54	127	1	254
221	Pumpkin Cheesecake	691	11	52	51	65	188	3	355
222	Pumpkin Cheesecake with Cranberry Glaze	432	7	48	24	49	135	2	246
223	Pumpkin Flan	210	5	24	9	39	131	1	146
224	Crème Brûlée	683	7	44	55	70	429	1	56
224	Strawberry Grand Marnier Sorbet	274	1	64	<1	2	0	3	2

NUTRITIONAL PROFILES

Pg #	Recipe Title (Approx Per Serving)	Cal	Prot (g)	Carbo (g)	T Fat (g)	% Cal from Fat	Chol (mg)	Fiber (g)	Sod (mg)
225	French Vanilla Ice Cream	608	4	43	49	70	178	0	62
225	Rich Homemade Vanilla Ice Cream	696	10	50	51	64	286	<1	282
226	Best-Ever Cream Puffs	200	5	17	13	58	112	<1	119
227	Profiteroles au Chocolat	228	4	29	12	47	71	<1	184
227	Chocolate Sauce	122	1	20	5	35	9	<1	70
228	Peach and Berry Shortcakes	621	6	50	46	65	178	4	265
228	Cream Sauce	374	2	11	37	87	129	0	31
229	Glazed Cardamom Pears with Honey Cream Sauce	370	2	59	17	38	45	4	70

[1]Nutritional profile does not include vegetable oil.

[2]Nutritional profile does not include milk.

[3]Nutritional profile does not include grenadine.

[4]Nutritional profile includes information for Butterscotch Pecan Rolls and Dinner Rolls combined; it does not include Sticky Buns.

[5]Nutritional profile does not include Pineapple Filling or Poppy Seed Filling.

[6]Nutritional profile does not include Confectioners' Sugar Glaze.

[7]Nutritional profile does not include butter for cooking the crepes.

[8]Nutritional profile does not include maraschino cherries.

[9]Nutritional profile includes Bacon Vinaigrette.

[10]Nutritional profile includes the entire amount of dressing.

[11]Nutritional profile includes the entire amount of marinade.

[12]Nutritional profile is per tablespoon.

[13]Nutritional profile does not include jalapeño jelly.

[14]Nutritional profile does not include olive oil for brushing chicken.

Food Photography Underwriters

Front Cover

The First Impressions *Cookbook Development Committee:*
Peg Ascherl
Ann Aulwes
Laura Dobson
Kathryn Marold Fain
Stacy Gary
Linda Hanson
Carol Heth
Margaret Kaliban
Anne Gallagher Nass
Becky Poe
Jeannie Robertson
Julie Westin

Back Cover

Roswitha Marold
Kathryn Marold Fain
Jeannie Robertson

Appetizers and Beverages

Ruth Buck
Susie Heaton
Carol Luce
Dorothy Sulentic Sullivan

Breads, Breakfast and Brunch

Junean Witham

Salads and Dressings

Cathy Gallagher
Mary L. Lichty
Tom and Becky Poe

Soups, Sandwiches and Condiments

Terri Jackson

Side Dishes

Carol, Kate, Grace, and Frances Williams

Pasta

The Bernhard Family—
Rudy, Jan, Christine, and Kim

Meat, Poultry and Seafood

Peg McGarvey
Anne Gallagher Nass

Desserts

Mary Liebscher
Amy Lockard
Doris Miller

THE JUNIOR LEAGUE *of Waterloo-Cedar Falls wishes to acknowledge and thank each of these persons whose generous donation made it possible for us to include in* FIRST IMPRESSIONS *the fine food photography.*

Recipe Contributors and Testers

THE JUNIOR LEAGUE of Waterloo-Cedar Falls wishes to acknowledge each of these members and friends who contributed and tested recipes. We extend our grateful thank you for giving us your valuable time, hosting testing parties, and providing your talent and expertise to make this book possible. It is our sincere hope that we have not inadvertently overlooked anyone who has contributed and supported our organization in making this cookbook a reality.

Kim Abbas
Beth Ahrenholz
Judy Alman
Roxanne Amhof
Peg Ascherl
Ann Aulwes
Kathy Bailey
Alberta Becker
Peggy Bernard
Carrie Bernhardt
Jackie Betts
Susan Bier
Vicky Samon Bjortomt
Ann Bostwick
Patricia Galloway Bowlsby
Deb Boyer
Kathy Breckunitch
Donna Brown
Jane Brown
Kathleen Brown
Sam Brungardt
Ruth A. Buck
Bridget Bunge
Celia R. Burger
Mary Burgess
Mary Ann Burk
Terri Burman
Natalie Williams Burris
Maureen Pray Burum
Laura Buser
Gina M. Carlson
Lois Catchpool
Laura Cerny
Jane W. Christensen
Laura Lagen Christensen
Marty Clark
Kevin Clasing
Kitty Clasing
Ron Coenen
Kathryn Coster
Chris Crews

Rosemary Curran
Peggy Dandy
Marilyn DeKoster
Gayle Price Denkinger
Vicki Dierks
Deb Dimond
Jean Marks Dobson
Laura M. Dobson
Shirley Doolen
Jerry Dreyer
Sharon Dreyer
Carol H. Driver
Brenda Durbahn
Sondra Dyer
Kay Ebetino
Tricia Elmer
Janis Dahlgren Engel
Cary Euchner
Kelly Evens
Kathryn Marold Fain
Jane R. Field
Debbie Fisher
Judy Fogdall
Patience Frankl
Stacy Gary
Dianne Gearhart
Jan D. Gibson
Kathy Gordon
Laurie Griffin
Onalee Green
Jan Guthrie
Diana Hansen
Linda Dougherty Hanson
Lynette Harter
Norma Hassman
Susie Heaton
Jane Helgeson
Anne Hennessey
Sandy Dobson Henry
Carol Heth
Pamela Hickman

Janet Rohlf Holden
Karol Rae Hoth
Betty Bergan Hurley
Claire Johnson
Lori Johnson
Marjorie Jones
Dee Jordan
Gina Jorgensen
Sharon Juon
Mary Kabel
Emily Kachulis
Margaret Kaliban
Kim Kalkhoff
Marion Karlin
Jeri Jenner Karr
Katinka Maloy Keith
Trenna King
Mimi MacKinnon Kingsbury
Lynn Klein
Mary Kay Klieman
Kerry Kloos
Kathryn Knaack
Lori Knapp
Deniene Kneeland
Ginny Knell
LuAnn Lasher-Gregg
Carlene A. Lawrence
Mary Liebscher
Carol Luce
Tim Luce
Lori Luthro
Roswitha Marold
Jaci McCann
Christine McConnell
Peg McGarvey
Sara McIntee
Donna McKay
Lisa McManus
Cathie Pederson Miehe
Jeanne Miller
Mary Miller

Mary Jane Miller
Sara Moe
Anne Gallagher Nass
Tom Nass
Chris Nelson
Trudy Neumann
Pam Noble
Yvonne Nutting
Becky Oelkers
Nikki Owens
Jean Parker
Connie Paul
Gloria Brunskill Paulsen
Wilma Paup
Barbara Paxson
Mary Petersen
Dorothy Plager
Becky Poe
Marty McNutt Port
Mary Esther Pullin
Jaymie Redfern
Mary Reidy
Ellen Reiley
Kelley Reis
Cindy Richards
Kendra Richman
Ann Christensen Richter
Julie Ritland
Stephanie Ritrievi
Lolly Roberts
Amy Robertson
Jeannie Robertson
Tricia Rooff
Norman W. Runge
Bryan Sands
Lori Sands
Peggi Sawyer
Susan W. Sawyer
Lori Schneider
Andrea Schoonover
Judy Schultz

Carol Schwickerath
Donna Sheldon
Nancy Shirey
Patty Siems
Margie Skahill
Sue Smith
Sherri Snow
Lisa Staebell
Linda Stamp
Mary Strattan
Sue Strever
Missie Sturch
Joan Summerhays
Kimberly Swanson-Huff
Jan Taylor
Linda Thompson
Kate Thorpe
Kay Waechter Thuesen
Sandie Ubben
Jane Walden
Rosemary Waldschmidt
Joan Walker
Katherine (Kate) Weidner
Janice Weilein
Marie Welton
Kathleen Wernimont
Kenneth Wernimont
Julie Westin
Carol Williams
Kate Williams
Dorothy Winter
Dwight Wirtz
Junean Witham
Carrie Worthington
Glynis Worthington
Janice Yagla
Jane Young

Special Thank You

THE JUNIOR LEAGUE *of Waterloo-Cedar Falls wishes to thank these contributors who have supported the production of* FIRST IMPRESSIONS *through their financial and in-kind donations, professional expertise, and technical assistance.*

Jan Anderson
Bernard W. Aulwes
Gary and Becky Bertch
Crystal Distribution Services
Glenda and Doug Dawson
Jerry Dreyer
Pam Echeverria
Cary Euchner
Dianne Gearhart
Allen Grooters
Investors Professional Services, Inc.
John Deere Waterloo Works
Eric Johnson, Attorney
Tim Luce, Attorney
McConville Communications
ME&V
Steve Muller
Tom Nass
Ann and John Nesbit
Diane Radack
Mary Reidy
Jayne Runge
Stephanie Shank
Marilyn Swenson
The Victoria Room
Kelly and Tammy Wentzel
Kate Williams

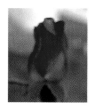

Index

m. – menu page reference
ph. – photograph page reference

Sources

"Epicurious Food." © 2000 CondéNet Inc. http://www.epicurious.com.
Herbst, Sharon Tyler. *The Food Lover's Companion, 2nd edition.* Barron's Educational Series, Inc. 1995.
MacMillan, Norma. *The Encyclopedia of Cooking Skills & Techniques.* Barnes and Noble Books, Inc. 1999.

Order Information

Name
_____

Street Address
_____

City   State   Zip
_____

Telephone
_____

Your Order	Quantity	Total
First Impressions $24.95 per book		$
Shipping & Handling $3.50 per book $1.00 each additional book		$
Total		$

Reduced rates available for orders of 6 or more books.
Please inquire by phone, fax, or mail.

Method of Payment: | | VISA | | MasterCard
| | Check payable to WCF Publications

Account Number   Expiration Date
_____

Cardholder Name
_____

Signature

Photocopies accepted

First Impressions
Dining with Distinction

To order by mail, send to:
The Junior League of
Waterloo-Cedar Falls, Iowa, Inc.
P.O. Box 434
Waterloo, Iowa 50704
319-232-8687
319-232-868711 Fax
(must dial all 12 digits)
jlwcf@cedarnet.org

255